Economy and Social Inclusion

Creating a Society for All

Series Editor

Akihiko Matsui, Tokyo, Japan

This series provides a forum for theoretical, empirical, historical, and experimental analysis of issues related to economy and social inclusion and exclusion. Included are the interconnected problems of alienation, deprivation, discrimination, economic inequality, polarization, and prejudices caused by or related to abusive behavior, aging, depopulation, disability, the educational gap, the gender gap, natural disaster, poverty, rare diseases, war, and various other economic and social factors.

The common theme of the series is to examine how we can create an inclusive society that accommodates as many people as possible and promotes their welfare. We believe this should be the main goal of economics as a discipline. Society need not passively observe its inequality, social exclusion, and decline. Policy, institutions, and our actions matter. The series aims to enrich academic discourse, influence economic and social policy, and enlighten a global readership.

Methodologies adopted in this series are mainly economic theory, game theory, econometrics, statistical analysis, economic experiments, and disability studies. Psychology, sociology, legal studies, and medical sciences, among other disciplines, are also considered important related fields of study.

The interdisciplinary research taken up in the series utilizes these existing methodologies for the common goal of creating a society for all. Furthermore, progress in such interdisciplinary studies will contribute new insights to the development of economic studies. The major geographical targets of the series are Japan and other Asian countries but are not restricted to those areas. At the same time, however, the goal is to amplify the findings therein to universally applicable insights and knowledge.

Sawako Shirahase
Editor

Social Stratification in an Aging Society with Low Fertility

The Case of Japan

Springer

Editor
Sawako Shirahase
Department of Sociology
The University of Tokyo
Tokyo, Japan

ISSN 2509-4270 ISSN 2509-4289 (electronic)
Economy and Social Inclusion
ISBN 978-981-19-3646-3 ISBN 978-981-19-3647-0 (eBook)
https://doi.org/10.1007/978-981-19-3647-0

This Springer imprint is published by the registered company Springer Nature Singapore Pte Ltd.
The registered company address is: 152 Beach Road, #21-01/04 Gateway East, Singapore 189721, Singapore

Preface

The edited book *Social Stratification in an Aging Society with Low Fertility: A Case of Japan* discusses how contemporary Japanese society is stratified based on empirical data analysis, and it is unique in its discussion of social inequality in relation to declining fertility and an aging population. Japan is the world's oldest society, with those aged 65 and over making up 29.1 percent of the population in 2021 according to the Statistics Bureau of Japan.[1] Simultaneously, a continuously declining number of children has been observed, particularly since the mid-1970s. Japan's total fertility rate was 1.34[2] in 2020, which has remained far below the replacement rate of 20.7 for more than four decades.

It is important to note that Japan has experienced a dramatic change in its demographic structure in a short period of time, and such rapid change could be closely associated with changes in how social stratification is generated. Japan was the first Asian society to achieve industrialization. In the 1970s and 80s, many social scientists, including sociologists and economists, paid close attention to Japan to see whether its pattern of industrialization and modernization was similar to that in Europe and North America. However, Japan tended to be defined by its peculiarities, such as a lack of socio-economic inequality and the high degree of societal homogeneity, although there is no consensus on this description. Japan shares a pattern and degree of social stratification that is somewhat similar to Europe and North America, although there are differences between them.

Currently, Japan is the most aged society in which a substantial number of the elderly have retired and do not have a spontaneous relationship with the labor market. Social stratification theory has been developed in close relation with the labor market, but we will need to make some amendments to examine the stratification of this very aged society in which a substantial number of people have no ties to the labor market. In this book, we discuss various aspects of stratification such as education, work, wealth, marriage, family, gender, generation, and social attitudes.

---

[1] *Statistics Topics No. 129* (Statistics Bureau of Japan, https://www.stat.go.jp/data/topics/topi1290.html).

[2] Vital statistics, Ministry of Health, Labour, and Welfare.

All arguments in this volume are based on the rigorous data analyses of the National Survey of Social Stratification and Social Mobility (hereafter, SSM), which has been conducted every 10 years since 1955. The SSM has been the leading source of quantitative empirical research in Japan attempting to reveal society's stratification structure and is one of the major large-scale social surveys in postwar Japan. The survey has been conducted every ten years since the mid-1950s, and the 2015 survey was the seventh. As an academic survey in a developed country, this large-scale nationwide survey that has been conducted consistently over a long period of time is a rare and valuable academic asset. In addition, the survey is of high academic value, as it exhibits the reality of people living through a 60-year period of major societal transformations in Japan after World War II.

The book consists of nine chapters, and the topics are roughly divided into five categories: (1) long-term trends in social inequalities, such as intergenerational mobility; (2) labor market and educational segregation between regular and non-regular employment, or between college graduates and others; (3) societal attitudes toward social stratification; (4) inequality measurement based on long-term work histories; and (5) wealth inequality as another aspect of social stratification. In summary, we will discuss Japan's high-speed demographic transformation, represented by an aging population with a declining fertility rate, from the perspective of social stratification. Some chapters do not directly refer to social inequality from a demographic perspective, but the phenomena argued in all chapters are closely related to the increase in the number of older people, the decrease in the number of young people, or the decrease in the number of married couples.

Finally, I would like to express my gratitude for the cooperation and dedication of all authors that contributed to this book. It was based on the book series *The Structure of Stratification in the Aged Society with Low Fertility*, published by the University of Tokyo Press, and I appreciate that the UTP agreed to publish the English language version of the book. The 2015 SSM project was supported by the Grant-in-Aid for Specially Promoted Research (Grant# 25000001) and the Grants-in-Aid for Scientific Research (A) (Grant# 18H03647) from the Japan Society for the Promotion of Science. Our project would not have been possible without this support. Finally, I would like to thank Ms. Juno Kawai for her patience and continuous support until this book is finally published.

Tokyo, Japan Sawako Shirahase

Contents

About the Editor

Sawako Shirahase is a Professor of Sociology at the Graduate School of Humanities and Sociology, the University of Tokyo. She received her D.Phil. in sociology from the University of Oxford, conducted post-doctoral research at the East Asian Institute, Columbia University as a junior researcher, and held positions of Senior Research fellow at the National Institute of Population and Social Security Research, and Associate Professor of Sociology at Tsukuba University. She is currently a director of the UTokyo Center for Contemporary Japanese Studies.

Dr. Shirahase's research interests include comparative social stratification and demographic transformation, gender and generational relations, and family change and social security system. She is the author of *Social Inequality in Japan* (Routledge, 2014) and *Demographic Change and Inequality in Japan* (ed.) (Trans Pacific Press, 2011), and her recent publications are "Social Stratification Theory and Population Aging Reconsidered," (*Social Science Japan Journal* 24(2): 277–288, 2021) and *The Structure of Social Stratification in the Late-stage of Life* (in Japanese) (ed., with S. Arita and N. Sudo) (University of Tokyo Press, 2021).

Dr. Shirahase is on the editorial board of *International Sociology* and *Contemporary Japan*, and on the advisory board of *Social Politics*. She currently serves as Vice President of the International Sociological Association and Vice President of the International Science Council. She was the principal investigator of the research project conducting the 2015 National Survey of Social Stratification and Social Mobility (SSM) Survey which has been conducted every 10 years since 1955.

Chapter 1
Introduction

Sawako Shirahase

1.1 Background for the Examination of Social Stratification Structure

Due to its achievement of miraculous economic development after World War II, Japan was the first nation to achieve industrialization in Asia. The first (National Survey of Social Stratification and Social Mobility (SSM)) survey conducted in the mid-1950s was an attempt led by the International Sociological Association to assess the validity of the theories of industrialization and modernization, which had been discussed mainly in the West, in Japan as the first industrialized Asian country. Since then, the SSM survey has been conducted every ten years without major changes to the survey's basic framework. It has been positioned as a core data source for studies of intergenerational and intragenerational mobility, collecting data on respondents' parental work and their own work history from their first job to their job at the time of the survey. Focusing on the pattern of inter- and intra-generational mobility studies, scholars have actively discussed whether Japan is peculiar or just another industrialized society (Cole & Tominaga, 1976; Erikson & Goldthorpe, 1992; Ishida, 1993). Previous studies from the 1970s to the 1990s derived the important finding that Japan was unusual due to its late but rapid industrialization process, but also similar to European and North American countries once the nation's peculiar pattern of social change is taken into consideration. Japan both differs from and is similar to Western societies regarding how they generate social inequality in intergenerational class mobility.

However, Japan's achievement of high economic growth has made people less sensitive to the existence of inequality. An OECD report published in the mid-1970s (Sawyer, 1976) that described Japan as the most equal country in the world became a favorable backup for this view of Japan as a country without class. However, is Japan

S. Shirahase (✉)
The University of Tokyo, Tokyo, Japan
e-mail: sshiraha@l.u-tokyo.ac.jp

S. Shirahase (ed.), *Social Stratification in an Aging Society with Low Fertility*, Economy and Social Inclusion, https://doi.org/10.1007/978-981-19-3647-0_1

truly such an equal country? Beginning in the late 1990s, when economist Toshiaki Tachibanaki (1998) first mentioned the growing economic disparity in Japan, the debate began in earnest. Since then, Japan's economy has remained stagnant for more than 20 years, a further extension of what is known as Japan's Lost Decade, and the Lehman Shock in the late 2000s also led to a global recession. Japan's employment system was hit hard, layoffs of temporary workers became a widespread problem, and much attention was paid to the increase in youth unemployment and unstable employment.

The other major change in Japan was the rapid shift in its demographic structure, exemplified by the declining birthrate and aging population. In the mid-1970s, when Japan entered a period of slow growth, its total fertility rate fell short of replacement level fertility. In 1989, the total fertility rate fell below 1.58, the lowest figure recorded since 1966, the year of *Hinoe-uma* (Fire Horse, so-called, is the 43rd combination of the sexagenary cycle and it has been told that girls born in that year would become very nasty and violent. The fertility rate dropped dramatically due to this superstition). This event was known as the 1.57 shock and served as an impetus for the Japanese government to take major steps towards reversing the declining birthrate. Since then, the total fertility rate has continued to decline, and in 2020, it was 1.36. This continuous downward trend in birthrate, in combination with increased longevity, has accelerated population aging. When the first SSM survey was conducted in 1955, those aged 65 years or older accounted for only 5.7 percent of the population, which significantly increased to 28.7 percent in 2020. We assume this rapid change in demographic structure impacts the distribution structure of the people that make up society. In the traditional theory of social stratification, social status is determined by position (occupation, industry, firm size, managerial position, remuneration, etc.) in the labor market, mainly of the head of the household in which they share basic levels of consumption and livelihood security. Sociology has been focused on the degree of inequality by comparing the social status of parents and children. If there is a high correlation between the class of origin exemplified by the social status of the father and the social status of the child, it is assumed that mobility over generations would be limited because a child's status is largely determined by their father's social status. In such a restrictive society, it is highly predictable that doctors' sons are much more likely to become doctors themselves. When there is no guarantee of equal access to different opportunities for all, this shows that a society is not open.

Social status here has been largely determined by its relationship with the labor market. However, social status is not fixed, but can change over the course of one's professional career. For example, under the seniority-based employment system, where employees are guaranteed to work for the same company in the future, social status (represented by the rewards and prestige of the position) increases steadily if they continue to work with the same organization. Today, however, the number of employees working under such a seniority-based long-term employment system is declining, and more importantly, women have been excluded from such fundamental social systems, regardless of how highly educated or how talented they are. In fact, women's work style has been closely associated with their family stage and spouse's social status, and the intermittent patterns of their work continue to be valid.

An aging population leads to an increase in the proportion of those who retire from the labor market, and the conventional framework of social stratification theory that has been focused on the working-age population can no longer account for how to generate and structure social stratification the same way as before. Thus, in the 2015 survey, the upper age limit for the study subjects was increased by 10 years to 79 years of age to reflect the aging of the overall population and to examine what kind of reform is needed in relation to the existing theory of social stratification when a society's population has aged.

1.2 Aging Population and Social Inequality in Different Life Stages

The main focus of this project is to consider Japan's aging population in an examination of social inequality. Previous studies on social stratification have focused on indices based on social status in the labor market. With one in four people aged 65 years or older at the time of the survey, social stratification cannot be observed solely from the labor market, even in Japan, where the employment rate for the elderly is relatively high compared to Europe. We had been examining economic indices with a particular focus on flows, which are compensation for labor. However, it has become increasingly important to focus on assets, which are concentrated among the elderly. A question on assets was already included in the 1995 survey, so it is not new as a question item. Nevertheless, the significance of the 2015 SSM survey is that it focuses on the aspects of socioeconomic status that cannot be explained simply by compensation for labor by including many elderly people who have retired from the labor market. I would like to explicitly consider such demographic transformation in examining the structure of Japan's social stratification.

This book explores social stratification by taking into account differences in life stages, that is, early, middle, and late life. For stratification in early life, educational opportunities, transition from education to the labor market, marriage and childbirth, and the period when people first leave their childhood home would be important for examining the structural mechanism by which disparity in early life is generated. For example, with respect to the family/household as a basic unit of social stratification, an individual's family background, the type of spouse they marry, and the type of family they form are important themes in the study of the basics of social stratification.

Midlife refers to the so-called mature years of life. It is the most orthodox framework, developed with a focus on the status of the working-age population, which has been the focus of previous SSM surveys. In response to the recent declining birthrate and aging population, and thus the relative shrinkage in the size of the working-age population, policy discussions have been conducted on labor shortage and productivity. However, the reality appears to be that there is no major change to the basic structure in which the head of the household, who is in his prime, supports the household, and his family members share his lifestyle. We adopted the traditional framework with extra attention to recent demographic changes, and consequently, the reality will not be captured by the same framework as before.

Finally, regarding the late stage of life, we posed the following research questions. For older people who are unrelated to or marginally related to the labor market, how is their social status related to that of their working years? Does their status from their working years continue to affect their socioeconomic status in old age? Because the SSM survey is a cross-sectional survey, its ability to capture dynamic changes throughout an individual's life is limited. However, retrospective information on an individual's career up to the time of the survey allows us to examine how frequently they changed jobs, how long they stayed in the same job, or when they left the labor force. This book includes the following discussions: lifetime income estimation in consideration of working years, retirement behavior in the elderly, class inequality in wealth such as housing and assets, and attitudes of the elderly, which may be different from those that are working age or younger.

1.3 The Structure of the Book

This volume includes eight chapters. The first chapter, "Long-term trends in intergenerational class mobility in Japan," was written by Hiroshi Ishida and examines whether Japanese society has become equal after World War II, focusing on patterns of international mobility since 1955. He concludes that there was no overall trend, such as an increase or decrease in the degree of inequality, and also that there was no trend in the pattern of intergenerational class mobility. There is not enough data to conclude that Japan has become a class-divided society due to less frequent intergenerational mobility. The second chapter, "Recent trends in intergenerational mobility through marriage," was written by Satoshi Miwa and examines whether Japanese society remains homogeneous through marriage, based on updating data from the 2015 SSM survey. Miwa claims that marriage has become less homogeneous than before, and an increasing number of married couples with different educational backgrounds exist. However, as mentioned in his chapter, we should not overlook the fact that the number of young people who delay or shy away from marriage has increased. Thus, it is important to assess the pattern of openness in society through marriage, taking into consideration declining marital rates.

The third chapter, "Relative indexes of educational attainment and trend analysis of inequality of educational opportunity using the 2015 SSM survey data," was presented by Takayasu Nakamura to examine whether the degree of inequality in educational opportunities has worsened or improved. He concludes that there was no specific trend in the inequality of educational opportunities over time, and there was no empirical evidence of an increase or decrease in inequality of educational opportunities across all generations, except for those in their 20s. Based on his analysis, Nakamura states that it is important to explore long-term trends in educational inequality. The fourth chapter, "Trends in Long-Term Employment in Japan," was written by Tsutomu Watanabe and examines when long-term employment has been regarded as a characteristic of the Japanese employment system. He took advantage of the long and detailed work histories in the SSM surveys from the 1920s to the 2010s and claims two important findings. First, the emerging long-term employment system was stabilized in the 1950s, and second, the deterioration of this system began in the 1980s.

The fifth chapter, "Intragenerational mobility between regular and non-regular employment sectors in Japan: From the viewpoint of the theory of mobility regimes since the mid-1950s," was written by Yoshimichi Sato. He tested his previous analyses based on the 2005 SSM data on segregation in the labor market between the core and peripheral sectors and concluded that the division between the two segments of the labor market has not improved but remained serious. Entry into the core segments has become more rigid, while the influx into the peripheral segment was more fluid.

The sixth chapter, "Gap in attitudes toward higher education between graduates and non-graduates: Growing educational disparity in younger cohorts," was written by Toru Kikkawa. He warns of the high possibility of widening the divide between college graduates and non-graduates in future generations. The reproduction of a favorable social status would be tightened by guaranteeing the intergenerational inheritance of higher education. The seventh chapter, "Effects of regional inequality on political attitudes: Social capital and support for redistribution and free competition," was written by Naoki Sudo. He investigates the effects of regional inequality on support for social policies and explores the relationships between support for social policies and social capital. He concludes that regional disadvantages generate social capital, but social capital does not have sufficient enough effects to offset the negative consequences of regional disadvantages.

The eighth chapter, "Explanation of socioeconomic inequality among the male elderly: An approach based on estimated income history," was written by Shin Arita. He concludes that position in the labor market is not a snapshot, but rather multidimensional. He proposes the use of more comprehensive indices, including various aspects of labor-market components over the life course, to examine the structure of social stratification in an aging society more accurately.

Finally, the ninth chapter, "Another aspect of social inequality, wealth, in a super-aged society, Japan: Re-examining the conventional framework of social stratification," was written by Sawako Shirahase to discuss socioeconomic inequalities in income and wealth. She particularly focused on wealth inequality, which has not received sufficient attention in social stratification studies. This chapter discusses three topics: (1) economic inequality in terms of income and savings, (2) the relationship between intergenerational class mobility and wealth inheritance, and (3) the determinants of the comprehensive economic well-being of the elderly, represented by the total value of household income and real savings. She paid attention to the rapidly aging population when examining social inequality to see whether it is necessary to revise conventional social stratification theory due to such a large demographic transformation. She concludes that the basic system of social stratification closely related to labor market positions has not dramatically changed, but demographic characteristics such as marital status, relations within the family, and education as a proxy for human capital should not be overlooked in determining the socioeconomic well-being of the elderly.

References

Cole, R. E., & Tominaga, K. (1976). "Japan's changing occupational structure, and its sinignificance. In: H. Patrick (Ed.), *Japanese Industrialization and Its Consequences*. Berkeley, C.A.: University of California Press.

Erikson, R., & Goldthorpe, J. H. (1992). *Constant Flux*. Clarendon Press.

Ishida, H. (1993). *Social Mobility in Contemporary Japan*. Stanford University Press.

Sawyer, M. (1976). Income distribution in OECD countries. *OECD Employment Outlook*.

Tachibanaki, T. (1998). *Nihon no Keizai Kakusa* (Economic Inequality in Japan). Tokyo: Iwanami Shoten (in Japanese).

Sawako Shirahase is Professor of Sociology at the Graduate School of Humanities and Sociology, the University of Tokyo. She received her D.Phil. in sociology from the University of Oxford, conducted post-doctoral research at the East Asian Institute, Columbia University as a junior researcher, and held positions of Senior Research fellow at the National Institute of Population and Social Security Research, and Associate Professor of Sociology at Tsukuba University. She is currently a director of the UTokyo Center for Contemporary Japanese Studies.

Dr. Shirahase's research interests include comparative social stratification and demographic transformation, gender and generational relations, and family change and social security system. She is the author of *Social Inequality in Japan* (Routledge, 2014) and *Demographic Change and Inequality in Japan* (ed.) (Trans Pacific Press, 2011), and her recent publications are "Social Stratification Theory and Population Aging Reconsidered," (*Social Science Japan Journal* 24(2): 277–288, 2021) and *The Structure of Social Stratification in the Late-stage of Life* (in Japanese) (ed., with S. Arita and N. Sudo) (University of Tokyo Press, 2021).

Dr. Shirahase is on the editorial board of *International Sociology* and *Contemporary Japan*, and on the advisory board of *Social Politics*. She currently serves as Vice President of the International Sociological Association and Vice President of the International Science Council. She was the principal investigator of the research project conducting the 2015 National Survey of Social Stratification and Social Mobility (SSM) Survey which has been conducted every 10 years since 1955.

Chapter 2
Class Structure, Education, and Social Mobility in Post-war Japan

Hiroshi Ishida

Abstract This chapter examines change and stability in the pattern of intergenerational class mobility and the role of education in mobility in post-war Japan. There is no clear tendency towards greater openness in post-war Japan nor is there an increase in intergenerational rigidity in the 1990s and 2000s. The results of trend analyses are consistent with the stability hypothesis which predicted that the strength and pattern of association between class origin and class destination remain stable in industrial societies. Similarly, the associations between class origin and education and between education and class destination show stability in the post-war period. Taking the results of absolute and relative mobility rates altogether, the Japanese postwar mobility experience can be understood as a remarkably stable relative mobility regime within the context of rapidly changing class structure and educational expansion during the 60-year postwar period.

This study was supported by the KAKENHI (grant numbers 25000001 and 18H05204) from the Japan Society for the Promotion of Science. I am grateful to Sho Fujihara and Satoshi Miwa for allowing me to use materials from our joint research (Fujihara & Ishida, 2016, 2017, 2018, 2021; Ishida & Miwa, 2009, 2011, 2012, 2017) and to Tsutomu Watanabe for providing me with invaluable references. The first part of this research is based on Ishida (2018), and the second part is based on Ishida (2021). Portions of this research were presented at the 2015 SSM Research Project workshops in 2017–18, the East Asian Studies Program Lecture series, Princeton University on 13 February, 2017, the Program on US-Japan Relations, Harvard University on 21 February, 2017, the Demography Seminar at the University of Wisconsin, Madison, on 9 May, 2017, the annual meeting of the American Sociological Association in Montreal, Canada, on 15 August, 2017, the annual meeting of the Japanese Sociological Society at the University of Tokyo on 4 November, 2017, the First Conference of the Comparative Social Research Network at Kyushu University on 27 January, 2018, Research on East Asian Demography and Inequality, Princeton University on 11 August, 2020, UTokyo-Princeton Demography & Inequality in East Asia Series, University of Tokyo Center for Contemporary Japanese Studies on 17 March, 2021, and the Second Congress of East Asian Sociological Association on 30 October, 2021. I am grateful to the participants of the meetings for comments and suggestions.

H. Ishida (✉)
Institute of Social Science, University of Tokyo, 7-3-1 Hongo, Bunkyo-ku, Tokyo 1130033, Japan
e-mail: ishida@iss.u-tokyo.ac.jp

S. Shirahase (ed.), *Social Stratification in an Aging Society with Low Fertility*, Economy and Social Inclusion, https://doi.org/10.1007/978-981-19-3647-0_2

2.1 Introduction

This chapter takes up the issue of social mobility. Social mobility has been a major concern in sociological investigations for decades. Researchers often examine intergenerational class mobility as a way to measure societal openness. By analyzing the trend of inheritance and mobility, we can understand the extent to which the society has become more open and fluid across time. Beginning in the late 1990s, the discourse on inequality emphasized the rising level of inequality in Japanese society. Japanese economists pointed out the trend of increasing income inequality in Japan since the late 1980s (Ohtake, 2005; Tachibanaki, 1998). The main cause of this increase is ascribed to the aging population (Ohtake, 2005; Ohtake & Saito, 1999). Since income inequality within the age group is higher among the elderly than among the younger population, as Japanese society ages, there is increased income inequality among the entire nation even though the extent of income inequality remains the same within different age groups. More recently, however, there has been a tendency for income inequality to increase among the younger population (Shirahase, 2005, 2006, 2014). A similar argument about an increasing rigidity in social mobility was reported. Sato (2000), for example, claimed that the upper non-manual class became more inter-generationally closed in the 1990s than in earlier decades. He reported increased barriers to mobility into the most advantaged class of professionals and managers.

Given this background, this chapter takes a long-term perspective in analyzing trends in intergenerational mobility. It analyzes empirical data on the trends in intergenerational class mobility in post-war Japan to test several hypotheses regarding long-term trends in mobility among industrial nations.

2.2 Trends in Intergenerational Mobility

This section presents four hypotheses about the long-term trends in intergenerational mobility in post-war Japan. These hypotheses are drawn from earlier studies on intergenerational mobility (see, Breen, 2004; Erikson & Goldthorpe, 1992a, b; Goldthorpe 1985; Vallet, 2001, 2004).

The threshold hypothesis is the first one we review. It claims that mobility rates increase dramatically when a society moves from the "pre-industrial" stage to the "industrial" stage (Lipset & Zetterberg, 1959; Davis, 1962). Migration from rural to urban areas and urbanization are the driving forces of increased mobility. Japan experienced rapid industrialization immediately following the end of World War II in the 1950s and 1960s (Tominaga, 1992; Yasuda, 1971). This hypothesis predicts rapid increase in absolute mobility rates, especially total and upward mobility rates during this period of dramatic transformation of the economy.

The second hypothesis is called the industrialism thesis hypothesis which argues a "continuous" increase in mobility rates both in absolute and relative mobility rates in the process of industrialization (Bell, 1973; Blau & Duncan, 1967; Treiman, 1970, 1990; Treiman & Yip, 1989). Accompanied by the expansion of the educational system, industrialization promotes meritocratic forms of selection by allocating social positions based on educational credentials rather than social background. Based on his analyses of social mobility data in the 1970s, Tominaga (1979) advocates the industrialism thesis by claiming that Japanese society has become increasingly more open during the period of high economic growth of the 1960s and 1970s. According to this hypothesis, all industrial societies converge towards a more fluid and open society as the level of industrialization increases. We would expect Japanese society to continue becoming more open while it experiences the process of rapid industrialization.

The third hypothesis claims "stability" in trends of intergenerational mobility. Sorokin (1959) argues that when we observe mobility rates over a short term, they fluctuate reflecting specific historical events and contingencies. However, when we take a long-term perspective, mobility rates tend to be stable and show "no perpetual trend in the fluctuations" (Sorokin, 1959, p. 63). More recently, Featherman et al. (1975) and Erikson and Goldthorpe (1992b) arrive at a similar conclusion. The shape of industrial structure as well as the distributions of class origin and class destination change as a result of industrialization, but the strength and pattern of the association between class origin and destination do not change and remain stable among industrial societies. According to this hypothesis, we would expect relative mobility rates to remain stable in post-war Japan despite rapid industrialization (see also Kanomata, 1987, 1997; Imada, 1989; Seiyama et al., 1990; Hara & Seiyama, 1999; Ishida, 2001; Ishida & Miwa, 2009, 2012, 2017).

The fourth hypothesis is derived from the work of Japanese economists and sociologists who claim that the level of inequality and rigidity in Japan increased following the collapse of the bubble economy in the 1990s. One of the most influential works was Tachibanaki (1998) who claimed that income inequality has increased from the late 1980s and that the level of income inequality has almost reached the level that of the United States. However, other research showed that the increased level of income inequality in Japan was driven primarily by the steady aging of the population (Ohtake, 2005; Ohtake & Saito, 1999). Sato (2000), a sociologist, argued that Japanese society became increasingly rigid and more closed in the 1990s. The upper non-manual class, or what he called the intellectual elite, was more likely to be recruited inter-generationally from the same class background in the 1990s than in the past, and the barriers to mobility into the upper non-manual class had increased. According to this increased rigidity hypothesis, we would expect a recent tendency of increasing rigidity and decreasing openness in Japan beginning in the 1990s. In the following sections, we will test these four hypotheses using empirical data.

2.3 Intergenerational Mobility and Education

The second objective of this study is to analyze trends in intergenerational mobility and education. Figure 2.1 presents the relationships among class origin, education, and class destination. As shown by the solid line in Fig. 2.1, education is a mediator that connects class origin to class destination. This relationship involving three variables is referred to as an OED triangle (Goldthorpe, 2014; Hout & DiPrete, 2006; Karlson & Birkelund, 2019). Education plays two conflicting roles as a mediating variable. One is the route by which people from disadvantaged classes acquire higher status by obtaining education. Here, education plays a role as a means of upward social mobility (Blau & Duncan, 1967). Another is the role of intergenerational reproduction through education, in which people from advantageous classes use their educational attainment to maintain advantageous positions (Ishida et al., 1995; Goldthorpe, 2014).

The thesis of industrialism discussed above assumes the former scenario. The hypothesis is that, as the level of industrialization progresses, (1) educational opportunities become more open to people from different backgrounds, weakening the origin and education (OE) association, and (2) social status is more likely to be defined by academic attainment than social background, thereby strengthening the education and destination (ED) association. On the other hand, when the reproductive function of education is strengthened, we predict that (1) the gap in educational opportunities by social background becomes larger, producing a stronger OE association, and (2) the link between education and class strengthens (the ED association becomes stronger). As the importance of the indirect path from class origin to destination through education increases, the portion of the direct path from origin to destination becomes smaller, indicating the weakening of the impact of ascriptive forces independent of education (Hout & DiPrete, 2006). It is therefore important to examine the components of the OED triangle. We will examine the relevant trends in the pairs of association: class origin and education (OE), education and class destination (ED), and class origin and destination (OD) after controlling for education. We will analyze the changing role surrounding education as a mediator in intergenerational class inheritance and mobility.

Education is not only a mediator that links the class people are born into and the class in which people end up, but also acts as a modifier that moderates the

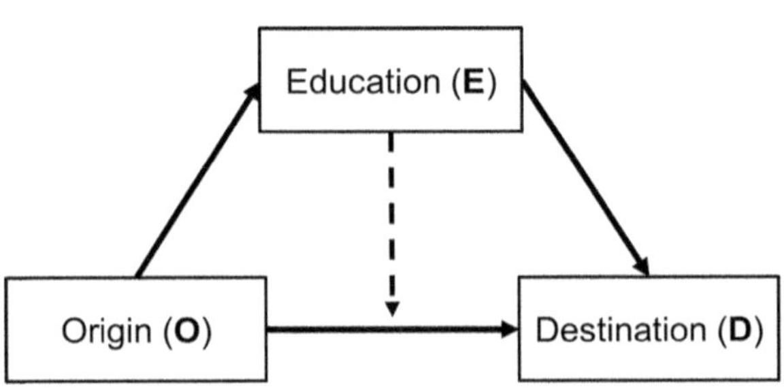

Fig. 2.1 Relationship among class origin, education, and class destination (OED Triangle)

association between class origin and destination as shown by the dashed line in Fig. 2.1. In other words, when education is a modifying/moderating factor, it means that the strength of the OD association varies depending on one's level of education. Hout (1984, 1988) found in the United States that the direct effect of the father's socio-economic status on the son's was much weaker among the college-educated population than among those with less education. Origin status affects destination status among people without a bachelor's degree, but among people who obtained a college degree, origin status had virtually no effect on destination status.[1] College education seems to cancel the influence of social background. This finding does not imply that college education eliminates inequality in a society because likelihood of attending college is strongly affected by social background factors including class origin. However, when people from disadvantaged backgrounds obtain college education, they are no longer affected by their disadvantaged backgrounds.

By extending Hout's research, Torche (2011) reported that intergenerational associations in terms of class, occupational status, earnings, and household income were strong among people without college education, while the same associations almost disappeared among college graduates. However, among those with graduate levels of education intergenerational associations were strong in the United States. Torche speculates that differences in college quality and field of study are responsible for stronger intergenerational associations among those with graduate levels of education.

A large body of research in Europe confirms a similar pattern of the modifying function of education: the association between class origin and destination is weaker or absent among people with college education. (Breen, 2004, 2010; Breen & Jonsson, 2007; Breen & Luijkx, 2007; Breen & Müller, 2020; Vallet, 2004). This finding is known as the "equalization effect" of college education. It suggests that graduating from university can free an individual from the influence of the class into which they were born. The equalization effect of college education has significant implications for trends in intergenerational mobility. Analyzing the French OED triangle, Vallet (2004) argued that the weakening of the OD association and the increased openness of society from the 1970s to the 1990s were due to the weaker OD association at the level of higher education and the greater proportion of people pursuing higher education. The society became more open from the 1970s to the 1990s because more people moved into the higher education sector. The impact of such an expansion of education on trends in OD associations is referred to as the "composition effect" which highlights the impact of the changing educational composition (Breen, 2010).

This chapter will examine the role of education as a modifying factor by analyzing whether OD associations differ by the levels of education in Japan. It specifically tests the "college as the great equalizer" hypothesis which states that the OD association is

[1] The finding that there is no effect of origin on destination among the highly educated implies that the socio-economic returns to education are greater among those from disadvantaged backgrounds. In other words, the ED association is stronger among people from disadvantaged class backgrounds, and this is sometimes called the "negative selection" hypothesis (Brand and Xie 2010).

weaker or absent among the college-educated population compared to those without college education. It will also examine the impact of educational expansion on the changing OD association in post-war Japan.

2.4 Data, Variables, and Methods

This section describes the survey data sets, variables, and analytical methods used in this study. The data sets are taken from the Social Stratification and Social Mobility (SSM) surveys conducted in Japan every 10 years since 1955. We restrict our analyses to men and women who were aged 25 to 64.[2] Female respondents were not included in the SSM surveys prior to 1985. We also restricted our analyses to respondents who had completed their educational attainment.

We use three variables: class origin, class destination, and education. Class origin refers to the class of the respondent's father when the respondent was growing up, and class destination refers to the respondent's class at the time of the survey.[3] We used the following four factors to determine class position: occupation, employment status, managerial status, and firm size. We used the six-category version of Erikson-Goldthorpe-Portocarero class schema (Erikson et al., 1979) developed by the Comparative Analysis of Social Mobility in Industrial Nations (CASMIN) project that allows for international comparison (Erikson & Goldthorpe, 1992a, b). The six categories are: the professional-managerial class or the "service class" (I + II); the routine non-manual class (III); the urban petty bourgeoisie (IVab); the farming class (IVc + VIIb); the skilled manual class (V + VI); and the unskilled manual class (VIIa).

The third variable is educational attainment. The SSM surveys collect information on the latest educational attainment of the respondents, and we use the following three categories: (1) compulsory education (elementary schools and senior elementary schools under the old pre-war system and junior high schools under the new post-war system), (2) secondary education (middle schools under the old system and senior high schools under the new system), and (3) higher education (senior high schools and universities under the old system and junior colleges, technical colleges, and universities under the new system). Table 2.1 presents distributions of class origin, class destination, and education by gender.

Next, we describe the methods of analysis. The analyses of trends in intergenerational mobility distinguish between two types of movement: absolute mobility and relative mobility. Absolute mobility uses three indices: the total mobility rate (the proportion of people who changed class positions between generations), the upward mobility rate, and the downward mobility rate. In the six-category class classification, three hierarchical groups are distinguished. The professional-managerial class is

---

[2] The age range is consistent with the previous cross-national studies on intergenerational class mobility (Breen 2004; Ishida and Miwa 2009, 2011, 2012, 2017).

[3] The father's class is determined by the father's main employment.

Table 2.1 Distribution of class origin, class destination, and education and indicators of absolute mobility by gender

	Men (survey year)							Women (survey year)			
	1955	1965	1975	1985	1995	2005	2015	1985	1995	2005	2015
Class origin											
I + II	7.2	10.9	13.7	16.5	20.3	20.7	25.5	15.0	21.0	19.8	25.0
III	3.9	4.1	5.1	5.8	5.2	8.6	9.6	7.2	6.4	9.0	9.9
IVab	22.9	25.0	25.5	27.0	27.1	26.2	23.7	25.5	25.4	23.1	23.6
IVc + VIIb	58.5	49.8	46.1	35.4	28.8	22.4	13.4	35.9	27.3	24.1	12.1
V/VI	2.6	6.4	5.1	9.0	10.9	12.6	15.0	10.4	11.1	14.3	16.0
VIIa	4.9	3.8	4.5	6.3	7.6	9.6	12.9	6.0	8.8	9.6	13.4
Class destination											
I + II	10.2	18.9	22.8	29.1	36.7	35.8	39.5	11.5	15.8	21.4	28.3
III	12.4	13.3	13.2	12.5	9.9	12.5	12.1	30.4	36.3	33.7	33.5
IVab	20.2	19.3	19.0	19.8	19.8	15.4	11.6	7.2	8.3	5.5	4.8
IVc + VIIb	40.4	21.4	15.5	6.6	4.8	4.7	3.5	12.1	6.6	4.0	2.5
V/VI	8.0	15.6	17.4	19.2	17.7	18.0	19.1	17.5	16.7	13.1	10.1
VIIa	8.8	11.5	12.1	12.8	11.0	13.5	14.4	21.3	16.4	22.3	20.8
Education											
Compulsory	71.7	60.3	45.5	31.2	20.9	12.0	4.5	37.7	22.2	10.6	3.9
Secondary	16.8	27.2	37.1	44.1	48.7	52.0	52.5	48.9	57.4	63.1	56.2
Higher education	11.5	12.5	17.4	24.7	30.4	36.0	43.0	13.4	20.4	26.3	40.0

(continued)

Table 2.1 (continued)

	Men (survey year)							Women (survey year)			
	1955	1965	1975	1985	1995	2005	2015	1985	1995	2005	2015
Absolute mobility indicators											
Dissimilarity index	20.8	34.0	37.2	36.0	31.3	28.5	22.0	45.7	43.1	39.0	34.4
Total mobility	48.1	62.5	67.1	69.3	68.8	68.8	68.4	78.5	79.8	78.8	78.5
Upward mobility	25.0	34.2	37.0	39.8	41.1	38.7	35.6	26.7	29.7	29.3	31.3
Downward mobility	7.1	9.3	10.4	11.6	11.8	14.5	17.2	20.3	21.7	21.7	26.3
(Ratio of Upward to Downward)	*3.53*	*3.68*	*3.56*	*3.45*	*3.47*	*2.66*	*2.07*	*1.32*	*1.37*	*1.35*	*1.19*
N	1591	1625	2044	1818	1716	1694	1825	685	1351	1478	1699

classified as the highest-ranking group, the unskilled manual class is classified as the lowest group, and the other four classes are classified into the middle group.[4] Movement into a higher-ranking group is defined as upward mobility, and movement into a lower-ranking group is defined as downward movement (Erikson & Goldthorpe, 1992b). The dissimilarity index indicates the degree of difference between the distributions of class origin and class destination and is used as an indicator of the extent to which the class structure change between generations. We will examine the trends in the total mobility rate, the upward and downward mobility rate, and the dissimilarity index.

Relative mobility represents differences in the opportunities for mobility among people of different class origins and measures the strength of the associations between class origin and class destination. As it is based on the comparison of mobility chances, changes in relative mobility rates are not influenced by changes in the distribution of class origin and destination. Relative mobility is used as an indicator of societal openness. By comparing multiple time points, it is possible to verify whether the strength of the association between class origin and class destination is constant or changing. If the strength of the association is weakened, it implies that the society has become more open. Conversely, if the association increased over time, it indicates that the society has become more closed.

We employ log-linear and log-multiplicative models to examine the trends in relative mobility. The conditional independence model is the baseline model where we assume no association between class origin and class destination. The model is written as the following multiplicative form:

$$F_{ijt} = \eta\, \tau_i^{O} \tau_j^{D} \tau_t^{Y} \tau_{it}^{OY} \tau_{jt}^{DY}, \tag{2.1}$$

where F_{ijt} refers to the expected frequency in cell (i, j, t) of the origin by destination by survey year table, η is a scale term, τ_i^{O} is the main effect of class origin, τ_j^{D} is the main effect of class destination, τ_t^{Y} is the main effect of survey year, and the two-way terms (τ_{it}^{OY}, τ_{jt}^{DY}) imply the association between origin and year and the association between destination and year, respectively. Given the origin and destination distributions, the model does not allow any association between class origin and class destination (τ_{ij}^{OD}). The model does not fit the data because we know there is significant association between origin and destination, but we use this model to evaluate how much other models improve the fit by computing the reduction in L^2 (the likelihood ratio chi-square) from the conditional independence model.

The second model is called the constant social fluidity (CSF) model. It sets the pattern of association in the mobility table the same across survey years. The CSF model allows the distributions of class origin and class destination to be different across survey years but imposes relative mobility rates or the odds ratio patterns to

[4] The only exception is the farming class which is classified as the middle group in terms of destination but the lowest group in terms of origin. This is because the changes in the scale and mechanization of farming shifted the position of the farming class from the bottom to the middle group between the two generations.

be the same value across years. The CSF model is written in the multiplicative form as follows:

$$F_{ijt} = \eta\tau_i^O\tau_j^D\tau_t^Y\tau_{it}^{OY}\tau_{jt}^{DY}\tau_{ij}^{OD}, \tag{2.2}$$

where the two-way terms ($\tau_{it}{}^{OY}$, $\tau_{jt}{}^{DY}$, $\tau_{ij}{}^{OD}$) imply the association between origin and year, destination and year, and origin and destination, respectively. The CSF model ensures the association between origin and destination to be the same across survey year and does not include the three-way term ($\tau_{ijt}{}^{ODT}$).

The third model is a log-multiplicative model of uniform difference or the "uni-diff model" (Erikson & Goldthorpe, 1992b; Xie, 1992). This model estimates the difference in the strength of the origin–destination association between a pair of two survey years by a single uniform difference parameter ($\varphi_t{}^Y$). Formally, the uni-diff model may be written as the following multiplicative form:

$$F_{ijt} = \eta\tau_i^O\tau_j^D\tau_t^Y\tau_{it}^{OY}\tau_{jt}^{DY}\exp(\psi_{ij}^{OD}\varphi_t^Y), \tag{2.3}$$

where the two-way association between origin and destination ($\psi_{ij}{}^{OD}$) is multiplied by a uni-diff parameter ($\varphi_t{}^Y$). The strength of association between class origin and class destination becomes either uniformly stronger or weaker across survey years. If the uniform difference parameter is greater than 1.0, the association is stronger, and if the parameter is smaller than 1.0, the association is weaker. We will examine the direction of the uniform difference parameter to evaluate the trend.

The associations between class origin and education as well as between education and class destination are analyzed using similar log-linear and multiplicative models described above to determine whether the strength of each association is constant or varies with time, controlling for the distributions of class origin, education, and class destination.

Finally, the three-way table of class origin by education by class destination is examined through log-linear and multiplicative models. We add the third dimension (education) to the models discussed above. We give below the multiplicative form for the uniform difference model:

$$F_{ijkt} = \eta\tau_i^O\tau_j^D\tau_k^E\tau_t^Y\tau_{it}^{OY}\tau_{kt}^{EY}\tau_{jt}^{DY}\tau_{ik}^{OE}\tau_{kj}^{ED}\exp(\psi_{ij}^{OD}\varphi_t^Y), \tag{2.4}$$

where the two-way associations between education and year ($\tau_{it}{}^{EY}$), between origin and education ($\tau_{it}{}^{OE}$) and between education and destination ($\tau_{it}{}^{ED}$) are added to Model (3). The uniform difference parameter ($\varphi_t{}^Y$) measures the difference in the strength of OD association across years, just like Model (3), but after controlling for OE and ED associations.

The last model is the log-multiplicative model allowing the uniform difference parameter to vary across educational levels, rather than survey years:

$$F_{ijkt} = \eta \tau_i^O \tau_j^D \tau_k^E \tau_t^Y \tau_{it}^{OY} \tau_{kt}^{EY} \tau_{jt}^{DY} \tau_{ik}^{OE} \tau_{kj}^{ED} \exp(\psi_{ij}^{OD} \varphi_k^E), \quad (2.5)$$

where the association between origin and destination ($\psi_{ij}{}^{OD}$) varies by level of education. The uniform difference parameter ($\varphi_k{}^E$) measures the difference in the strength of the OD association across three levels of education.

We will examine the goodness of fit of various models and determine which model best describes the data. We are particularly interested in the comparison of the constant social fluidity model and the uniform-difference model. The parameters of the uniform difference model will indicate the direction of mobility: whether society is becoming more open or more closed.

2.5 Trends in Absolute Rates of Intergenerational Class Mobility

We analyze in this section the trends in absolute rates of intergenerational class mobility that have occurred in post-World War II Japan over a long period of 60 years between 1955 and 2015. Table 2.1 presents the changing distributions of class origin, class destination and education as well as absolute mobility measures by gender. We begin with a discussion of men's mobility.

Before focusing on the mobility measures, let us look at class distributions. Class destination represents the class structure of the Japanese society in each year when the survey was conducted. First, the most fundamental change in the class structure is the shift from rual to urban population reflecting the rapid course of industrialization. The farming class contracted dramatically during the economic growth period: from 40% in 1955 to 21% in 1965, and further to 16% in 1975. Second, the professional-managerial class increased rapidly during the high growth period: from 10% in 1955 to 29% in 1985, and further to 40% in 2015. The share of the professional-managerial class was already the largest in the class destination distribution in 1975. Third, the skilled manual working class expanded from 8% in 1955 to 19% in 1985, but thereafter remained about the same until 2015. These changes in the distribution of class destination suggest that the contraction of the farming class was accompanied by the expansion of both thc blue-collar sector (the skilled manual class) and the white-collar sector (the professional-managerial class), unlike the experience of early industrializing nations where the expansion of the blue-collar sector preceded that of the white-collar sector. Because the process of industrialization in Japan took place in a compressed time period, the rapid pace of industrialization resulted in the simultaneous expansion of the white-collar and blue-collar classes. This trajectory has implications for the changes in absolute mobility rates which will be discussed below.

Other features of the trend in class destination include the persistence of the urban petty bourgeoisie class and the stable shares of the routine non-manual class and the unskilled manual class. The urban self-employed sector constituted about

20% of the class destination distribution consistently from 1955 to 1995, and there was no clear sign of declining importance of this sector in the process of economic development. The decline only began in the late 1990s when the value of the property assets declined sharply during the recession. The share of the unskilled working class remained the same at about 12% although there has been a slight increase in the last two decades. This class never developed into a demographically significant group in the Japanese class structure, in contrast to the early industrializing nations that contained a fairly substantial non-skilled working class at a relatively early stage in industrial development.

The changes in the distribution of class origin parallel in many ways those of class destination. Continuous reduction of the farming population was observed throughout the 60-year period. The professional-managerial class expanded gradually during this period. The urban petty bourgeoisie continued to occupy a fourth of the distribution even in 2015. The changes observed in the class origin distribution are generally in the same direction as those in the class destination distribution, but the pace of change is slower and the magnitude of change between any two surveys is much more modest in the class origin distribution than in that of class destination. It should be noted that the distribution of class origin does not represent the class structure of any given time because fathers were of different ages and there is differential fertility by class (Blau & Duncan, 1967).

The last panel of Table 2.1 reports absolute mobility indicators for the seven survey years. The trend in total mobility rates is characterized by two stages. The first stage is the rapid increase during the period of high economic growth from 1955 to 1975. The second stage is the stagnation period since 1985 when the total mobility rate plateaued at about 69%. This trend is closely related to the changing shape of the class origin and class destination distributions. In 1955 the proportion of parents and children who remained in the same class (52%) was higher than the proportion who moved to another class (48%). In 1975 the rate of intergenerational mobility increased to two-thirds (67%). The farming class accounted for a large share of the class distribution in both origin and destination in 1955, and this resulted in a high proportion of inheritance among the farming class, which pushed down the overall mobility rate. The rapid economic growth after the 1960s resulted in a sharp decline in the agricultural population, leading to differences in the class distribution between parents and children, and the outflow from the farming class pushed up the overall mobility rate. This finding is consistent with the threshold hypothesis advocated by Lipset and Zetterburg predicting a historic increase in mobility rate when a society enters a mature industrial stage.

The dissimilarity index represents the proportion of cases that must be moved to make the two distributions identical. In 1955, 21% of cases needed to be moved to make the class origin and destination distributions exactly the same because of a large share of the farming class in both distributions. Just like the total mobility rate, the dissimilarity index increased rapidly from 21% in 1955 to 37% in 1975, as the share of the farming class rapidly reduced in the class destination distribution. The dissimilarity index stayed about the same from 1975 to 1985. However, the index dropped from 31% in 1995 to 22% in 2015, indicating that fathers' and sons' class distributions are becoming more similar in recent times. Indeed, the index has continued to drop from 37% in 1975, suggesting that major structural changes in Japanese class structure took place in previous decades and that the recent period is characterized by an increasing similarity in class distributions between the two generations. The implication of this change is that there is steadily less mobility in Japanese society due to changes in the class structure. In summary, the Japanese class structure as reflected in the class destination distributions appeared to have reached a mature and stable stage in the 2000s (Ishida & Miwa, 2009).

So, is the high overall rate of total mobility due to upward mobility or downward mobility? According to Table 2.1, the upward mobility rate is higher than the downward mobility rate in every survey year. We find a substantial increase in the opportunities of upward mobility from 25% in 1955 to 41% in 1995. The increase is particularly salient in the early stage of industrialization from 1955 to 1965. Because of the continuous expansion of the professional-managerial class in the latter half of the twentieth century, opportunities for upward mobility continued to climb during this period. However, the increasing trend in upward mobility rates was put on hold in 2005 due to the lack of expansion of the professional-managerial class from 1995 to 2005. The share of the professional-managerial class reached 36% in 1995 and remained the same in 2005. It seemed that the share of this class hit a peak in the 1990s, but it increased slightly again in 2015. Downward mobility rates, in contrast, did not change substantially and remained low at around 10% from 1965 to 1995. However, the rate increased during the last two decades reaching 17% in 2015. At the bottom of the class structure, the percentage of unskilled manual working class members increased to 14% in 2015 after it had been stable at around 11% for several decades between 1965 and 1995.

Perhaps the most interesting of the trends in absolute mobility is the ratio of upward to downward mobility. Until 1995, it was stable at about 3.5. The chances of upward mobility were more than three times greater than those of downward mobility, and people were able to aim to improve their class position. This is attributed to two significant changes in class structure up until 1995. The first is the rapid shrinkage in the farming class, and the second is the expansion of the professional-managerial class. The shift from primary to secondary industries resulted in large-scale migration from rural to urban areas which resulted in upward class mobility. Since all inflows from the other classes to the professional-managerial class are regarded as upward mobility, the increase in the "size of the pie" occupied by the professional-managerial class implies increased opportunities for upward mobility.

Since 1995, the ratio between upward and downward mobility has declined significantly, reaching 2.1 in 2015. Opportunities for upward mobility are still greater than those for downward mobility, but when compared with earlier periods, upward mobility rates are clearly decreasing. The main reason is that the expansion of the professional-managerial class has stagnated since 1995. On the other hand, while the size of the unskilled manual class is small, it has shown a trend toward increasing its share since 1995. The increase in the size of this class leads to increased opportunities for downward movement since all flows from other classes into the unskilled manual class are downward movements except for flows from the farming class.

The ratio of upward to downward mobility is closely related not only to the trends in the distribution of class destination, but also to those in the distribution of class origin. People from the professional-managerial class can experience only horizontal movement (class inheritance) or downward movement (movement to other classes which are in lower hierarchical levels) by definition. This segment reached 20% of the class origin distribution in 1995. Conversely, the farming class can by definition experience only horizontal or upward movement. Because the share of people born into the farming class has declined significantly since 1975, the number of people who can experience upward mobility has shrunk year by year. In summary, the changes in the distribution of both class origin and destination affected the changing ratios of upward to downward mobility.

Next, we examine the trends in class distributions and absolute mobility rates for women. The SSM surveys before 1985 did not include female respondents, so Table 2.1 shows the distributions and rates only for the 30 years between 1985 and 2015. Because of the difference in time periods covered by the data set, the extent of the changes in the class distributions among women is much smaller in scale than that among men. Nonetheless, there are similar shifts in the class distribution. The farming class was reduced from 12 to 3% in the class destination distribution and from 36 to 12% in the class origin distribution during the 30-year span. Just like men, the share of the farming class in the class structure in 1985 was already small, while the same share in the class origin distribution was substantial in 1985 and shrank rapidly after then. Following the rapid course of industrialization, massive migration from rural to urban areas was observed even among women.

There are several features in the class destination distribution among women that are clearly different from those among men. First, the largest share in the women's class structure is the routine non-manual class (clerical and sales workers): about a third of women belonged to this lower white-collar sector. Due to the extensive feminization of clerical work, female workers in the sector were not often promoted to managerial positions. It was not unusual for female workers to withdraw from the labor market after marriage and childbirth especially prior to the 2000s. Only very recently have there been clear signs of work continuation among women after family events. Second, there is a substantial share of the unskilled manual working class comprising about 20% of the women's class structure. This is a result of married women working part-time on the manufacturing production lines and lower service work. Third, the share of the upper white-collar sector (the professional-managerial class) is much smaller among women than men although it is expanding steadily and reached 28% in 2015. More women are moving into professional work, but women continue to be disadvantaged in access to managerial positions.

When we shift our attention to absolute mobility rates, we observe that women's total mobility rates are consistently high at values close to 80%, which are clearly higher than those of men. This reflects not only the differences between generations, but also differences between men and women regarding jobs in which they engage in the labor market because class origin is measured by the fathers' class, not by the mothers' class. Total mobility rates imply that only 20% of women stayed in the same class as their fathers.

Similarly, women's dissimilarity indices are higher than those of men, due in part to the differences between fathers and daughters. However, they have declined over the past 30 years, and the class distributions of parents and children have become similar. This is not only due to the fact that there have been fewer structural changes in the class structure between generations, but also to the fact that the jobs that women can engage in have become similar to those of men.

The upward mobility rate among women rose from 1985 to 1995, then leveled off, before rising again from 2005 to 2015, exceeding 30%. This trend is associated with a consistent upward trend in the size of the professional-managerial class for women over the last 30 years, unlike men. Downward mobility also shows similar trends, especially from 2005 to 2015. During the past three decades, the rates of both upward and downward mobility increased while the extent of horizontal movement that is neither upward nor downward decreased. This is related to the fact that the classes belonging to the middle level (the urban self-employed, farming, and skilled manual classes) are shrinking in the class destination distribution among women.

Finally, looking at the ratio of upward to downward mobility, the ratios for women are generally much smaller (on average 1.31) than those for men (on average 3.20). The opportunities for upward mobility are lower among women than men while the chances of downward mobility are higher among women than men, producing smaller ratios of upward to downward mobility among women. The ratios for women were almost stable from 1985 to 2005 at about 1.35, and slightly decreased to 1.19 in 2015, reflecting the large increase in the percentage of downward mobility from 2005 (21.7) to 2015 (26.3). This recent trend is almost parallel to that among men.

In summary, the results of examining absolute mobility rates suggest the following conclusions. First, total mobility rates increased rapidly during the period of the high economic growth following the sharp decline in the agricultural population and increased migration to urban areas while the rates plateaued at about 69% after 1985 among men. Total mobility rates of women were even higher than those of men reaching close to 80% from 1985 to 2015 because of the difference by gender between the fathers' generation and the daughters' generation. The changing total mobility rates during the period of high economic growth are consistent with the threshold hypothesis which predicts historic increase in mobility rate when a society enters a mature industrial stage. Second, the trends in the chances of upward and downward mobility rates are heavily influenced by the changing class distributions of both class origin and class destination. Opportunities for upward mobility were always greater than those for downward mobility for both men and women throughout the post-war era in Japan. However, men possessed more chances for upward mobility than women primarily due to the more rapid expansion of the professional-managerial class. Women were also disadvantaged by their greater chances of downward mobility than men. With regard to the changing ratio of upward to downward mobility chances, men and women showed a similar trend: there has been a recent reduction in the ratio of upward to downward mobility. The relative abundance of chances for upward mobility compared to those for downward mobility has clearly reduced in the most recent period. Both men and women now face grimmer prospects of moving upward in the class structure than in the past.

2.6 Trends in Relative Mobility (Social Fluidity) in Intergenerational Class Mobility

We analyze in this section the trends in relative mobility, that is the extent of association between class origin and class destination. The extent of association is used as the measure of societal openness, and we examine whether the Japanese society became more open between 1955 and 2015.

Table 2.2 presents the results of testing trends regarding the association between class origin and class destination in postwar Japan by fitting the log-linear and log-multiplicative models described above to the mobility table at seven points in time for men and four points in time for women. We begin with the results for men. The conditional independence model does not fit the data at all, but it is used as the baseline. The constant social fluidity (CSF) model allows class origin and class destination to be associated but keeps the association constant across survey years. This model fits the data fairly well; the likelihood ratio chi-square statistic (L^2) is 190.5 and the associated p-value is 0.014 with 150 degrees of freedom. The CSF model misclassifies (Δ) only 4.1% of cases, and the reduction in the L^2 value from

Table 2.2 Trends in the association between class origin and class destination by gender

	L^2	*df*	*p-value*	Δ	*Reduction in* L^2	BIC	
Men							
Conditional indepenence model	3189.659	175	0.000	0.200	–	1541.21	
Constant social fluidity model	190.542	150	0.014	0.041	94.026	-1222.41	
Uniform-difference model	184.458	144	0.013	0.040	94.217	-1171.98	
Uniform-difference parameters	1955	1965	1975	1985	1995	2005	2015
	1.000	0.955	0.952	1.063	0.965	1.056	0.917
Women							
Conditional indepenence model	671.634	100	0.000	0.132	–	184.26	
Constant social fluidity model	110.717	75	0.005	0.051	83.515	-531.20	
Uniform-difference model	106.284	72	0.005	0.049	84.175	-509.96	
Uniform-difference parameters	1985	1995	2005	2015			
	1.000	1.245	1.250	1.047			

Notes Δ indicates the degree of difference between the observed frequencies and the expected frequescies under the model

Reduction in L^2 indicates the change in L^2 between that of independence model and the model fitted

BIC indicates the baysian information criterion

the conditional independence model is 94%. The uniform difference model allows the association between origin and destination to vary across seven survey years (using six degrees of freedom over the CSF model), but it does not significantly improve the fit over the CSF model: the difference in the L^2 value is 6.1 with six degrees of freedom, and the associated p-value is 0.414. The Bayesian Information Criteria (BIC) statistics can be used to compare the fits of the three models. The smaller the BIC value, the better the fit. The CSF model shows the smallest BIC statistic, and it is our preferred model. Both the difference in the L^2 value and the BIC statistics arrive at the same conclusion: there is constancy in the strength of association between class origin and class destination in postwar Japan.

The last row presents the uniform difference parameters. The 1955 survey year is used as the base year and set at 1.000. The value for 1965 is 0.955, indicating that the association is slightly weaker than in 1955 because it is smaller than 1. The value for 1975 (0.952) is almost the same as that for 1965, implying no change in the strength of the association between these two years. The value for 1985 is 1.063, indicating that the strength of the association became much stronger than in 1975, but the difference is not statistically significant. The uni-diff value became smaller in 1995 (0.965), implying that the association became weaker than in 1985. The uni-diff value in 2005 (1.056) is larger than that in 1995, implying a strengthening of the association. This observation is consistent with the post-industrial rigidity hypothesis which predicted a trend of increasing rigidity and decreasing openness in recent years in Japan. Although there is a trend of increasing rigidity judging from the uni-diff values, the difference is not statistically significant. Finally, the uni-diff value in 2015 (0.917) was smaller than that of 2005, but again the difference is not significant at the 0.05 level of significance. Therefore, these changes should not be taken seriously. We observed a small trendless fluctuation, but the dominant trend throughout the 60-year period is basic stability and constancy.

When we shift our attention to women, a very similar picture emerges. Among the three models we fitted, the constant social fluidity model is our preferred model based on both the BIC statistics and the difference in L^2 values. It misclassifies only five percent of the cases and improves the fit over the independence model by 84%. Looking at the estimates of uniform difference parameters, the association between class origin and class destination became stronger from 1985 to 1995, stayed about the same from 1995 to 2005, and became weaker from 2005 to 2015. Like men, however, these changes are not statistically significant, and over the past three decades women's relative mobility has remained stable, with social fluidity neither rising nor falling consistently.

To summarize the trends in relative mobility, our analysis did not provide any clear evidence to support the industrialism hypothesis which predicted a continuous increase in societal openness or the increased rigidity hypothesis which predicted widening disparity and entrenched class stratification since the 1990s. Looking at the long-term time period from 1955 to 2015, the strength of the association between class origin and class destination has been extremely stable since the end of World War II, with no clear trends observed. These results are consistent with the stability hypothesis which predicted the trendless fluctuation in the relative mobility regime.

People's class background affects where they end up in the class structure, and the extent of the effect of social background has not weakened or strengthened over time.

2.7 Trends in the OED Triangle

We will examine in this section the relevant trends in the pairs of association: class origin and education (OE), education and class destination (ED), and class origin and destination (OD) after controlling for education. We will analyze the changing role surrounding education as a mediator in intergenerational class inheritance and mobility.

2.7.1 Associations Between Class Origin and Education (OE) and Between Education and Class Destination (ED)

To understand the association between class origin and class destination within the OED triangle framework, the relationship between class origin and education (OE) as well as between education and class destination (ED) must first be examined. As mentioned in the "Data, Variables, and Methods" section, education is divided into three levels: (1) compulsory education, (2) secondary education, and (3) higher education.

The results of applying log-linear and log-multiplicative models for trends in the OE association are reported in Table 2.3.[5] Based on the BIC statistics (the smaller, the better), the constant social fluidity model is adopted as the most favorable model for both men and women. The tests for the difference in the likelihood ratio chi-squared values between models yield a similar conclusion.[6] Disparities between classes regarding educational opportunities are stable without significant changes in post-war Japan. According to the uniform difference parameters, in the case of men, there is little variation with only slight fluctuations around the 1955 baseline value. In the case of women, the association between class origin and education was strengthened between 1985 and 2005, with a slightly weakening trend between 2005 and 2015. However, these changes are not statistically significant.

As is apparent from the trends in educational distribution shown in Table 2.1, in post-war Japan, the secondary and higher education sectors were gradually expanded, leading to a significant increase in educational attainment. Young people increasingly

---

[5] As OE is analyzed further in other chapter in this book, the OE analysis is positioned here just as a preliminary analysis to capture the relationship among the three OED variables. The chapter by Nakamura in this book and Fujihara and Ishida (2016) used relative measurement of education to analyze the OE trends, so their results are not exactly the same as those reported in this chapter.

[6] The difference in the likelihood ratio chi-squared values between the constant fluidity model and the uniform difference model is 3.182 (difference in degrees of freedom = 6), p-value = 0.786 for men, and 5.720 (difference in degrees of freedom = 3), p = 0.126 for women.

Table 2.3 Trends in the association between class origin and education by gender

	L^2	*df*	*p-value*	Δ	*Reduction in* L^2	BIC	
Men							
Conditional indepenence model	2238.140	70	0.000	0.158	–	1578.85	
Constant social fluidity model	82.907	60	0.027	0.026	96.296	–482.20	
Uniform-difference model	79.725	54	0.013	0.024	96.438	–428.87	
Uniform-difference parameters	1955	1965	1975	1985	1995	2005	2015
	1.000	0.981	0.959	0.919	1.023	1.025	1.057
Women							
Conditional indepenence model	832.945	40	0.000	0.145	–	490.59	
Constant social fluidity model	57.784	30	0.002	0.029	93.063	-198.98	
Uniform-difference model	52.064	27	0.003	0.028	93.749	-179.03	
Uniform-difference parameters	1985	1995	2005	2015			
	1.000	1.195	1.377	1.242			

Notes see Table 2.2

graduated from high school and went on to higher education institutions. However, such an expansion of education was not accompanied by a narrowing in disparities of educational opportunities by class origin. Opportunities for obtaining education vary according to the father's class, and such disparities persisted throughout the post-war period.

The trends in the ED association are presented in Table 2.4. When we compare models based on the BIC statistics, the constant social fluidity model is our preferred model for both men and women. However, according to the tests of the differences in the likelihood ratio chi-squared values between models, the uniform difference model significantly improves over the constant social fluidity model for both men and women.[7] Judging from the parameters of the uniform difference model, among men, 1955 was the outlier (the ED association was stronger in 1955); there was no significant difference between 1965 and 2015, and the constant social fluidity model fits the data. Among women, the effect of education on class destination was significantly smaller in 2015, but for the rest of the years there was no significant change. Therefore, the overall model fitting exercises suggest that the trend in the ED association is essentially stable, with no major changes. In the following 3-variable

[7] The difference in L^2 is 34.634 (with the associated p-value < 0.01) for men and 15.845 (with the associated p-value < 0.01) for women.

Table 2.4 Trends in the association between education and class destination by gender

	L^2	*df*	*p-value*	Δ	*Reduction in* L^2	BIC	
Men							
Conditional indepenence model	3700.834	70	0.000	0.210	–	3041.55	
Constant social fluidity model	120.367	60	0.000	0.032	96.748	-444.74	
Uniform-difference model	85.733	54	0.004	0.025	97.683	-422.86	
Uniform-difference parameters	1955	1965	1975	1985	1995	2005	2015
	1.000	0.794	0.689	0.741	0.696	0.744	0.671
Women							
Conditional indepenence model	1017.929	40	0.000	0.154	–	675.57	
Constant social fluidity model	48.559	30	0.017	0.034	95.230	-208.21	
Uniform-difference model	32.714	27	0.207	0.026	96.786	-198.38	
Uniform-difference parameters	1985	1995	2005	2015			
	1.000	1.085	1.242	0.831			

Notes see Table 2.2

analysis of the OED triangle, we assume that the ED association is constant across survey years.[8]

As previously mentioned, in post-war Japan, there has been an increase in educational attainment and an upshift in its distribution. It has been argued that the relative increase in the proportion of highly educated people could lead to educational inflation and reduce the socio-economic returns to education. Indeed, after 1995, the rate of enrollment in higher education rose sharply. However, the 18-year-old population peaked at 2 billion in 1992 and then declined sharply. As a result of shrinking youth population, the absolute number of people who attended higher education remained between 700,000 and 800,000 without ever rising above this level. Therefore, educational inflation among university graduates did not take place. These labor supply trends are likely to be related to the stability of the ED association (Mugiyama and Toyonaga, 2021).

[8] We could estimate an ED association model controlling for O. However, the same trends are observed after controlling for O, so we do not report the results here.

2.7.2 Association Between Class Origin and Class Destination (OD) and Education (E)

Table 2.5 reports the trends in the association between class origin and class destination (OD) after controlling for education using the O by E by D three-way cross-tabulated table for each survey year. The constant social fluidity model implies that the OD association is constant over time after the associations between O and E and between E and D are set constant. The uniform difference model (by survey year) allows the strength of the OD association to differ from one survey year to the next. Based on the BIC statistics, the constant social fluidity model is our most preferred model for both men and women. As with the analysis when there was no control for education (Table 2.2), we conclude that the OD relationship is stable and has been constant since the end of World War II. For men, there is no difference in the trends in the uniform difference parameters whether one controls for education or not. For women, the trends in the uniform difference parameters are slightly different after controlling for education, with 1985 showing the greatest degree of closure after the control. However, these differences are not statistically significant and should not be taken seriously.

Table 2.5 also shows the fit of the uniform difference model (by education) where the strengths of the OD association differ by educational level, not by survey year. When we compare this model with the constant social fluidity model in which the OD association does not vary by educational level, the constant social fluidity model is the preferred model using the BIC statistics for both men and women.[9] Nonetheless, the parameters of the uniform difference model are of interest. For men, the OD association is strongest among those who have the highest level of education, whereas for women, the association is weakest among those who received higher education.

In the case of women, acquiring higher education appears to weaken the influence of class origin on class attainment, a pattern similar to those observed in other industrial societies. Conversely, men who have obtained higher education are more likely to be affected by their class origin in their attainment than men with lower education. However, to reiterate, given the fact that the constant social fluidity model is our preferred model for both men and women, these differences in the strength of OD association by levels of education should be interpreted with caution. In short, our results suggest that class origin and class destination are associated within the same level of education and that the extent of the association is about the same across all three levels of education. Our results are not consistent with the "college as the great equalizer" hypothesis which states that the OD association is weaker or absent among the college-educated population compared to those without college education.

---

[9] The difference in L^2 between the constant social fluidity model and the uniform difference model are 13.684 (with the associated p-value = 0.001) for men and 3.423 (with the associated p-value = 0.181) for women.

Table 2.5 Trends in the association between class origin and class destination after controlling for education by gender

	L^2	*df*	*p-value*	Δ	*Reduction in* L^2	BIC	
Men							
Conditional indepenence model	8281.260	665	0.000	0.313	–	2017.50	
Constant social fluidity model	716.157	620	0.004	0.075	91.352	-5123.74	
Uniform-difference model (by survey year)	710.137	614	0.004	0.075	91.425	-5073.25	
Uniform-difference model (by education)	702.473	618	0.010	0.074	91.517	-5118.59	
Uniform-difference parameters by survey year	1955	1965	1975	1985	1995	2005	2015
	1.000	0.961	0.961	1.113	1.036	1.160	1.046
Uniform-difference parameters by education	Compulsory	Secondary	Higher education				
	1.000	1.170	1.331				
Women							
Conditional indepenence model	3867.910	380	0.000	0.292	–	537.59	
Constant social fluidity model	409.268	335	0.003	0.081	89.419	-2526.67	
Uniform-difference model (by survey year)	395.838	332	0.009	0.078	89.766	-2513.81	
Uniform-difference model (by education)	405.845	333	0.004	0.080	89.507	-2512.56	
Uniform-difference parameters by survey year	1985	1995	2005	2015			
	1.000	0.926	0.771	0.559			
Uniform-difference parameters by education	Compulsory	Secondary	Higher education				
	1.000	1.092	0.813				

Notes see Table 2.2

2.8 Summary and Conclusion

This chapter examined changes and stability in the pattern of intergenerational class mobility in Japan in the late 20th and early twenty-first centuries. Japan experienced rapid economic development in the 1960s and early 1970s, followed by a recession and then sustained economic growth until the early 1990s when the nation was hit by a serious recession. In the 2000s, the country was on the path toward moving out of the phase of the recession. These changes had direct implications for the changing class structure in postwar Japan. The path of late but rapid industrialization caused a massive shift in population out of the farming sector that was accompanied by the expansions of both the blue-collar sector and the white-collar sector at almost the same time. Total mobility rates increased rapidly during the period of high economic growth of the late 1950s and 1960s and continued to increase modestly until 1985. Upward mobility rates also climbed sharply during the initial phase of industrial development in the 1950s and 1960s. These findings are consistent with the threshold hypothesis advocated by Lipset and Zetterburg (1959), predicting a historic increase in mobility rates when a society enters a mature industrial stage.

With regard to relative mobility rates, we observed a very different picture. Even though Japan experienced a process of late but rapid industrialization and stagnation of its economy, the relative mobility rates or social fluidity patterns were remarkably stable throughout the postwar period. No systematic trend was observed. There was no clear sign of continuous societal openness in postwar Japan, contrary to the prediction of the industrialism thesis (Treiman, 1970, 1990; Treiman & Yip, 1989). Our results are not consistent with the post-industrial rigidity hypothesis (Sato, 2000), either. There was no clear tendency of increasing intergenerational rigidity in the 1990s and 2000s. Japanese society did not seem to become more closed during this recent period. The results of trend analyses are consistent with the stability hypothesis (Sorokin, 1959) which predicted that the strength and pattern of association between class origin and class destination would remain stable in industrial societies.

We would like to speculate on why there was a resurgence of interest in economic gaps and discourse on inequality recently in Japan despite there being little evidence of declining openness in trends of intergenerational mobility. We claim that relative mobility rates are very difficult to observe because they involve a comparison of mobility chances for people from different class origins. In contrast, absolute mobility rates, especially upward and downward mobility rates, are relatively more discernible because they are related to the changing size at the top and bottom of the class structure. We have already pointed out that the expansion of the professional-managerial class was put on hold in the 2000s for the first time in the postwar period. Similarly, the share of the unskilled manual working class increased modestly but steadily in the 2000s after being stable for several decades. These changes are easier to observe. It is possible that the people's perceptions and discourse are more likely to be driven by these changes in absolute rates. However, the underlying mobility regime represented by relative rates remained stable within the context of changing absolute rates.

Taking the results of absolute and relative mobility rates altogether, we arrive at the following conclusion: the Japanese postwar mobility experience can be understood as the combination of rapidly changing absolute rates at a time of fast economic growth and remarkably stable relative mobility rates throughout the 60-year postwar period. Class origin continues to affect class destination to a similar extent, even though there was a rapidly changing context of class structure. This conclusion is not unique to Japan. Recent work analyzing new data from Great Britain (Bukodi et al., 2015) arrives at a similar conclusion.

The second objective of this chapter was to examine the role of education in intergenerational class mobility within the framework of the OED triangle. Specifically, the relationship between class origin and class destination was decomposed into the direct path and the indirect path through education. We focused on the role of education as a factor mediating the process of intergenerational class mobility and examined the indirect path components: the associations between class origin and education and between education and class destination. When the trends in these two pairs of associations are examined, there were no clear changes in the associations over the 70-year period after World War II.

In post-war Japan, more young people graduated from high school and went on to higher educational institutions, with great strides made toward improving levels of education. However, such expansions of educational attainment did not accompany a clear reduction in disparities in access to educational opportunities by class origin, nor did they weaken the association between education and class destination. These findings suggest that education plays a role in mediating class inheritance and intergenerational mobility, and that there have been no major changes in its role over time. Furthermore, class origin and class destination are directly related without the mediation by education, with no significant changes in this relationship.

Finally, we examined the role of education as a factor modifying the OD association by analyzing whether the strength of the relationship between class origin and class destination differs depending on the level of education. For both men and women, there was no clear difference in the extent of the OD association across three levels of education. Unlike in the United States and some European nations (Breen, 2004, 2010; Breen & Jonsson, 2007; Breen & Luijkx, 2007; Hout, 1984, 1988; Torche, 2011; Vallet, 2004), the attainment of higher education does not ensure that the highly educated are independent of the influence of class origin on their class attainment in Japan. People with higher education are almost equally likely to have their socio-economic attainment affected by their class origin as those with less education. In the United States, for example, people with less education including high school graduates and dropouts tend to rely on parental resources because they lack superior educational qualifications (Fiel, 2020), so the influence of parents was most visible among the least educated. However, in Japan, the extent of the effect of class origin among high school graduates is not stronger than that among college graduates. One reason is that Japanese high schools play an active role in assisting students in finding jobs after graduation. Japanese employers delegate the selection of students to high schools and hire students who were recommended by schools. The institutionalized linkage between high schools and Japanese firms tends to weaken the influence of family background on occupational destination because the assistance of schools is available to all high school students regardless of their background (Ishida, 2022).

Another reason why a strong effect of class origin is apparent among college-educated people in Japan is related to the institutional features of the labor market for college graduates. Large Japanese firms tend to adopt an employment practice of recruiting school graduates who are still in school, train them on-the-job, and promote them internally (Kato, 2001; Ono, 2010). Although the long-term employment practice is in decline (Kawaguchi & Ueno, 2013), Japanese firms still focus on recruiting college seniors and select them on the basis of trainability. College seniors compete among themselves for entry-level jobs, with little variation in their skill levels. It is possible that family resources such as parental networks and social capital are used to gain advantage in the process of job searching. These institutional features of the labor market for high school graduates and college graduates may contribute to the fact that the OD association is not weaker among college-educated people than those without college education, thereby not providing support for the "college as the great equalizer" hypothesis in Japan (Fujihara & Ishida, 2021).

References

Bell, D. (1973). *The Coming of Post-industrial Society*. Basic Books.

Blau, P. M., & Duncan, O. D. (1967). *The American Occupational Structure*. Wiley.

Brand, J. E., & Xie, Y. (2010). Who benefits most from college? Evidence for negative selection in heterogeneous economic returns to higher education. *American Sociological Review, 75*, 273–302.

Breen, R. (Ed.). (2004). *Social Mobility in Europe*. Oxford University Press.

Breen, R. (2010). Educational expansion and social mobility in the 20th century. *Social Forces, 89*, 365–388.

Breen, R., & Jonsson, J. O. (2007). Explaining change in social fluidity: Educational equalization and educational expansion in twentieth-century Sweden. *American Journal of Sociology, 112*, 1775–1810.

Breen, R., & Luijkx, R. (2007). Social mobility and education: A comparative analysis of period and cohort trends in Britain and Germany. In: S. Scherer, P. Reinhard, G. Otte, & M. Gangl (Eds.), *From Origin to Destination: Trends and Mechanisms in Social Stratification Research* (pp. 102–24). Campus Verlag.

Breen, R., & Müller, W. (Eds.). (2020). *Education and Intergenerational Social Mobility in Europe and the United States*. Stanford University Press.

Bukodi, E., Goldthorpe, J. H., Waller, L., & Kuha, J. J. (2015). The mobility problem in Britain: New findings from the analysis of birth cohort data. *British Journal of Sociology, 66*, 93–117.

Davis, K. (1962). The role of class mobility in economic development. *Population Review, 6*, 67–73.

Erikson, R., & Goldthorpe, J. (1992a). The CASMIN project and the American Dream. *European Sociological Review, 8*, 283–305.

Erikson, R., & Goldthorpe, J. (1992b). *The Constant Flux: A Study of Class Mobility in Industrial Societies*. Clarendon Press.

Erikson, R., Goldthorpe, J., & Portocarero, L. (1979). Intergenerational class mobility in three Western European societies. *British Journal of Sociology, 30*, 415–441.

Featherman, D., Jones, F. L., & Hauser, R. M. (1975). Assumptions of social mobility research in the United States: The case of occupational status. *Social Science Research, 4*, 339–360.

Fiel, J. E. (2020). Great equalizer or great selector? Reconsidering education as a moderator of intergenerational transmissions. *Sociology of Education, 93*, 353–371.

Fujihara, S., & Ishida, H. (2016). The absolute and relative values of education and the inequality of educational opportunity: Trends in access to education in postwar Japan. *Research in Social Stratification and Mobility, 43*, 25–37.

Fujihara, S., & Ishida, H. (2017). Socio-economic returns to university education in Japan: Estimating the causal effects of vertical and horizontal stratification in education. In: Paper presented at the International Sociological Association RC28 meeting, University of Cologne.

Fujihara, S., & Ishida, H. (2018). Class origin, education, and class destination: Analyzing the OED triangle in Japan. In: Paper presented at the XIX International Sociological Association World Congress, Toronto, Canada.

Fujihara, S., & Ishida, H. (2021). College is not the great equalizer in Japan: An alternative approach to the OED triangle. University of Tokyo Panel Survey Project Discussion Paper Series No. 146, pp. 1–55.

Goldthorpe, J. H. (1985). On economic development and social mobility. *British Journal of Sociology, 36*, 549–573.

Goldthorpe, J. H. (2014). The role of education in intergenerational social mobility: Problems from empirical research in sociology and some theoretical pointers from economics. *Rationality and Society, 26*, 265–289

Hara, J., & Seiyama, K. (1999). *Shakai Kaiso (Social Stratification)*. University of Tokyo Press.

Hout, M. (1984). Status, autonomy, and training in occupational mobility. *American Journal of Sociology, 89*, 1397–1409.

Hout, M. (1988). More universalism, less structural mobility: The American occupational structure in the 1980s. *American Journal of Sociology, 93*, 1358–1400.

Hout, M., & DiPrete, T. A. (2006). What we have learned: RC28's contributions to knowledge about social stratification. *Research in Social Stratification and Mobility, 24*, 1–20.

Imada, T. (1989). *Shakai Kaiso to Seiji (Social Stratification and Politics)*. University of Tokyo Press.

Ishida, H. (2001). Industrialization, class structure, and social mobility in postwar Japan. *British Journal of Sociology, 52*, 579–604.

Ishida, H. (2018). Long-term trends in intergenerational class mobility in Japan. In: T. Yoshida (Ed.), *SSM Research Report 3: Social Mobility and Health* (pp. 41–64). Tokyo: The 2015 SSM Research Committee.

Ishida, H. (2021). Sedaikan Kaiso Ido to Kyoiku no Susei (Trends in Intergenerational Class Mobility and Education). In: T. Nakamura, S. Miwa, & H. Ishida (Eds.), *Jinsei Shoki no Kaiso Kozo* (The Structure of Social Stratification in the Early-stage of Life) (pp. 19–36). Tokyo: University of Tokyo Press.

Ishida, H. (2022). Understanding transition from high school to work using three samples the Japanese life course panel surveys: The 2007 continuous, the 2010 supplementary, and the 2019 refresh samples. University of Tokyo Panel Survey Project Discussion Paper Series No. 149, pp. 1–14.

Ishida, H., & Miwa, S. (2009). Kaiso Ido Kara Mita Nihon Shakai, (Japanese Society as Seen from Class Mobility) *Japanese Sociological Review, 59*, 648–662.

Ishida, H., & Miwa, S. (2011). Shakaiido no Susei to Hikaku (Trends and Comparisons of Social Mobility). In: H. Ishida, H. Kondo, & K. Nakao (Eds.), *Gendai no Shakai Kaiso 2: Kaiso to Ido no Kozo* (Structure of Inequality and Mobility) (pp. 3-19). Tokyo: University of Tokyo Press.

Ishida, H., & Miwa, S. (2012). Intergenerational mobility and late industrialization. In: Paper presented at the RC28 Meeting at the University of Virginia.

Ishida, H., & Miwa, S. (2017). Social mobility in post-war Japan: Long-term trends and cross-national comparisons. In: Paper presented at the Annual Meeting of the American Sociological Association.

Ishida, H., Muller, W., & Ridge, J. (1995). Class origin, class destination and education: A cross-national study of ten industrial nations.. *American Journal of Sociology, 101*, 145–193.

Karlson, K. B., & Birkelund, J. F. (2019). Education as a mediator of the association between origins and destinations: The role of early skills. *Research in Social Stratification and Mobility, 64*. https://doi.org/10.1016/j.rssm.2019.100436.

Kanomata, N. (1987). Shakai Kaiso to Ido Kenkyu ni okeru Sangyoka Meidai no Saikento (Re-evaluation of Industrialism Thesis in the Study of Social Stratification and Mobility). *Gendai Shakaigaku, 13*, 156–181.

Kanomata, N. (1997). Sengo Nihon niokeru Sedaikan Ido no Hendo (Changes of Intergenerational Mobility). *Kodo Keiryogaku, 24*, 20–27.

Kawaguchi, D., & Ueno, Y. (2013). Declining long-term employment in Japan. *Journal of the Japanese and International Economies, 28*, 19–36.

Kato, T. (2001). The end of lifetime employment in Japan? Evidence from national surveys and field research. *Journal of the Japanese and International Economies, 15*, 489–514.

Lipset, S. M., & Zetterberg, H. L. (1959). Social Mobility in Industrial Societies. In: S. M. Lipset, & R. Bendix (Eds.), *Social Mobility in Industrial Society* (pp. 11–75). Berkeley: University of California Press.

Mugiyama, R., & Toyonaga, K. (2021). Role of cohort size in class and occupational returns to education at first job: The case of Japan. *European Sociological Review* jcab037. https://doi.org/10.1093/esr/jcab037.

Ohtake, F. (2005). *Nihon no Fubyodo* (Japan's Inequality). Tokyo: Nihon Keizai Shinbunsha.

Ohtake, F., & Saito, M. (1999). Shotoku Fubyodo no Haike to Sono Seisakuteki Imi (Background of Income Inequality and Its Policy Implications). *Kikan Shakaihosho Kenkyu, 35*, 65–76.

Ono, H. (2010). Lifetime employment in Japan: Concepts and measurements. *Journal of the Japanese and International Economies, 24*, 1–27.

Sato, T. (2000). *Fubyodo Shakai Nippon* (Japan as an Unequal Society). Tokyo: Chuokoron Shinsha.

Seiyama, K., Naoi, A., Sato, Y., Tsuzuki, K., & Kojima, H. (1990). Gendai Nihon no Kaiso Kozo to sono Susei (The Structure of Stratification in Contemporary Japan and its Trends). In: A. Naoi, & K. Seiyama (Eds.), *Gendai Nihon no Kaiso Kozo* (The Structure of Stratification in Contemporary Japan) (pp. 15–50, Vol. 1). Tokyo: University of Tokyo Press.

Shirahase, S. (2005). *Shoshi Korei Shakai no Mienai Kakusa (The Unseen Gaps in an Aging and Low Birth-rate Society)*. University of Tokyo Press.

Shirahase, S. (Ed.). (2006). *Henka Suru Shakai no Fubyodo (Inequality in a Changing Society)*. University of Tokyo Press.

Shirahase, S. (2014). *Social Inequality in Japan*. Routledge.

Sorokin, P. A. (1927). *Social and Cultural Mobility*. Glencoe, Il.: The Free Press.

Tachibanaki, T. (1998). *Japan's Economic Inequality*. Tokyo: Iwanami Shoten.

Treiman, D. (1970). Industrialization and Social Stratification. In: E. O. Laumann (Ed.), *Social Stratification: Research and Theory for the 1970s* (pp. 207–34). Indianapolis: Bobbs-Merrill.

Treiman, D. (1990). Industrialization and social stratification. *Sociological Inquiry, 40*, 207–234.

Treiman, D., & Yip, K. (1989). Educational and occupational attainment in 21 countries. In: M. L. Kohn (Ed.), *Cross-national research in sociology* (pp. 373–94). Newbury Park: Sage.

Tominaga, K. (1979). Shakai Kaiso to Shakai Ido no Susei Bunseki (Trend Analysis of Social Stratification and Social Mobility). In: K. Tominaga (Ed.), *Nihon no Kaiso Kozo* (The Structure of Stratification in Japan (pp. 33–87). Tokyo: University of Tokyo Press.

Tominaga, K. (1992). Sengo Nihon no Shakai Kaiso to sono Hendo: 1955–1985 (Social Stratification and its Changes in Post-war Japan: 1955–1985). In: Gendai Nihon Shakai (Ed.), Vol. 6, (Contemporary Japanese Society) Institute of Social Science, University of Tokyo (pp. 429–495). Tokyo: University of Tokyo Press.

Torche, F. (2011). Is a college degree still the great equalizer? Intergenerational mobility across levels of schooling in the United States. *American Journal of Sociology, 117*, 763–807.

Vallet, L. A. (2001). Forty years of social mobility in France: Change in social fluidity in the light of recent models. *Revue Francaise De Sociologie, 42*(Supplement), 5–64.

Vallet, L. A. (2004). Change in Intergenerational Class Mobility in France from the 1970s to the 1990s and Its Explanation: An Analysis Following the CASMIN Approach. In: R. Breen (Ed.), *Social Mobility in Europe* (pp. 115–48). Oxford: Oxford University Press.
Xie, Y. (1992). The log-multiplicative layer effect model for contingency mobility table. *American Sociological Review, 57*, 380–395.
Yasuda, S. (1971). *Shakai Ido no Kenkyu (The Study of Social Mobility).* University of Tokyo Press.

Hiroshi Ishida is University Professor at the University of Tokyo. He received his Ph.D. in sociology from Harvard University and held academic appointments at Columbia University and the University of Michigan. He served as the Director of the Institute of Social Science and the Director of the Center of Social Research and Data Archives at the University of Tokyo. Ishida's research interests include comparative social stratification and mobility, school-to-work transition, family formation, and social inequality over the life course. He is the author of *Social Mobility in Contemporary Japan* (Macmillan and Stanford University Press) and the co-editor of *Social Class in Contemporary Japan* (Routledge). He was the editor-in-chief of *Social Science Japan Journal* published by Oxford University Press, and he currently directs the Japanese Life Course Panel Surveys.

Chapter 3
The Changing Marriage Market and Status Homogamy

Satoshi Miwa

Abstract This chapter examines the relationship between marriage and social stratification in contemporary Japanese society, with a focus on status homogamy, and how this relationship has changed over time. The SSM survey data support the fact that the trend toward non-marriage and late marriage has been increasing. It has also been confirmed that the reason for meeting a spouse has changed to a more free-love style. In the midst of such changes, homogamy has also become less likely to occur, but this is a reflection of the fact that marriage itself has become less likely to occur, and it is not a phenomenon unique to homogamy. When we examined the structure and trends of status homogamy by focusing only on married couples, we found that homogamy decreased when the indices of status were occupation and education. In addition, in terms of professional relationships and friendships, which account for the majority of opportunities to meet, there was a decrease in status homogamy during this period, and these results contributed to the overall declining trend of status homogamy.

3.1 Introduction

There is a trending proposition called the romantic love hypothesis (Smits, 2003). It implies that as time goes on and love marriages become more common, the hierarchical bonding through marriage becomes weaker. This chapter focuses on whether this hypothesis is valid and empirically examines the relationship between marriage and social class in contemporary Japan.

Broadly speaking, marriage can be a hierarchical issue on two fronts. The first is that the opportunities for marriage may differ depending on one's hierarchical status. In other words, this means that in the marriage market, social class becomes a constraint on the choice of spouse. The second is that the hierarchical status of those who marry can be similar. In this case, the marriage sphere is divided by social class.

S. Miwa (✉)
University of Tokyo, Akamon-sogo-kenkyu-tou, 7-3-1 Hongo, Bunkyo-ku, Tokyo, Japan
e-mail: miwa@iss.u-tokyo.ac.jp

S. Shirahase (ed.), *Social Stratification in an Aging Society with Low Fertility*, Economy and Social Inclusion, https://doi.org/10.1007/978-981-19-3647-0_3

The disparity in marital opportunities has been studied not only in sociology, but also in economics, demography, and many other fields. Studies have found that factors such as education, employment status, and economic power affect the ease of marriage (e.g., Mizuochi, 2006; Tsuya, 2009; Yamada, 2010). Recent studies have shown that class of origin, as represented by parental occupation and other factors, influences the timing of first marriage (Shirahase & Ishida, 2018). However, there is still no clear answer to the question of how hierarchical status, including class of origin, relates to the likelihood of status homogamy, and this remains an unexplored question.

Status homogamy is the tendency or structure in which people with the same or similar characteristics in terms of hierarchical status are united through marriage. As Breen and Jonsson (2005) point out, status homogamy has been treated as an important indicator for measuring social openness, along with social mobility and educational attainment. Simply put, the fact that the marriage sphere is not free from social stratification is seen as proof of its closed nature. Previous SSM[1] studies have repeatedly reported that there is a tendency for homogamy to establish itself in relation to educational background and occupation (e.g., Watanabe & Kondo, 1990; Shida et al., 2000; Shirahase, 2011). However, conclusions about the long-term trend of status homogamy in Japan are not necessarily unanimous. Some studies state that the trend of status homogamy as measured by educational background is stable over time (e.g., Shida, 2000; Shirahase, 2011), while others claim that it has been decreasing[2] (Miwa, 2007b; Raymo & Xie, 2000; Uchikoshi, 2018, etc.). Therefore, it is necessary to re-examine the trend of status homogamy based on new data.

Some points should be considered while examining marriage and social stratification from these perspectives. The overall social context of marriage and the reason for meeting one's spouse must be fully considered. What is important about the former is the phenomenon known as non-marriage and late marriage. The marriages examined in this chapter generally occurred between the late 1950s and the mid-2010s, and it is clear from multiple indicators and documents that the number of people who did not marry and the age of first marriages increased during this period. The fact that a time when most people of the same generation experienced marriage have already finished should be taken into account, when reading the results of the empirical analysis regarding the association between marriage and social stratification. In terms of the latter, it is known that the opportunity to meet has been transforming from arranged marriages to love marriages, and from professional relationships (meeting at work) to friendships (meeting through friends), and that this has been related to the trend toward non-marriage and late marriage (Iwasawa & Mita, 2005). However, the relationship between opportunities to meet and status homogamy has not been fully clarified[3] and still needs to be examined.

In short, the purpose of this chapter is to explore the factors that make status homogamy more likely to occur, to understand the structure and trends of homogamy, and to elucidate the relationship between the opportunities to meet and status homogamy. If the romantic love hypothesis is correct, opportunities to meet in relation to free love should have increased in the last half century, which will lead to a decrease in status homogamy. In Sect. 3.2, we present the results of our basic analysis of the trend toward non-marriage, late marriage, and changes in the opportunities to meet. In Sects. 3.3 and 3.4, we analyze the likelihood of status homogamy in first marriages and the trends of status homogamy, respectively. After synthesizing these findings, we conclude in Sect. 3.5 that as love marriages have become mainstream, non-marriage and late marriage have become more common, and at the same time, class cohesion through marriage has weakened.

3.2 Data on Trends in Non-Marriage, Late Marriage, and Opportunities to Meet

(1) Data and variables

We use data from The National Survey of Social Stratification and Social Mobility (SSM) as a source for empirical analysis. The SSM survey has already been conducted 7 times, beginning in 1955. In this study, we mainly use the dataset from the 2015 survey and sometimes merge it with supplemental data from the 2005 survey.[4]

Particularly important variables were the hierarchical statuses of the husband and wife. This is because we measured status homogamy by combining them. The hierarchical statuses addressed were education and occupation. Education is one of the most important hierarchical indicators, as it has the function of displaying status in itself, as well as being an important position as a factor that influences the attainment of other social resources and status (Amano, 1983). Furthermore, occupation is a central hierarchical indicator that continues to be a major source of income and prestige in post-modern societies (Yasuda & Hara, 1982). Therefore, we decided to include both of them in our analysis.

To operationalize the social strata, we used four categories of educational background (middle school/high school/junior college and technical college/university or higher) and four categories of occupation at the time of marriage (upper nonmanual/lower nonmanual/manual/farming).[5] In practice, therefore, the analysis of homogamy was based on the relationship between the husband's education and the wife's education, and the husband's occupation and the wife's occupation.

Table 3.1 is a cross-tabulation table showing educational and occupational homogamy. The numbers in the cells are relative to the overall frequency, and only the characteristic parts[6] are in bold. Bolded areas are concentrated in the diagonal cells, and the total rate of intra-marriage was about 56% for educational homogamy and about 47% for occupational homogamy. The results of this table show a structure that should be called status homogamy.

(2) Trends in age at first marriage

Let us examine the age during first marriage from Fig. 3.1. Here, we display the 10th, 50th, and 75th percentile values of age during first marriage for each birth cohort.[7] The 10th percentile can be interpreted as the age during first marriage for those who

Table 3.1 Joint distribution of couple's education and occupation

(A) Educational homogamy (in-marriage rate 0.559, N = 6,371)

Wife's education

		Middle	Hige school	Jr. College	University
Husband's education	Middle	**0.076**	0.065	0.002	0.001
	High School	0.049	**0.370**	0.059	0.022
	Jr. College	0.001	0.014	**0.006**	0.002
	University	0.006	0.134	**0.086**	**0.107**

(B) Occupational homogamy (in-marriage rate 0.474, N = 5,003)

Wife's occupation

		Upper nonmanual	Lower nonmanual	Manual	Farming
Husband's occupation	Upper Nonmanual	**0.070**	0.080	0.016	0.000
	Lower Nonmanual	0.065	**0.253**	0.043	0.003
	Manual	0.052	0.232	**0.138**	0.009
	Farming	0.004	0.013	0.009	**0.013**

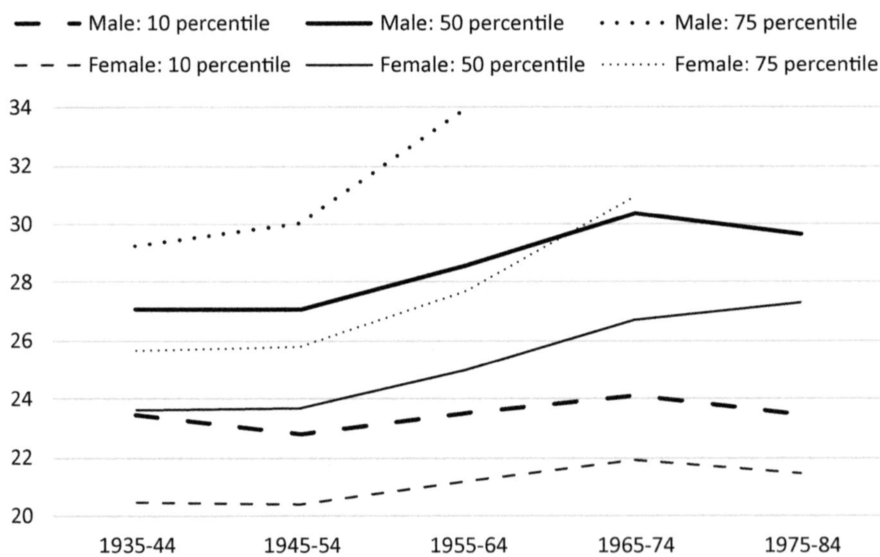

Fig. 3.1 Age of first marriage by birth cohort

married much earlier in their generation, followed by the 50th percentile for standard marriages, and the 75th percentile for slightly late marriages.

The figure clearly shows that more people are marrying later in life. For men, the 50th percentile increased by about 3 years during this period, from about 27.1 years in the 1945–54 birth cohort to about 30.4 years in the 1965–74 birth cohort. The same is true for women; comparing the same cohorts, the 50th percentile increased by 3 years, from about 23.7 years (1945–54 birth cohort) to about 26.7 years (1965–74 birth cohort).

The increase in the age of first marriage is particularly pronounced for those who marry later in life. The slope of the increase in the 75th percentile value appears to be much steeper than the earlier values. Furthermore, the 10th percentile value, which indicates the earliest marriage among the three, does not differ much between cohorts. For some cohorts, the 75th percentile value is not shown because the number of those who have experienced marriage has not yet reached 75% of the cohort (Fig. 3.1).

(3) Trends in opportunities to meet

Now, let us examine the transition of the contents of matching in the marriage market, using the opportunity to meet a partner as the key. Figure 3.2 displays the distribution of reasons behind meeting in a band graph that can be compared for each marriage cohort. The reason why we chose to use the marriage cohort instead of the birth cohort is that the purpose of the analysis is to understand the nature of the reasons behind meeting that led to the marriage at the time it occurred.

Figure 3.2 shows that the reasons for meeting a marriage partner have shifted over time. In the 1955–1969 marriage cohort, family/relatives were the most frequent source of introductions at over 30%, followed by meeting through work and friends

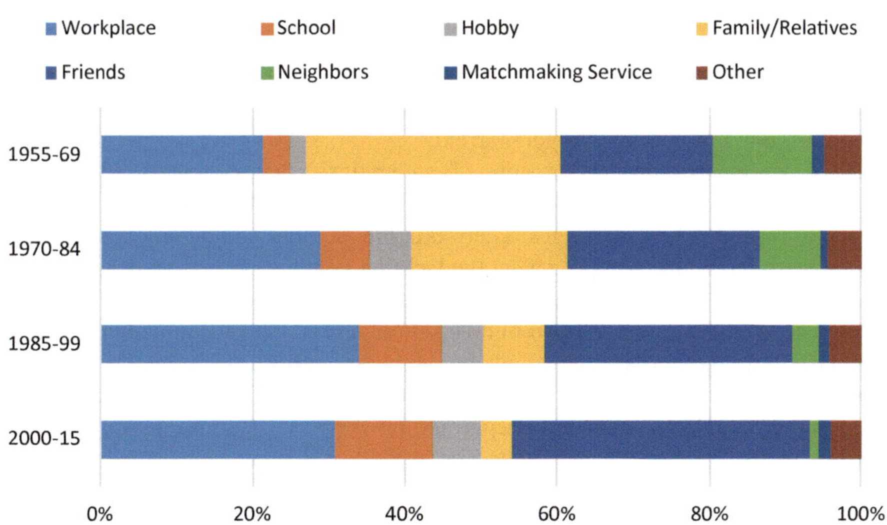

Fig. 3.2 Opportunity to meet by marriage cohort

at around 20%, and meeting through neighbors at just over 10%. Subsequently, the number of encounters triggered by family/relatives and neighbors declined to just 4% and 1%, respectively, in the 2000–2015 marriage cohort. Contrarily, the number of those who met through friends, work, or school increased during this period. In the 2000–2015 marriage cohort, they each accounted for approximately 40%, 30%, and over 10%, respectively. The rise and fall of job-related marriages can be seen here, just as how the opportunities to meet through work increased and then slightly declined.

Of these, which triggers are most often associated with what we should call romantic love? There are relatively more encounters through friends, at school, and through hobbies and lessons than there are through introductions from family, relatives, and neighbors. If we assume that this is the case, we can see that the number of cases similar to free love has been on the rise.

3.3 The Effects of Social Background on Homogamy

As shown in the previous section, the trend of late marriage or non-marriage has been progressing in Japan. Therefore, this section examines which types of people were more likely to marry, and which types of people were more likely to marry a partner of the same status.

Table 3.2 shows the results of a Cox regression analysis on the factors that affect the ease of marriage.[8] Note that the dataset used here was a merger of the 2015 SSM survey data and the 2005 SSM survey data. The numbers in the table are regression coefficients; a positive value means that marriage is more likely to occur, and a negative value means that marriage is less likely to occur.

Table 3.2 shows that the ease of first marriage is related to birth cohort. This is because the coefficients are negative for the relatively young cohorts of both men and women born after 1965. For men only, it is clear that those with a higher level of education are more likely to get married.[9]

Next, let us examine the results of an analysis that considers educational homogamy as an event.[10] The pattern of coefficients for birth cohorts was generally similar to those for first marriages. Therefore, the fact that homogamy is less likely in younger cohorts may simply reflect the fact that younger cohorts are less likely to marry in the first place. Men were found to be more likely to engage in educational homogamy at the high school and middle school levels. Upper nonmanual workers were also more likely to engage in educational homogamy. Educational homogamy was less likely to occur among women in junior colleges and technical colleges, but was more likely to occur in colleges and universities. In addition, only women were found to be more likely to engage in educational homogamy if their father's occupation was farming class.

For occupational homogamy, the pattern of coefficients for the birth cohort did not differ much from the pattern in the analysis of first marriages. In terms of the coefficients of educational background, it was common for both men and women to

Table 3.2 Estimates of cox regression analysis for predicting first marriage

	First marriage				Educational homogamy				Occupational homogamy			
	Male		Female		Male		Female		Male		Female	
Birth Cohort (base: 1935–44)												
1945–54	0.012		0.097		–0.002		0.122		0.006		0.014	
1955–64	−0.478	*	–0.222	*	–0.486	*	–0.198	*	–0.675	*	–0.273	*
1965–74	–1.105	*	–0.738	*	–1.174	*	–0.639	*	–1.180	*	–0.846	*
1975–84	–0.960	*	–0.831	*	–1.023	*	–0.750	*	–1.052	*	–0.944	*
Education (base: University)												
Middle	–0.350	*	0.118		0.355	*	–0.324	*	–0.138		–0.105	
High school	–0.183	*	0.113		0.854	*	–0.218	*	–0.273	*	–0.223	*
Jr. College	0.047		0.053		0.259		–2.866	*	–0.140		–0.156	
First job (base: Upper Nonmanual)												
Lower nonmanual	–0.016		–0.018		–0.278	*	0.029		0.399	*	0.228	*
Manual	–0.101		–0.109		–0.284	*	–0.031		–0.360	*	0.427	*
Farming	0.007		0.266	*	–0.140		0.438	*	–0.052		0.611	*
Father's Job (base: Upper Nonmanual)												
Lower Nonmanual	0.028		0.017		–0.149		0.084		–0.100		–0.104	
Manual	0.075		0.054		–0.076		0.114		–0.050		–0.100	
Farming	0.076		0.146	*	–0.073		0.279	*	–0.145		0.009	
Number of events	2700		3636		1487		2055		1310		1724	
N	3287		4075		3287		4075		3287		4075	

Note * $p < 0.05$ (two tailed test)
Self evaluation of economic status at the age of 15, the number of siblings, same-sex first-child, and the age of first job employment are included as control variables.
The risk start of the male was assumed to be 18-year-old. For the female, it was assumed to be 16-year-old. The observation was censored at the age of 50

find that occupational homogamy was somewhat less likely to occur for high school. For men, nonmanual workers were more likely to engage in occupational homogamy, while manual workers were less likely to do so. For women, occupational homogamy was most likely to occur in farming, followed by manual, lower nonmanual, and upper nonmanual occupations.

Let us compare the effects of the cohorts. Even after controlling for a variety of factors, we found that the younger the cohort, the less likely they were to get married or engage in homogamy. Again, the pattern of coefficients across cohorts was generally similar regardless of whether the results were for first marriages or homogamy. The results show that homogamy is becoming less likely to occur, but this is in line with the fact that marriages themselves are becoming less likely to occur, and not at a faster or slower pace than the normal rate of late marriage and non-marriage.

3.4 The Structure and Trends of Status Homogamy

(1) Model selection on the trend of status homogamy

Here, we examine married couples and clarify how marriage has combined wives' and husbands' hierarchical statuses and how they have changed. We focus on the long-term trend of educational and occupational homogamy.

A cross-tabulation table of marriage cohort, husbands' classes, and wives' classes was created, and Table 3.3 shows the goodness of fit of the loglinear model for educational and occupational homogamy, respectively. Model 1 is a conditionally independent model, which means that there is no relationship between the husbands' and wives' hierarchies, although there are differences in the hierarchical composition of husbands and wives between cohorts. Model 2 assumes that there is an association between the husbands' and wives' hierarchies, but that it is constant across cohorts. In Model 3, the pattern of association between the husbands' and wives' hierarchies is the same, but the strength of the association differs between cohorts. We examine which model fits the best among these models.

Model 3 is considered to be the best for the analysis of the trends in educational attainment. The value of the information criterion BIC (Bayesian Information Criteria) is the smallest among all the models, and the value of goodness of fit (G^2) though not statistically significant, is at an acceptable level. In addition, the index of dissimilarity (I.D.) is only about 1.5%, and multiple statistics confirm that it is a good fit. The parameter-uniform difference in Model 3 indicates that the strength of educational homogamy has been declining since the 1980s.

The same examination was subsequently conducted for occupational homogamy, and Model 3 is still the best choice. Although the BIC in Model 3 is comparable or slightly inferior to that in Model 2,[11] G^2 is not statistically significant in Model 3 and the I.D. is small enough at 1.7%. Therefore, we can see that occupational homogamy also changed between cohorts. The trend of the strength of occupational homogamy

Table 3.3 Fitting indices of log-linear/multiplicative models

(A) Educational homogamy

	G^2	df	*p*-value	I.D	BIC
Model 1: Conditiona indeendence	2697.8	36	0.000	0.219	2372.1
Model 2: Constant homogamy	74.3	27	0.000	0.027	−170.0
Model 3: Unidiffed homogamy	**34.5**	**24**	**0.076**	**0.015**	**−182.6**

(Unidiff parameter in Model3)

		1955–69	*1970–84*	*1985–99*	*2000–15*
		1	*1.14*	*0.98*	*0.75*

(B) Occupational homogamy

	G^2	df	*p*-value	I.D	BIC
Model 1: Conditiona indeendence	979.7	36	0.000	0.138	665.0
Model 2: Constant homogamy	41.4	27	0.038	0.022	-194.7
Model 3: Unidiffed homogamy	**24.0**	**24**	**0.462**	**0.017**	**-185.8**

(Unidiff parameter in Model3)

		1955–69	*1970–84*	*1985–99*	*2000–15*
		1	*0.99*	*0.71*	*0.72*

according to the uniform difference parameter in Model 3 shows that there was a fault line after the 1980s and that it also decreased.

In other words, we examined the cohort trends in educational and occupational homogamy among couples who married between the 1950s and the 2010s, and found a downward trend. Previous research has been divided between those that view the trend in Japan's status homogamy as stable and those that indicate a declining trend, but the results of a reanalysis using high-quality data covering new generations suggest that the latter view should be more appropriate.[12]

(2) Opportunities to meet and status homogamy

Figure 3.3 shows how the relationship between the opportunities and strength of the propensity for homogamy has changed among the marriage cohorts based on the uniform difference parameter for each type of main reason for meeting.[13]

The tendency of homogamy differs greatly depending on the reason for meeting. In terms of the uniform difference parameters, meeting at school was the most common in terms of educational homogamy, followed by introduction by neighbors and family members/relatives. In terms of occupational homogamy, the opportunities to meet through work was outstandingly high. The lowest values for both were opportunities to meet through hobbies and lessons.

The strength of homogamy for each trigger also varied among the marriage cohorts. The trend of decreasing educational homogamy is particularly pronounced in relation to opportunities to meet through friends and work. Although there were only two of six, the percentage of responses for those was on an upward trend as shown in Fig. 3.2, so it is likely that they were linked to the overall decrease in

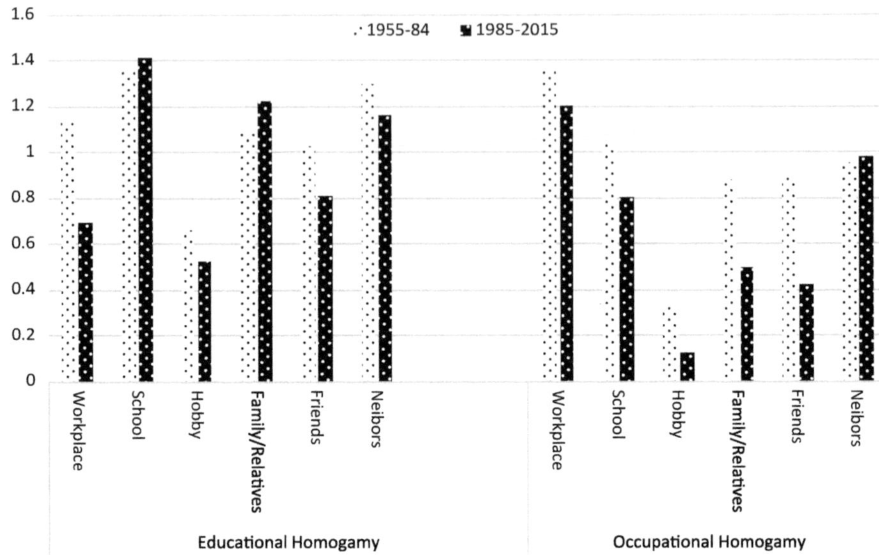

Fig. 3.3 Unidiff parameter estimates about the degree of homogamy

educational homogamy seen in the previous section. Occupational homogamy has been declining across the board in many of the opportunities to meet.[14] However, it is clear that occupational homogamy has also been on a downward trend in terms of meeting through friends and work, which has been on the rise especially since the 1980s. In this sense, the pattern is similar to the downward trend of educational homogamy.

Looking through the postwar period to recent years, we have seen a shift from an era in which opportunities to meet was mainly through family and neighbors to an era in which opportunities to meet is mainly through friends and work. Furthermore, the content of the downward trend in overall status homogamy was found to consist of a decrease in status homogamy in the two latter groups.

3.5 Summary and Conclusion

This chapter examines the relationship between marriage and social stratification in contemporary Japanese society, with a focus on status homogamy, and how this relationship has changed over time. The SSM survey data support the fact that the trend toward non-marriage and late marriage has been increasing. It has also been confirmed that the reason for meeting a spouse has changed to a more free-love style. In the midst of such changes, homogamy has also become less likely to occur, but this is a reflection of the fact that marriage itself has become less likely to occur, and it is not a phenomenon unique to homogamy. When we examined the structure and trends of status homogamy by focusing only on married couples, we found that homogamy decreased when the indices of status were occupation and education. In addition, in terms of professional relationships and friendships, which account for the majority of opportunities to meet, there was a decrease in status homogamy during this period, and these results contributed to the overall declining trend of status homogamy.

These results are generally consistent with predictions based on the romantic love hypothesis.[15] Our findings are more robust than previous findings, as we found that attainment of status homogamy declines when we manipulate not only the educational background of married couples but also their occupation at the time of marriage. The shift from arranged marriages to love marriages, and the change in the opportunity to meet from familial and territorial relationships to professional relationships and friendships, led to the undoing of the hierarchically closed nature of marriage spheres.

However, these changes in marriage and opportunities to meet have led to a decline in marriage itself. It has been a long time since it was shown that the decline of arranged marriages and workplace marriages was the cause of non-marriage in Japan (Iwasawa & Mita, 2005), and the marriage cohorts covered in this chapter were living in the midst of this transformation. It must be pointed out that the decline in the probability of experiencing a first marriage has been even more significant than the phenomenon of the decline in status homogamy among those who got married. The weakening of the system for matching prospective spouses, first of all through introductions from people with territorial and familial relationships, and then through the weakening of the function of professional relationships, has unintentionally created a major trend toward non-marriage and late marriage. However, among those who did marry, the result was that they were freer to choose a potential spouse from their hierarchical status than in previous eras. This concludes this chapter.

Will this trend continue in the future of Japanese society? It is very difficult to predict, but there are signs of change. In recent years, there have been two notable developments in the area of love and marriage. First, romantic relationships among young people may be becoming more inactive (Kobayashi and Kawabata 2019; The Japanese Association for Sex Education 2019). Second, new opportunities to meet, such as so-called "marriage activity sites" and matching apps, are becoming more widespread (Kobayashi & Nochi, 2016; Suzuki et al., 2018). Of these, the former may encourage non-marriage and late marriages, while the latter, which is an online matching system based on attributes, characteristics, and preferences, is likely to encourage more homogamy. Through these factors combined, the number of non-marriages may continue to increase and the number of status homogamy may start to increase. We will have to keep a close eye on this from the perspective of marriage and social stratification.

Notes

1. "SSM" stands for the national survey of Social Stratification and Mobility.
2. However, because the cohorts, data, and methods of analysis are different, the findings must be carefully compared and generalized.

3. Shirahase (2011) examines the relationship between the reasons for meeting and the respondents' educational background, and Yamamoto (1988) and Watanabe (1989) examine whether the degree of status homogamy changes depending on love or arranged marriage.
4. The 2015 SSM survey is very valuable for empirical analysis of marriage, as it was able to collect information on first marriages even for those who were separated, bereaved, or remarried, and even asked how they met their spouse at the time of their first marriage. However, there was a concern that the number of cases to be analyzed would be insufficient, so we decided to merge data from the 2005 SSM survey, which covers roughly the same generation and has the same survey methodology, according to the needs of the analysis.
5. The reason for adopting the occupation at the time of marriage instead of the current occupation is only because we want to capture the hierarchical status of the marriage when it occurred. In order to look at the phenomenon of marriage as an aspect of hierarchical cohesion, we thought it would be more appropriate to base our analysis on the information available at the time of marriage.
6. This means that where the adjusted cell residuals are statistically significant at the one-tailed test with a significance level of 1%, they are observed significantly more often than when the statuses of the husband and wife are independent.
7. The percentile value is a statistic that indicates the percentage of the population in the rankings, counting from the lowest value. For example, the 10th percentile value means that the position corresponds to the top 10% in order of decreasing value.
8. The statistical analysis of the ease of marriage requires some strategies. Some of the respondents (1) know how old they were married and (2) know they have not been married until their age at the time of the survey. In order to make an unbiased estimate of the likelihood of marriage in such circumstances, the application of a technique called event history analysis is key. The Cox regression analysis used in this chapter is one of the methods that belong to this category. For more information on event history analysis, see Yamaguchi (1991) and other publications. Blossfeld and Timm (2003) provide results of an important project that used event history analysis in an international comparative study of educational homogamy. In addition, Uchikoshi (2018) makes an important contribution in the form of a Japanese study that applied this method to elaborate on the trend of educational homogamy while also taking into account the increase in unmarried couples.
9. The difference in educational attainment is opposite to that in Shirahase (2011), but this is largely due to the fact that the analysis in this chapter controlled for the age of entry into first jobs, which changed the meaning to "how soon after entry into the workforce does marriage occur?"
10. Only marriages in which the couple had the same level of education were treated as event occurrences, while other marriages were treated as censored. The same procedure was used for the analysis of occupational homogamy.

11. However, if the model is subjected to equality constraints on the parameter-uniform difference, such that the values of the 1955–69 and 1970–84 marriage cohorts are equal, and the values of the 1985–99 and 2000–15 marriage cohorts are equal, the BIC is calculated to be –203.3. Therefore, even when we focused on this criterion, we judged that it was not unreasonable to claim that it supported the change in trend.
12. Even in overseas empirical studies, the results of trend analysis vary depending on the target country. In a comparative analysis of 10 Asian countries, there was a downward trend in educational homogamy (Smits & Park, 2009).
13. Here, we fixed the association pattern of homogamy (density parameter) to the result obtained in Model 3 in Table 3.3 of the previous section, and then estimated the uniform difference parameter as a free parameter. However, in order not to create estimation problems due to sparse cell frequencies, we merged the categories of marriage cohorts into two categories, 1955–1984 and 1985–2015.
14. Estimates of the uniform difference parameter for neighborhood referrals show an exceptionally invariant trend, but it is a relatively rare category and its impact on the total will be limited.
15. It would not be sufficient to test the hypothesis unless we also observe a decrease in the number of homogamy based on birthplace. This point has been confirmed by Miwa (2007a), although only for the marriage cohort from the 1950s to the 1990s.

Acknowledgements Permission was received from the 2015 SSM research committee for use of the SSM survey datasets.

References

Amano, I. (1983). Kyoiku no Chii Hyouji Kinou ni tsuite (Materialization Function of Educational Credential). *Kyoiku Shakaigaku Kenkyu (The Journal of Educational Sociology), 38*, 44–49. (in Japanese).

Blossfeld, H. P., & Timm, A. (Eds). (2003). *Who Marries Whom?: Educational Systems as Marriage Markets in Modern Societies*. Kluwer Academic Publishers.

Breen, R., & Jonsson, J. O. (2005). Inequality of opportunity in comparative perspective: recent research on educational attainment and social mobility. *Annual Review of Sociology, 31*, 223–243.

Iwasawa, M., & Mita, F. (2005). Shokuen Kekkon no Seisui to Mikonka no shinten (Trends in Job Marriages and the Progress of Unmarried Marriage). *Nohon Rodo Kenkyu Zasshi (The Japanese Journal of Labour Studies), 535*, 16–28. (in Japanese).

Kobayashi, J., & Kawabata, K. (Eds). (2019). *Henbou suru Renai to Kekkon (Transforming Love and Marriage)*, Shinyosha (in Japanese).

Kobayashi, J., & Nochi, C. (2016). Konkatsu ni okeru Kekkon no Kitei Youin ha Nanika? (What are Determinants of Marriage in Marriage Hunting?). *Riron to Houhou (sociological Theory and Methods), 31*(1), 70–83. (in Japanese).

Miwa, S. (2007a). "Long-term Trends in Status Homogamy," Yoshimichi Sato ed., *Deciphering Stratification and Inequality*, Trans Pacific Press, 140–160.

Miwa, S. (2007b). Nihon to Kankoku ni okeru Kaisou Douruikon no Hendou (The Variation of Status Homogamy in Japan and Korea). *Shakaigaku Kenkyu (The Study of Sociology), 81*, 67–92. (in Japanese).

Mizuochi, M. (2006). Gakusotsu Tyokugo no Koyou Joutai ga Kekkon Taimingu ni Ataeru Eikyou (The Impact of Employment Status Right After Graduation on Marriage Timing). *Seikatsu Keizaigaku Kenkyu (journal of Personal Finance and Economics), 22–23*, 167–176.

Nihon Seikyouiku Kyoukai (Ed). (2019). *Wakamono no Sei Hakusho: Dai 8 Kai Seishounen no Sei Koudou Zenkoku Tysousa Houkoku (White Paper on "Sexual Behavior in Youth": Report of the 8th National Survey on Sexual Behavior in Youth)*, Shougakukan (in Japanese).

Raymo, J. M., & Yu, X. (2000). Temporal and regional variation in the strength of educational homogamy. *American Sociological Review, 65*(5), 773–781.

Shida, K., Seiyama, K., & Watanabe, H. (2000). "Kekkon Shijou no Henyou (Transformation in Marriage Market)," In: Seiyama, K. (Ed.), *Nihon no Kaisou Shisutemu 4: Jenda, Shijou, Kazoku (Strara System in Japan 4: Gender, Market, Family)* (pp. 159–176). Tokyo Daigaku Shuppankai (in Japanese).

Shirahase, S. (2011). Shoshika Jidai no Kaisou Kouzou: Kaisou Ketsugou to shiteno Kekkon ni Chakumoku Shite (Strata Structure in the Era of Low Birth Rate: Focusing on Marriage as Status Homogamy). In: H. Ishida, H. Kondo, & K. Nakao (Eds.), *Gendai no Kaisou Shakai 2: Kaisou to Idou no Kouzou (Strata Socity in Contemporary Japan 2: Structure of Stratification and Mobility)* (pp. 317–333) Tokyo Daigaku Shuppankai (in Japanese).

Sawako, S., & Ishida, H. (2018). Shoushi Kourei Shakai ni okeru Shakai Kaisou to Raifu Kosu (Social Stratification and Life Course in an Aging and Low Birth Rate Society). *Riron to Houhou (sociological Theory and Methods), 33*(2), 185–201. (in Japanese).

Smits, J. (2003). Social closure among the higher educated: trends in educational homogamy in 55 countries. *Social Science Research, 32*, 251–277.

Smits, J., & Park, H. (2009). Five decades of educational assortative mating in 10 East Asian societies. *Social Forces, 88*(1), 227–255.

Suzuki, S., Sudo, K., Terada, Y., & Oguro, M. (2018). Gakureki, Shunyu, Youshi ga Seikon to Haiguusha Sentaku Koudou ni Ataeru Eikyou (The Effects of Educational Attainment, Income, and Appearance on Success in Marriage Hunting and on Behavior of Partner Selection). *Riron to Houhou (sociological Theory and Methods), 33*(2), 167–181. (in Japanese).

Tsuya, N. (2009). Gakureki to Koyou Anteisei no Paatonaashippu Keisei heno Eikyou (Education, Regular Employment, and Partnership Formation in Japan). *Jinko Mondai Kenkyu (journal of Population Problems), 65*(2), 45–63. (in Japanese).

Uchikoshi, F. (2018). Mikonka Jidai ni okeru Kaisou Ketsugou (Assortative Mating in the Age of Marriage Decline). *Riron to Houhou (sociological Theory and Methods), 33*(1), 15–31. (in Japanese).

Watanabe, H. (1989). Haigusha Sentaku ni okeru Shokugyou Renkan (Association between Husband's and Wife's Occupation in Partner Selection). In: 1985-nen Shakai Kaisou to Idou Zenkoku Chousa Iinkai (ed.), *1985-nen Shakai Kaisou to Idou Zenkoku Chousa Houkokusho 4: Josei to Shakai Kaisou (Report of the 1985 National Survey of Social Stratification and Mobility 4: Women and Social Stratification)* (pp. 97–116) (in Japanese).

Watanabe, H., & Kondo, H. (1990) Kekkon to Kaisou Ketsugou (Marriage and Status Homogamy). In: H. Okamoto, & M. Naoi (Eds.), *Gendai Nihon no Kaisou Kouzou 4 Josei to Shakai Kaisou (Strara Stracture in Contemporary Japan 4: Women and Social Stratification)* (pp. 119–145) Tokyo Daigaku Shuppankai (in Japanese).

Yamada, M. (Ed). (2010). *Konkatsu Gensyou no Syakaigaku (Sociological Thinking about Phenomenon of Marriage Hunting)*, Touyou Keizai Shinpou Sha.

Yamaguchi, K. (1991). *Event History Analysis*, Sage (in Japanese).

Yamamoto, T. (1988). Kaisou Naikon ni tsuite no Kiso Bunseki (Basic Analysis about Status Endogamy). In: 1985-nen Shakai Kaisou to Idou Zenkoku Chousa Iinkai (ed.), *1985-nen Shakai Kaisou to Idou Zenkoku Chousa Houkokusho 1: Shakai Kaisou no Kouzou to Katei (Report of*

the 1985 National Survey of Social Stratification and Mobility 1: The Structure and Process of Social Stratification) (pp. 179–194) (in Japanese).
Yasuda, S., & Hara, J. (1982). *Shakai Chosa Handobukku (Handbook of Social Research) (Third edition)*, Yuuhikaku (in Japanese).

Satoshi Miwa is Professor of Sociology in the Institute of Social Science at the University of Tokyo, Japan. He received his Ph.D. in Behavioral Science from Tohoku University in 2006. He is involved in the Social Science Japan Data Archive (SSJDA) of the University of Tokyo, the largest data archive in Japan distributing survey data for scientific use. His research interests include social stratification and mobility, sociology of education, family sociology, longitudinal data analysis, and quantitative sociological methodology including survey methods. He is editor of *Jinsei shoki no Kaisou Kouzou (Social Stratification Structure at the Early Stage of Life), Nihon no Shakai Kaisou to sono Mekanizumu (Social Stratification and its Mechanism in Japan)*, and more.

Chapter 4
Relative Indices of Educational Attainment and Trend Analysis of Inequality of Educational Opportunity Using the 2015 SSM Survey Data

Takayasu Nakamura

Abstract This study was an examination of some of the relative indices of educational attainment and analyses the long-term trend of inequality of educational opportunity in Japan using those indices. The data revealed four points, as follows: (1) Three indices were mainly used to describe the trend of inequality of educational opportunity in Japan for this study. SYS was found to be the best choice as a relative index of educational attainment. (2) According to these three indices, the trend of educational opportunity in Japan is stable, but the youngest cohort of men revealed a growing disparity of educational opportunity among social classes. (3) These trends were confirmed by an analysis using a generalized ordered logit model, although the trend among males in their 20 s needs to be closely examined by further research. (4) It was found that a simple description of the inequality trend according to the relative education index presented a rough picture of the reality of inequality of educational opportunity.

4.1 Introduction

There are various analytical perspectives from which to examine issues of education and social class, among which "inequality of educational opportunity" has become one of the most typical research themes. Of course, as many studies in the sociology of education have shown, it is realistically difficult to attain complete equality of educational opportunity; research has therefore taken the existence of inequalities in educational opportunity as given, and focused its discussion on such topics as (1) what kind of mechanisms produce inequalities in educational opportunity, and (2) whether educational opportunities have become, as a trend, more open or closed. (1)

This chapter, a slightly modified and translated version of the original article (Nakamura, 2018), was reproduced with the original publisher's permission.

T. Nakamura (✉)
Graduate School of Education, The University of Tokyo, 7-3-1 Hongo, Bunkyo-ku, Tokyo 113-0033, Japan
e-mail: tnaka@p.u-tokyo.ac.jp

S. Shirahase (ed.), *Social Stratification in an Aging Society with Low Fertility*, Economy and Social Inclusion, https://doi.org/10.1007/978-981-19-3647-0_4

has produced studies based on so-called reproduction theory (Bourdieu & Passerron 1970, Bowles & Gintis, 1976, etc.) and rational choice theory (Boudon, 1973; Breen & Goldthorpe, 1997, etc.); (2) has yielded an accumulation of quantitative trend analyses.

In particular, the trend analysis of educational opportunity, as in (2), has been an obligatory topic that appears without fail whenever a survey is conducted for the SSM (Social Stratification and Social Mobility) project, which has produced data on social class over a long period in Japan (Imada, 1979, Fujita, 1979, Ojima, 1990, Aramaki, 2000, Kondō & Furuta, 2009, 2011; Hirasawa, 2011, etc.). In keeping with that, in this paper, I will examine this issue from various perspectives using the latest SSM survey data from 2015.

Such trend analyses of educational opportunity have long found that class differences are stably maintained even across countries (Shavit & Blossfeld, Eds., 1993). However, the finding that inequality of educational opportunity has narrowed, as indicated by the international comparative analysis of Breen et al., has invited debate in recent years (Breen et al., 2009).

One of the issues raised in critical arguments against Breen et al. is the point that in trying to understand levels of education categorically, we may be failing to grasp changes in their relative meaning (Shavit & Park, 2016), i.e., the importance of adequately considering the changes in the relative meaning of educational attainment caused by the expansion of education. This is because educational opportunity can display different trends depending on how it is approached. It is understandably out of such concerns that *Research in Social Stratification and Mobility* compiled a special feature called "Education as a positional good." Certainly, for researchers from European countries, which have seen the rapid expansion of higher education in recent years and changes in the relative meaning of educational attainment, this perspective must have had a corresponding reality.

Kondō and Furuta (2009, 2011) have conducted a trend analysis of educational opportunity using data from Japan that takes into account what is being discussed internationally, as well as changes in the relative value of educational attainment. However, an excellent study by Fujihara and Ishida (2016) goes further by using a comparative examination of the value of relative educational attainment and absolute educational attainment to clearly show the differences in the results obtained by each measure. They examined trends in educational opportunity using data from the SSM and JLPS surveys until 2005. The results of their analysis show that inequality declines over the long term when an index of educational attainment that has an absolute meaning is used, such as years of schooling, but when a relative index of educational attainment is used, it changes from stable to slightly growing.

Like Kondō and Furuta (2009, 2011), Fujihara and Ishida (2016) conducted a trend analysis of educational opportunity that takes into account the relative meaning of educational attainment using a generalized ordered logit model, whose threshold can be assumed to differ with each cohort. Their results clearly show the model's effectiveness in approaching this problem.

Some have analyzed the trends in educational opportunity using the 2015 SSM Survey. According to Nakazawa, who analyzed the trends in educational opportunity a traditional way by merging the data from the 2015 SSM Survey and JLPS data and using the generalized ordered logit model, social class inequality of educational opportunity was basically persistent (Nakazawa, 2017).

Fujihara and Ishida (2017) examined the trends in educational opportunity within the OED triangle structure. They also indicated that the association between O and E was stable in general both in a categorical analysis (loglinear model) and in a quantitative analysis (structural equation model). On the other hand, Fujihara (2018) examined the trends in educational opportunity through several approaches, including a general trend analysis using the ordered logit model. Only the male data are used here, but he argued that although inequality of educational opportunity caused by father's academic background and inequality of educational opportunity caused by father's occupation are stable depending on what indexes to use, they tend to decrease in the long term, confirming the findings by Breen et al. (2009) and Kondo and Furuta (2009, 2011). At the same time, he points out that inequality tends to widen among the youngest generation.

However, as its complex statistical processing can make it difficult to read the meaning of changes in numerical values, intuitive and simple indices like a "university-level education" dummy variable and years of schooling are also useful in another sense. If we consider the need to incorporate changes in the relative meaning of educational attainment into the analysis, it would arguably be worthwhile to examine indices of educational attainment that are simple yet reflect changes in meaning, even in research tasks independent of trend analyses of educational opportunity like these.

To that end, in this study, I will illustrate trends in educational opportunity in a simple way and conduct a fundamental trend analysis by examining multiple indices of educational attainment that indicate relative position. In addition, I will conduct a generalized ordered logit model analysis and OLS to ascertain if the trends found therein are substantiated by other methods. This will show that the general outline of trends can be described effectively with simple indices.

4.2 Education System and Educational Opportunity in Post-War Japan

Before getting into the specifics of the relative indices of educational attainment and the trend analysis of educational opportunities in Japan, I want to explain the social context of Japan. This is because the analysis of educational opportunities based on relative educational attainment indicators has a more realistic context in contemporary Japan than in the West.

The context is the hierarchical structure of the university system and the long-term rise in the percentage of students going to university.

In Japan, it has long been pointed out that social benefits differ depending on the type of university one graduates from. For example, according to Ozaki, starting salaries for university graduates in the pre-war period differed depending on the university, and there was also a large disparity in employment opportunities among universities (Ozaki, 1967). Although such overt disparities have been eliminated in modern times, there are still considerable differences in the opportunities for initial employment and in the social evaluation associated with being a graduate of a particular university. And because of these differences, "which university you attend" is still considered to be of great value to high school students and prospective students. Universities with higher status are more popular, which inevitably leads to fiercer competition in the entrance examinations and higher difficulty in admission. This index of difficulty in entering universities ("Hensachi",[1] in Japanese) has also been the index for ranking universities. In Japan, therefore, it has been practiced for a long time to consider the academic background as "school background" (Amano, 1982), and attempts have been made for a long time to incorporate this inter-university gap as a variable in the analysis of educational opportunities and status attainment (Ando, 1979, Ojima, 1990, Nakanishi, 2000, Hirasawa, 2011, Fujihara and Ishida, 2017 etc.). As will be explained later, the use of university classification in the analysis of this chapter is also due to this background.

At the same time, the value of a university degree itself has changed significantly over the long term, as Japan was the first country to popularize higher education after the U.S., even earlier than Europe. In the mid-1960s, Japan's university enrollment rate reached the mass stage pointed out by Trow (1974), and in the 1990s, it entered the universal stage. Therefore, the meaning of a college degree has changed dramatically over time, and more specifically, its relative value has declined. There are three factors behind this.

The first is that the high economic growth of the postwar period provided households with the financial means to send their children to university.

The second is the declining birthrate. The total fertility rate as of 2020 is 1.36, and the number of school-aged children is expected to continue to decline. This trend of declining birth rates is a major problem for society as a whole, but from the perspective of educational opportunities alone, it is a good thing. Even if the number of children decreases, the number of educational institutions will not decrease drastically, making it easier for students to go on to higher education. This is a factor that has pushed up the rate of higher education.

The third is education policy. In 1991, the Japanese government deregulated the establishment of universities, and the number of universities jumped from 514 in 1991 to 803 in 2021, a roughly 1.6-fold increase. In other words, the number of universities was increased on a policy basis even though it was known that the birthrate would

---

[1] Hensachi is calculated using the following equation.

$$\text{Hensachi} = 10 \times \{(\hat{\imath} - \text{mean})/\text{standard deviation}\} + 50.$$

Statistically speaking, this is the application of the Z score. This calculation was contrived by a junior high school teacher, Shouzou Kuwata, and has been used in Japan since the 1960s. Most mock examinations for high school and university entrance continue to use it today to calculate the probability of passing the examination. Most applicants for high school and university focus a great deal of attention on raising their hensachi. This index is used to calculate the average score of successful applicants to the entrance exam and is used to rank many schools.

decline. As the declining birthrate generation reached the age of college enrollment, this policy spurred an increase in the college enrollment rate.

Figure 4.1 shows the changes in the number of students and the university enrollment rate in postwar Japan. This graph shows the rapid and long-term decline in the number of children in postwar Japan and the large increase in the rate of university enrollment. Japan has always had a university system with a hierarchical structure that does not allow the issue of educational opportunities to be discussed only in terms of the difference between school stages (ex. high school graduates/university graduates), but at the same time, there has been an expansion of the university enrollment rate that has reduced the value of university graduates over the long term. This is why it has been taken for granted in research to consider the meaning of education

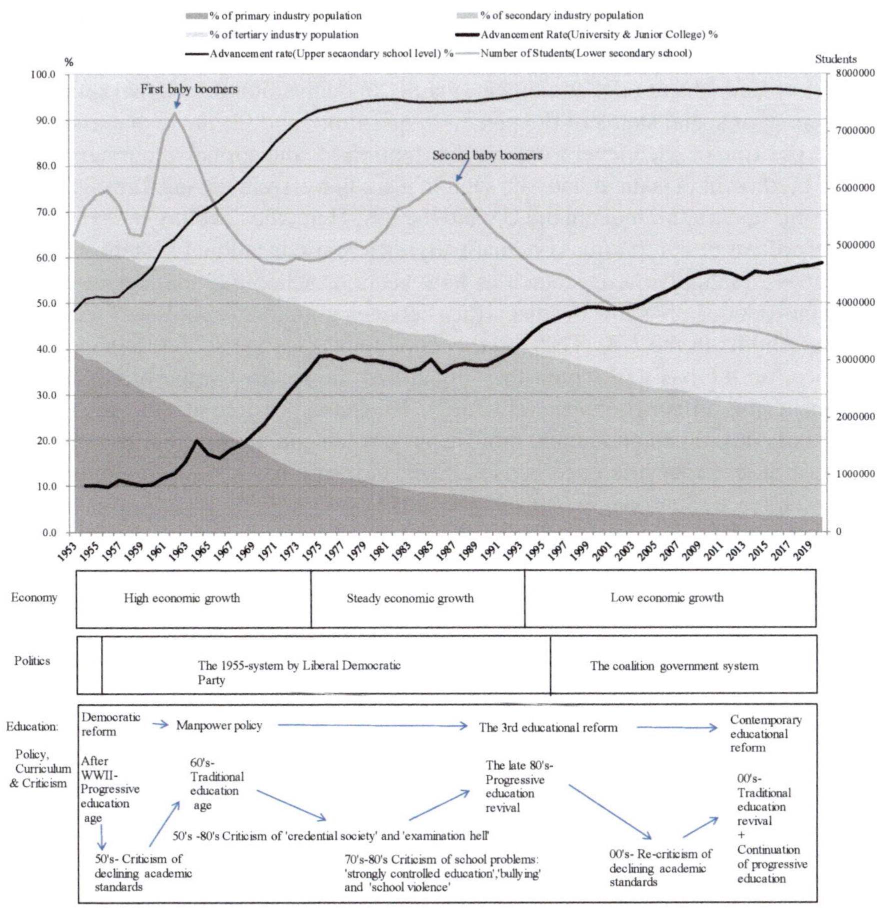

Fig. 4.1 Social change and education in Post-War Japan. *Data Sources* Ministry of Education, Culture, Sports, Science and Technology. *School Basic Survey*. Statistical Survey Department, Statistics Bureau, Ministry of Internal Affairs and Communications. *Labour Force Survey*

relative to the same education and the changes in its value over time when dealing with issues of educational opportunity and education, and this has been the case long before the rise of the view of education as "positional goods" in international discussions. One proof of this is the fact that concepts such as "the symbolic values of education" by Havighurst (1961) and "the status-indicating function of education" by Amano (1983) have often been used in the sociology of education in Japan. It is in the Japanese context that the issue of relative educational attainment is most relevant.

4.3 Examining Relative Indices of Educational Attainment

Different studies take different approaches to indexing educational attainment, but they can be broadly divided into two categories: (1) those that evaluate the relative position of said educational attainment, mainly in connection to external references (the income or social status of the person in question), and (2) those that assign the relative position of each level from the distribution of educational attainment itself.

The method in (1) can already be seen in a study by Treiman and Terrell (1975), comparing status attainment in the US and the UK. Here, they explore indexing from the perspective of comparing systematically different educational system variables and discuss qualitative issues, such as how years of schooling and school-leaving age cannot adequately show the disparities between grammar schools and secondary modern schools in the UK. They used occupational prestige scores as an external reference, on the basis of which they quantified the relative value of educational attainment (the "effect-proportional scale"). Thus, it is possible to show the relative position of educational attainment more clearly, when comparing countries or points in time if an external reference is used. Such indexing has also been attempted in recent years (e.g., Schröder & Ganzeboom, 2014); however, its usefulness is limited, as an analysis that incorporates subjects' process of status attainment ends up using the variable to be explained in the first place to index the explanatory variable. Therefore, in this study, I will examine indices of educational attainment from the orientation in (2).

In recent years, the PSI (Positional Status Index, Tam, 2007) is sometimes referred to as one such distribution-based index. According to Tam, the PSI is shown by a simple equation like the one below.

$$\mathrm{PSI}_k = \frac{P_k}{1 - P_k}$$

k represents a certain level of educational attainment, and P_k represents the proportion of those whose educational attainment has not reached k. The denominator $1 - P_k$ is therefore the proportion of those with educational attainment of k or greater. In essence, if we look at someone's educational attainment in terms of rankings, this is an index of the odds that someone else is lower than them versus being equal to or higher than them. According to Tam himself, this index has several convenient properties. For example, the PSI is more palpably understandable than indices that create latent variables, as it shows the average number of people who must compete with each other to attain *k*, and it gives meaning to values of 0, among others. It also has properties that are convenient for statistical work—for example, lnPSI, the natural log of PSI can be freely input into regression equations to perform interval regression analysis (Tam, 2007, 2013). As such, I would also like to try to describe trends using the PSI in this study. However, in this case, it is necessary to note that this strongly assumes that it is possible to rank various categories of educational attainment in a unified way.

Besides PSI, other examples of indexing the relative meaning of educational assessment include studies that use percentile rank (PR) (Bukodi & Goldthorpe, 2013). PR simply quantifies the percentage of people below a given person. For example, if 30% of people are college graduates, then the PR of a college graduate is 70. The index seems difficult to understand at first glance, but it does show the relative position of the category in question and is also sometimes used to display TOEFL and GMAT results, so it may be familiar in the West as well. In any case, as it is a simple index that is easy to work with, and there are examples of its use, I will try to examine it in this study also. Note that this index is also based on the premise that it is possible to rank categories of educational attainment in a unified way.

In this study, I will also consider a novel method of standardizing years of schooling for each generation (Standardized Years of Schooling, SYS) and attempt to use it as an index.

$$\mathrm{SYS}_k = \frac{Y_k - \overline{Y}}{s}$$

Y_k represents years of schooling at category k, and $\overline{Y}$ represents the total average of years of schooling. S means standard deviation of them. This is exactly the standardization of years of schooling.

Using years of schooling has the merit of providing different information than categorical indices for education. At the same time, I have considered the fact that assigning a point value yields a variable that is easy to work with and also useful for analyses for various purposes. I will describe specifically how the index was created in the next section.

4.4 Data, Variables, and Method

The tertiary distribution of the 2015 SSM survey data (SSM2015_v070_20170227.sav) was used for this study. The subjects of the 2015 SSM survey, which was conducted between January and July 2015, were men and women of Japanese nationality between 20–79 years old (born between 1935 and 1994) living in Japan at the end of December 2014. A total of 7,817 valid responses were received, resulting in a valid response rate of 50.1% (Shirahase, 2018).

Variables used in the analysis include, firstly, the father's level of education, which is used as an index of original social class. It is represented as one of three levels in reference to the classifications that are sometimes used to describe trends. I will describe the extent to which this affects educational attainment by sex and age group.

The indices used for educational attainment were the relative indices of (1) PSI, (2) lnPSI, (3) PR, and (4) SYS and, for comparison, the absolute indices of (5) years of schooling, (6) three levels of educational attainment, (7) four levels of educational attainment, and (8) six levels of educational attainment.

For (1)–(4), it is necessary to define the group (generation) from which to calculate the variable. As the expansion of education is a trend that varies by sex, these must be calculated separately for males and females. In addition, in the interest of ensuring a fixed sample size, people up to five years younger and older (a total span of eleven years) were included in the calculation for each sex, and the result of the calculation was assigned to the center of that age group. Specifically, PSI, PR, and SYS were calculated for each sex with a target group from n–5 years to $n + 5$ years, and those results were assigned to all n-year-old samples of the group. (2) lnPSI is simply the natural log of (1) PSI. All of the educational attainment categories used in the calculations were taken from six categories, namely, those who have completed or graduated from (a) middle school or lower, (b) high school, (c) vocational school, (d) junior or technical college, (e) general university, and (f) prestigious university, medical school, or graduate school.[2] In ascending order, the years of schooling used for (4) and (5) were 9, 12, 14, 14, 16, and 18. (4) SYS is the standardized value of these numbers of years of schooling within the 11-year age group that includes the samples in question. As the value changes ever so slightly with each year of age difference even between people with the same educational attainment, it is thus an extremely fine-grained index. The same is true for (1)–(3). However, as (4) is standardized, the average educational attainment within that generation is expressed as 0, with positive numbers indicating above-average and negative numbers indicating below-average attainment. That is to say, it makes it possible to intuitively understand changes in the relative position of educational attainment from the plus or minus sign and absolute value of the variable.

[2] What was coded as the "prestigious university" level corresponds to the "universityI" category in Fujihara and Ishida (2016) and specifically includes national and public universities as well as private research universities. The "general university" level consists of those who did not attend a "prestigious university," were not in a graduate program, and did not study medicine. The private research institutions, which the aforementioned paper does not mention by name, are as follows: Aoyama Gakuin University, Keio University, International Christian University, Sophia University, Chuo University, Tsuda University, Tokyo University of Agriculture, Tokyo University of Science, Nippon Medical School, Japan Women's University, Hosei University, Meiji University, Rikkyo University, Waseda University, Doshisha University, Ritsumeikan University, Kansai University, and Kwansei Gakuin University. This information was provided directly by Shō Fujihara, co-author of the aforementioned paper. For that, as well as for giving me valuable advice about previous research and the generalized ordered logit model, I would like to take this opportunity to express my thanks.

(6)–(8) indicate educational attainment in terms of categories. (6) consists of those who have completed (a) compulsory education, (b) secondary education, and (c) higher education, the same three levels used for the father's level of education. (7) further divides (6c) higher education into (a) short-term higher education and (b) university or above. (8) divides (7b) university or above into two further levels and consists of the same six categories of educational attainment as those used to calculate the PSI.

Using the above variables, I will proceed with my analysis below as follows. First, I will provide an overview of the distribution and features of the data with regard to relative indices of educational attainment (1)–(4). Secondly, I will use indices (1)–(5) to describe trends in the effect of inherited social class on educational opportunity by sex and age group. In addition, I will examine indices intended for simple trend descriptions. Thirdly, in order to more clearly describe trends in disparities in educational opportunity among social classes with a single index, I will use the $\eta 2$ (eta-squared) correlation coefficient to examine continuous variables and the γ (gamma) coefficient to examine categorical variables. Finally, I will examine the extent to which the trends in disparities in educational opportunity, thus discovered, agree with the results produced by an international-level multivariate analysis method (specifically, the generalized ordered logit model). I would like to confirm the robustness of this trend analysis and show the effectiveness of the relative indices of educational attainment used in this study.

4.5 Features of Each Relative Index of Educational Attainment

4.5.1 Distribution of PSI and Its Changes

Figures 4.2 and 4.3 show the frequency distributions of PSI and lnPSI and make it possible to grasp the characteristics of these indices. As is clear from Fig. 4.2, PSI is an index that can easily produce a distribution concentrated around 0. The calculation assigns people with the lowest level of educational attainment a value of 0, and in a country like Japan, where there are very few people at the lowest level (middle school graduate), the next highest level, i.e. high school, is also close to 0. If we consider tendencies such as this, we may be hesitant to use PSI for simple trend descriptions.

Compared to PSI, lnPSI (in Fig. 4.3) follows a normal distribution and looks like it can be included as an explanatory variable in OLS without issues, as Tam explains. However, it must be noted that if PSI is concentrated around 0, as in Japan's case, values of lnPSI will be distributed with a concentration at a certain low value.

Figure 4.4 shows the change in the relative meaning of educational attainment, with age along the horizontal axis, by calculating PSI for each education level. It also shows that having completed university or above was an extremely rare case for

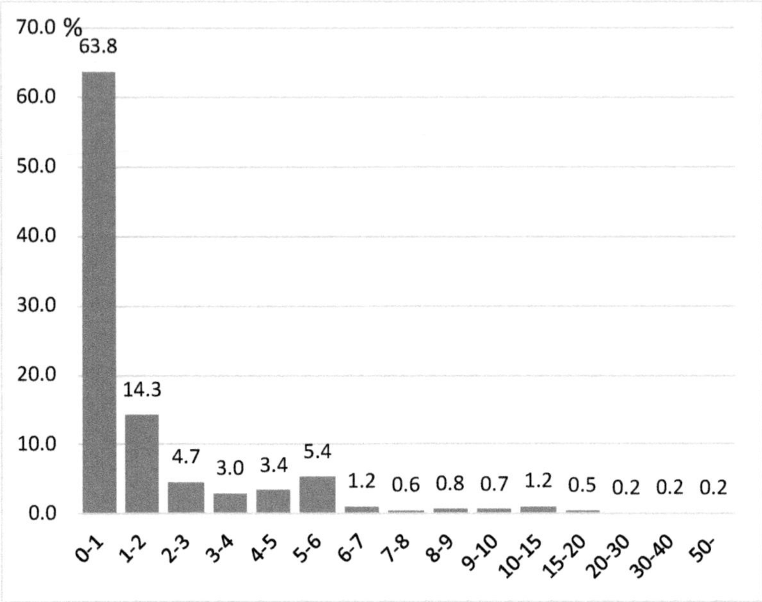

Fig. 4.2 PSI frequency distribution

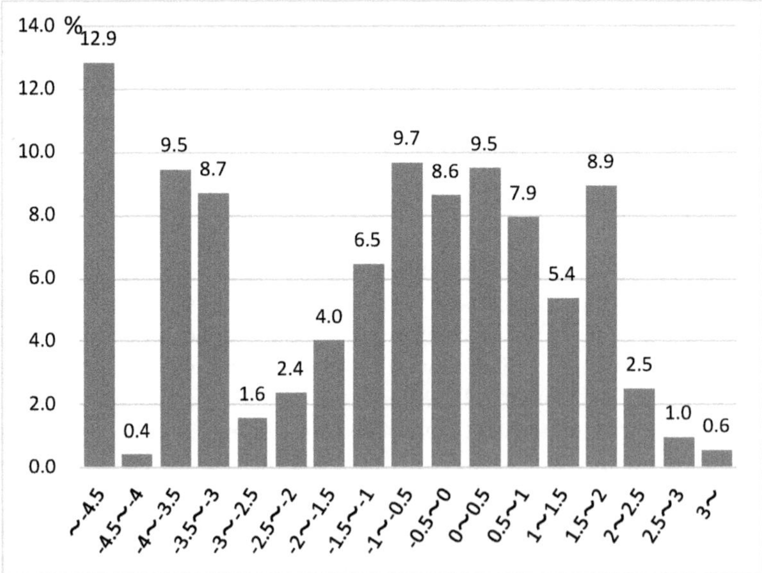

Fig. 4.3 ln PSI frequency distribution

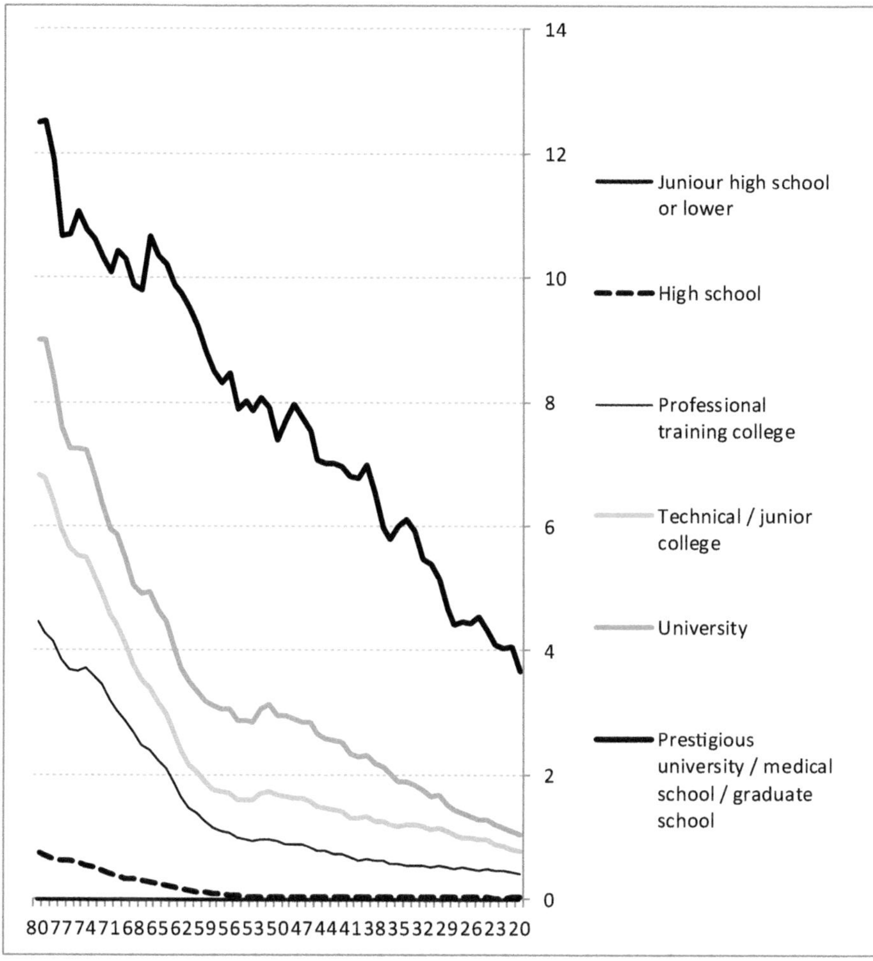

Fig. 4.4 Changes in PSI by level of education

higher age groups. It can also be seen from this graph that the relative value of each educational level decreases as age decreases.

4.5.2 Distribution of PR and Its Changes

Figure 4.5 shows the frequency distribution of PR. PR is scattered in terms of numerical values, though as expected, the calculation produced a value of 0 for the lowest level of education and a value close to 0 for the next higher level as well, if there

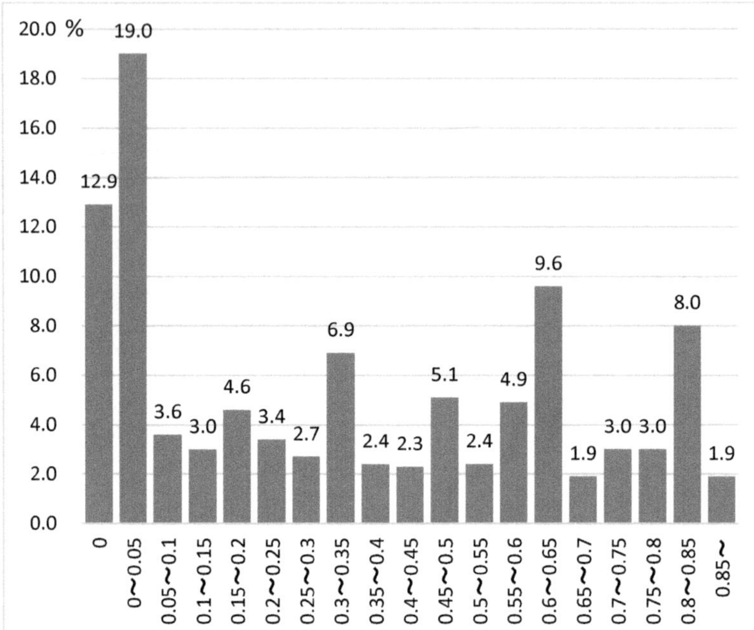

Fig. 4.5 PR frequency distribution

were few samples at the lowest level. This can be considered a demerit with regard to trend description.

Figure 4.6 shows the trends in changes in PR. Here, it once again shows that the position of a university or higher level of education used to be relatively high. Meanwhile, it is problematic that as the PR of high school graduates is close to 0, high school graduates, who occupy a certain proportion of the population, could only be assigned a value of nearly 0. It is the same situation as PSI.

4.5.3 Distribution of SYS and Its Changes

Figure 4.7 shows the frequency distribution of SYS, which can be seen to approach a standard distribution overall, being a standardized variable to begin with. For this reason, SYS, by its nature, can arguably be incorporated relatively freely into various analyses.

Figure 4.8 shows changes in aggregate standardized years of schooling (SYS) by age. As the number of years of schooling for both technical/junior college and vocational school were coded as 14 for this analysis, their graphs overlap completely,

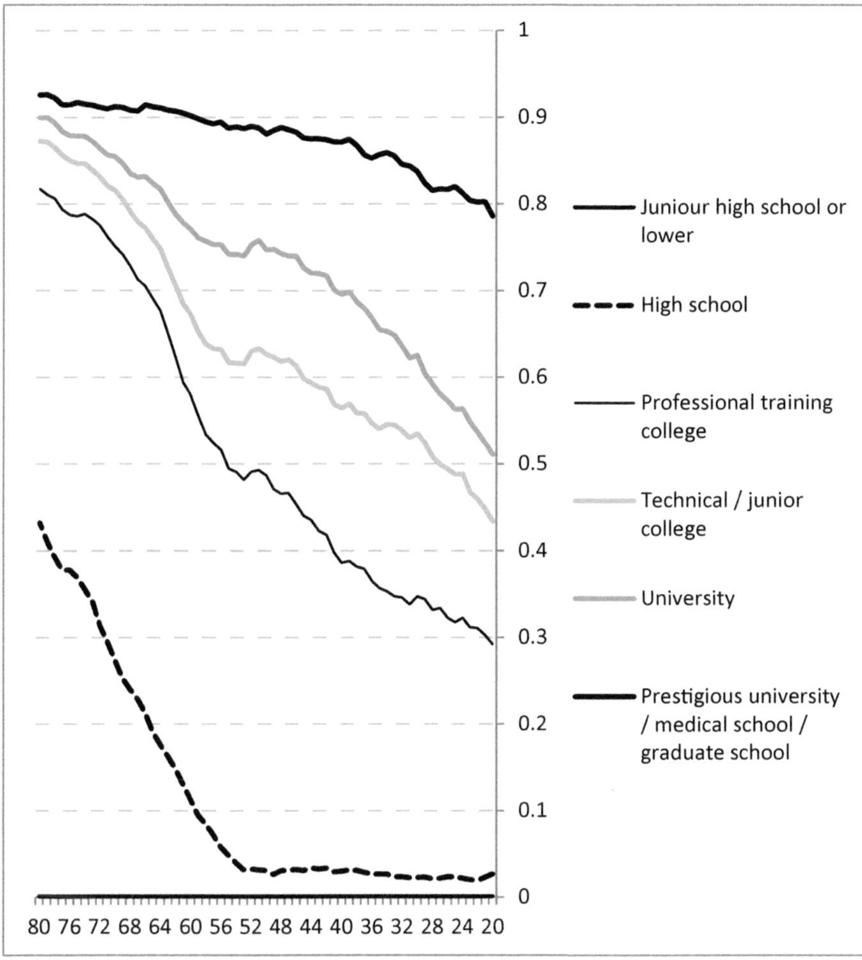

Fig. 4.6 Changes in PR by level of education

which is problematic.[3] The distance *between* educational levels is more difficult to understand through SYS than PSI and PR, due to the process of standardization, but what distinguishes SYS is that because 0 indicates the average level of education of each age group, it is possible to understand the relative position of each level by looking at it in terms of how far it is from 0. For example, it can be seen that high school education was about average for people in the 72-year-old age group, but far below average for younger; and it is also easy to understand that the expansion of higher education has lowered the positions of all levels of educational attainment

[3] However, technically speaking, it is possible to aggregate years of schooling at the individual level from SSM data, so that should also be followed up on and indexed in the future. I have done only a provisional treatment of the data for this study, but I would like to make this a future research task.

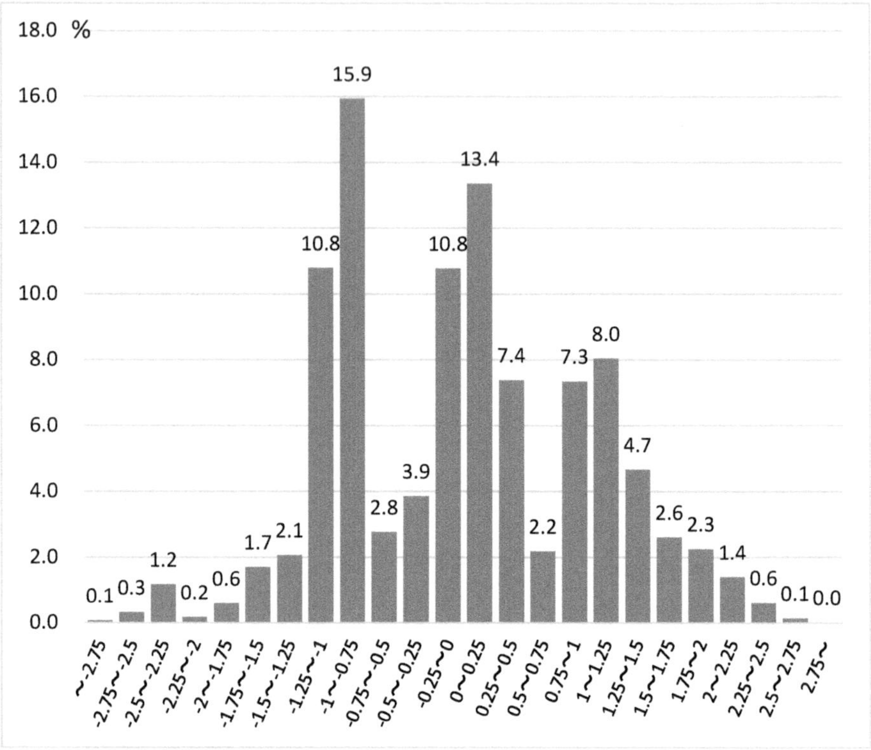

Fig. 4.7 SYS frequency distribution

across the board, including junior high school-only, which could not be analyzed by PSI and PR. Lastly, if we compare the SYS position of high school with its PSI and PR, they have a tendency to be slightly underestimated, as high school graduates in younger age groups are assigned a value close to that of junior high school graduates. On this point, SYS corresponds more closely to reality.

4.6 Trends in Educational Opportunity Shown by Each Relative Index of Educational Attainment

Moving on, let us take a look at how each index illustrates the trend in educational opportunity for each of the inherited social classes defined by the three categories for father's level of education (compulsory, secondary, and higher education).

Disparities in PSI between generations cannot be said to have sharply reduced based on Fig. 4.9. As we will see below, this is because such reductioncan be denied by other indices, analyses, or previous studies. Consequently, it is considered inappropriate to use PSI to describe disparities between social classes. Meanwhile, it

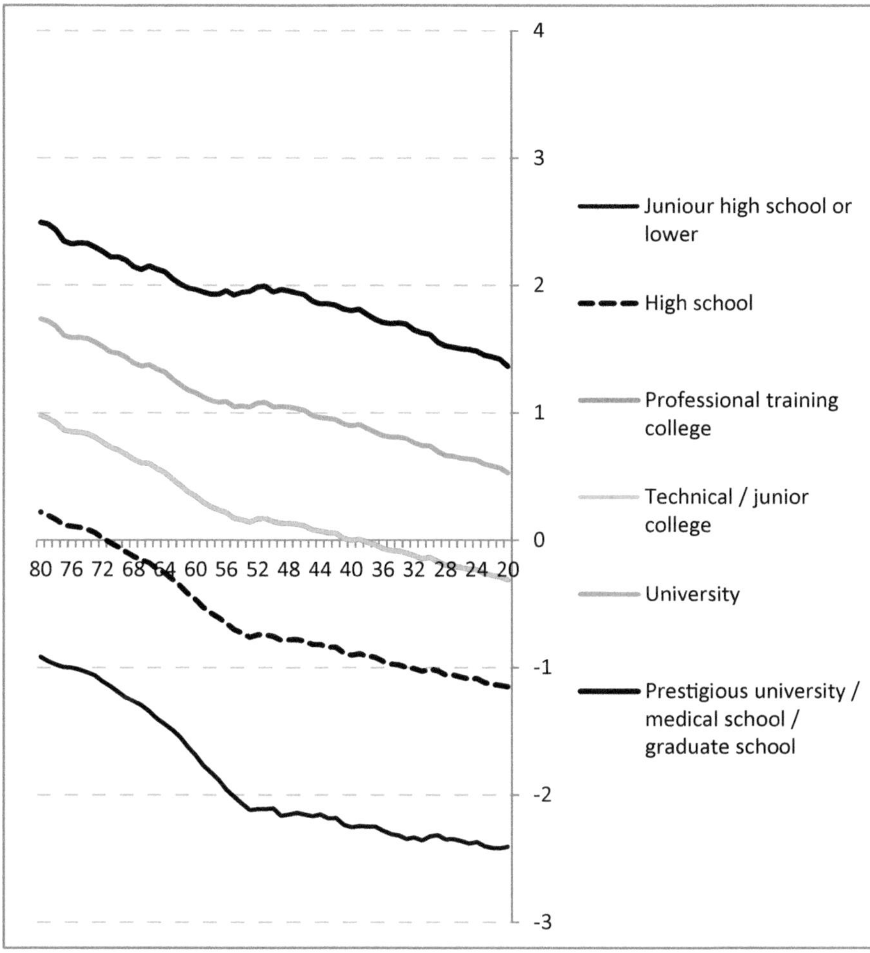

Fig. 4.8 Changes in SYS by level of education

appears that lnPSI (Fig. 4.10) may yield a more reasonable description. However, converting to logs makes the meanings of the numbers themselves very difficult to understand, and furthermore, the graph of the compulsory education level fluctuates widely, so the extent to which a trend can be read from it is questionable.

The shapes of the PR and SYS graphs in Figs. 4.11 and 4.12 look quite similar. In both graphs, the values themselves can be interpreted concretely, and the graphs express a stable trend in class disparities in educational opportunity over the medium and long-term (i.e., the distance between the three lines is constant to a large extent), while at the same time showing that the relative position of educational attainment has decreased overall due to the expansion of education. Both PR and SYS seem to show that in particular, educational attainment among people in their twenties (the youngest age group) whose fathers have only completed compulsory education,

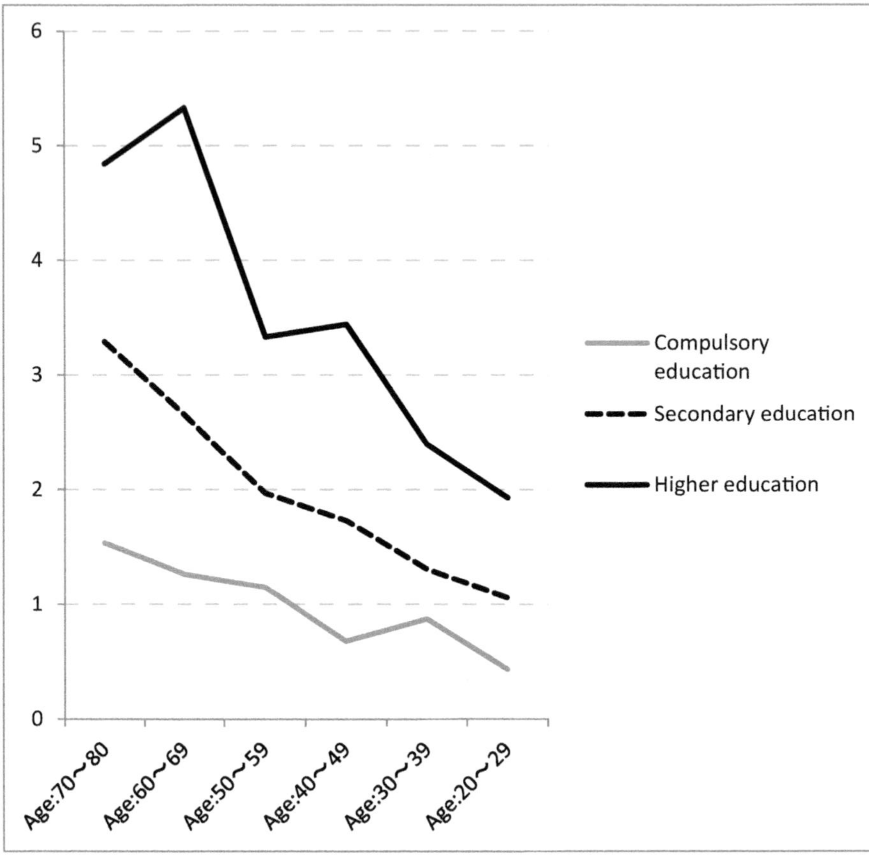

Fig. 4.9 Changes in PSI by father's level of education

has dropped more dramatically than that of other groups. While the response rate from that age group was itself low and the data should therefore only be used as a reference, a growth in disparity can also be read from its pattern. Also, since an SYS value of 0 indicates average educational attainment, it can be seen that among people in their twenties, the educational attainment of those whose fathers have a high school education falls below average, and the relative educational attainment of those whose fathers completed only compulsory education is rather low. In that sense, SYS can be considered an easy-to-use index.[4]

[4] In addition to father's education, I conducted a similar trend analysis using the Japanese Socio-Economic Index (JSEI) of fathers (Fujihara 2019). The results show that the gap in educational opportunities between social classes is stable and slightly widens for those in their 20 s, which is similar to the results of father's education.

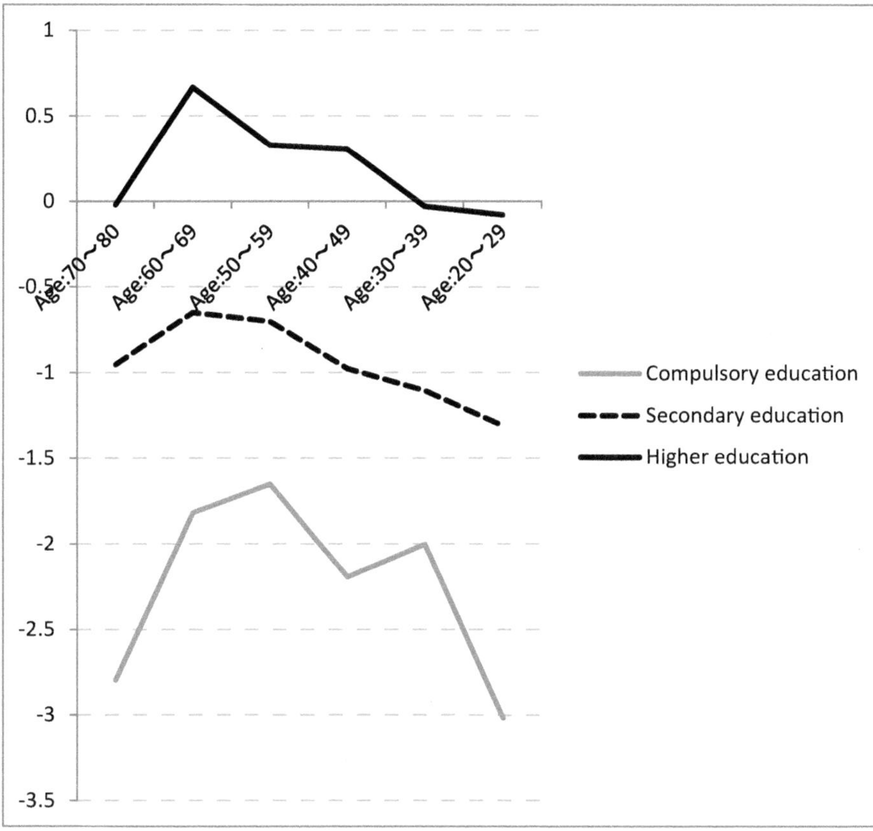

Fig. 4.10 Changes in lnPSI by father's level of education

4.7 Further Simplification and Comparison of Indices Using η^2 and γ Coefficients

Trends in disparities in educational opportunity among different social classes can be summarized in an easy-to-understand way by using a single index to aggregate them. Of course, this entails a considerable amount of simplification, but because the reason we are interested in trends in disparities in educational opportunity is very often to answer the simple question of whether the disparities are growing or not, it is worth attempting a single-index trend description.

To that end, in this paper, I have taken the preceding analyses, calculated the father's average level of education for each generation, and tried to plot the relative indices of educational attainment PSI, lnPSI, PR, and SYS for each generation, with the η2 correlation coefficient of each index as a single index of disparity. As a further target of comparison, I have (1) created a simple cross tabulation of (a) the categories of educational attainment used in calculating the relative indices and (b) the three

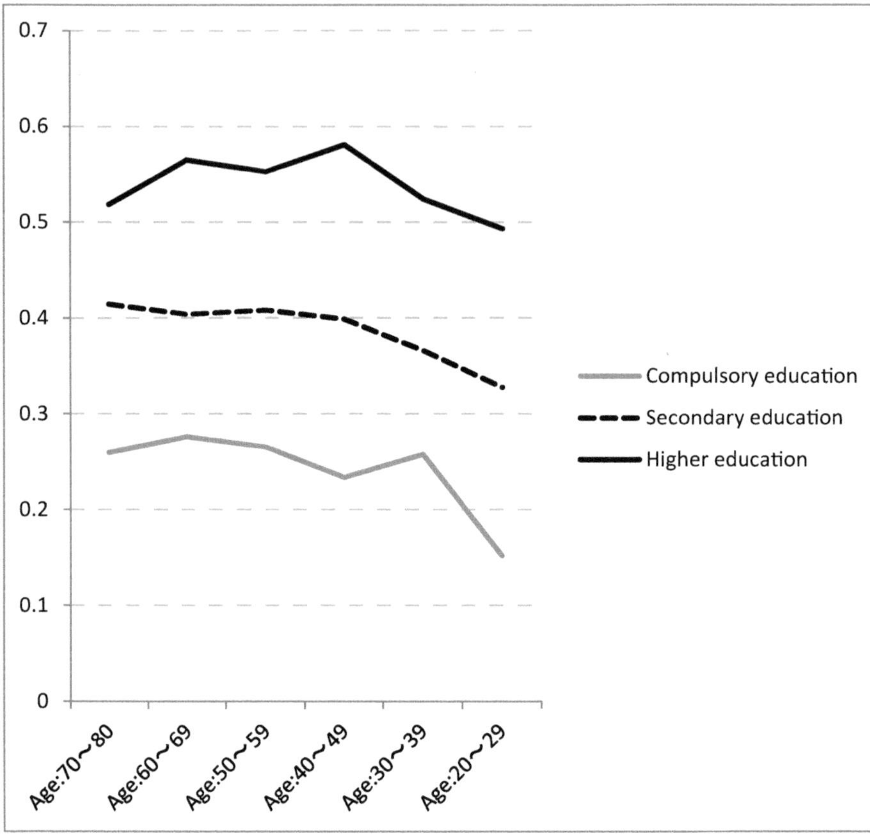

Fig. 4.11 Changes in PR by father's level of education

categories of father's level of education; (2) calculated the γ coefficient for each generation, which is an index that looks at the strength of their correlation; and (3) tried to plot them in a similar way to describe their trends (three-category index = $\gamma 3$, four-category index = $\gamma 4$, and six-category index = $\gamma 6$). The resulting graphs are Figs. . 4.13 (male) and 4.14 (female).

Looking at these graphs, it can be confirmed that the basic trends are stable, though there is a noticeable trend that looks like a growth in disparity for males in their twenties. However, it is difficult to read the trend from these graphs alone. In parallel, we conducted a two-way analysis of variance with the four relative education indices as dependent variables and father's education and age group as explanatory variables and confirmed the effect of the interaction terms of father's education and age group. We confirmed that the interaction terms were not significant in all cases except for the PSI for women. Therefore, as shown in previous studies and previous analyses, the basic trend here was confirmed to be stable.

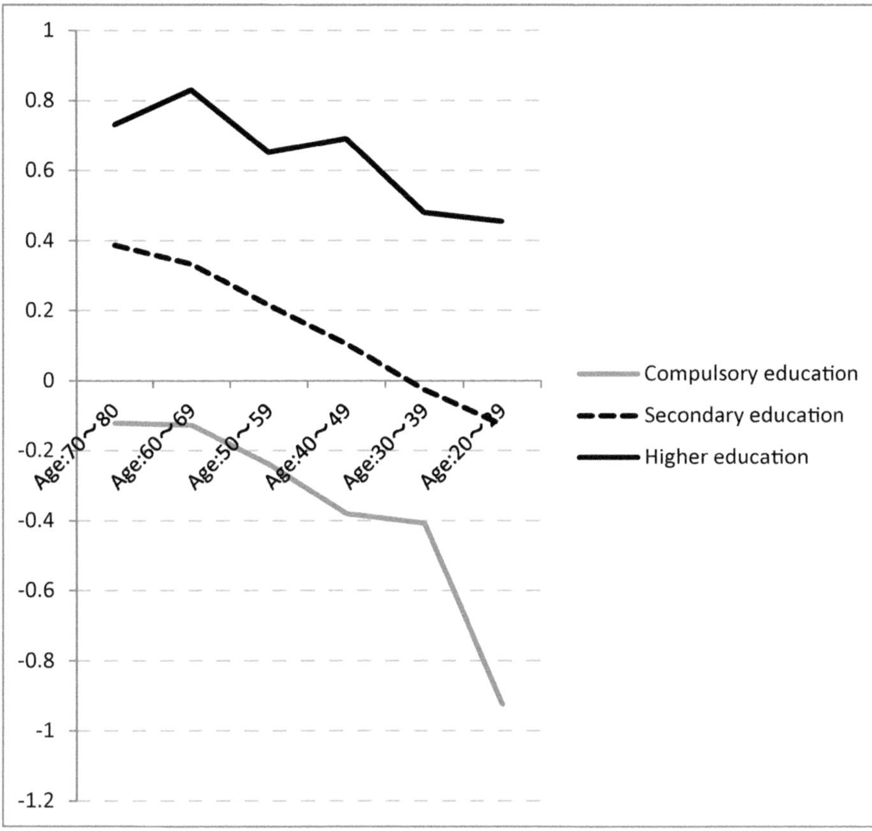

Fig. 4.12 Changes in SYS by father's level of education

On the other hand, we are concerned about the trend that the gap seems to be widening among men in their 20 s. This trend is common to all indicators. However, it is necessary to interpret this trend for men in their 20 s more carefully. The reason is that when we conducted a similar analysis of the 2005 SSM survey, the correlation ratios of the four relative education indices for females in their 20 s in 2005 and 30 s in 2015 (i.e., the same generation) were fairly consistent, but for males, there was some variation and the correlation ratios for males in their 20 s in 2005 and 30 s in 2015 were not consistent. It is important to keep in mind the possibility of sample distortion specific to the 20 s.

Additionally, It must be noted that sometimes the values of the γ coefficients themselves are large, which causes the movements from generation to generation to look exaggerated; however, the relative indices of educational attainment (the group of overlapping lines toward the bottom) all display reasonable movements in comparison. There is a considerable amount of overlap among lnPSI, PR, and SYS, with seemingly none of them affecting the interpretation of the trend, though PSI

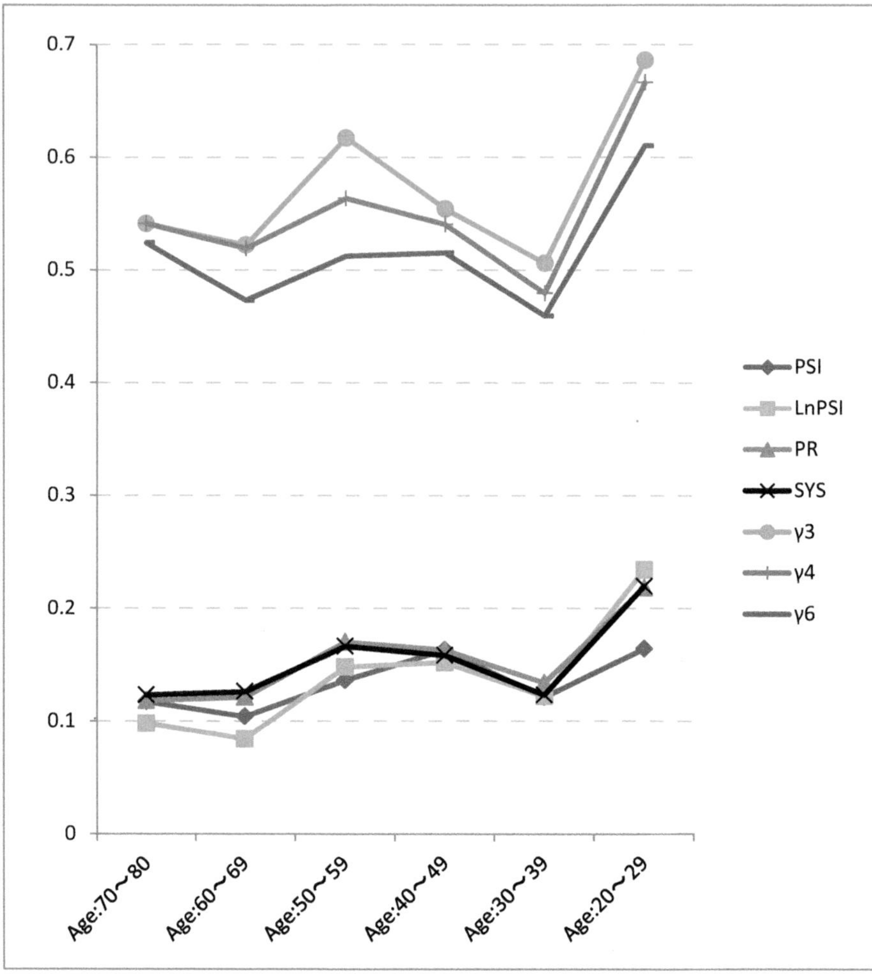

Fig. 4.13 (left). Trends in disparities of educational opportunity based on a single index of educational attainment (males)

shows movements that deviate somewhat (particularly on the graph for females) and can be thought of as an index with slightly different characteristics than the other three. In any case, as the relative indices of educational attainment covered in this paper all exhibit restrained movements, they may be better suited to making cautious trend judgments.[5]

---

[5] As in the previous section, the same trend was also confirmed in the analysis using the JSEI (Fujihara, 2019).

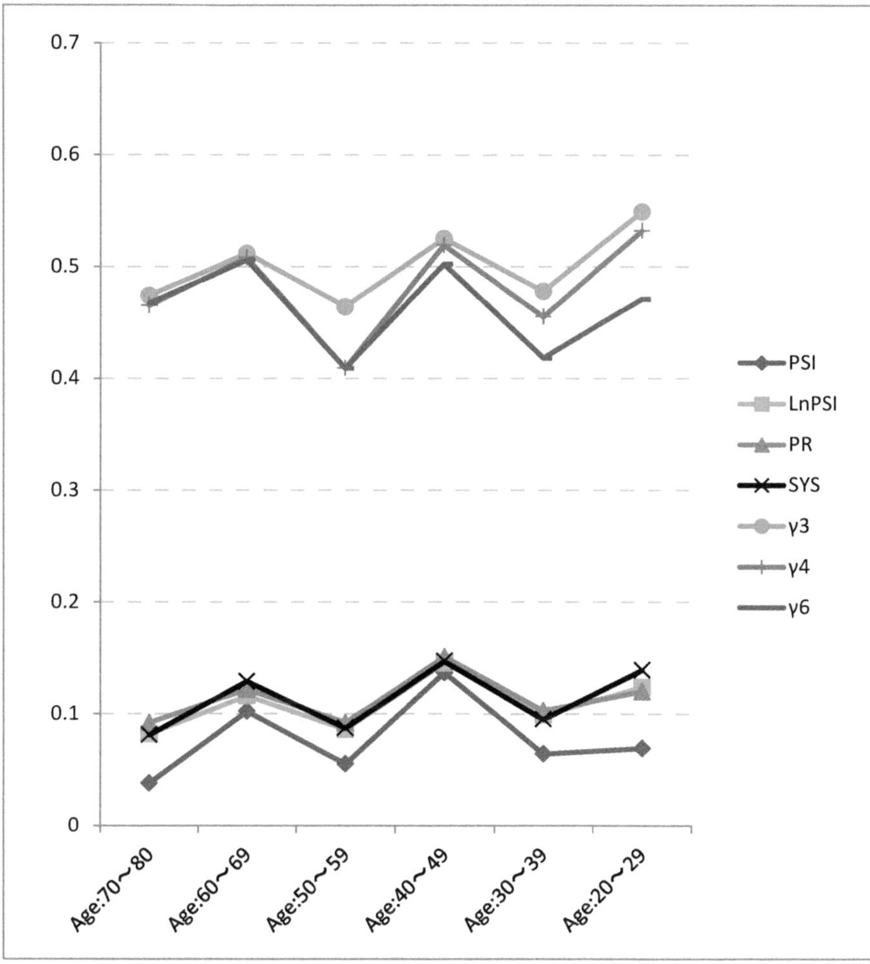

Fig. 4.14 (right). Trends in disparities of educational opportunity based on a single index of educational attainment (females)

4.8 Verification with a Generalized Ordered Logit Model

Let us verify the general tendencies indicated thus far—i.e., (1) that the effect of inherited social class, as represented by father's level of education, on educational opportunity is demonstrably stable over the long term, and (2) that disparities may be growing among males in their twenties, the youngest age group—using a different method. As stated above, trend analyses of changes in the relative value of education, such as this, have made use of generalized ordered logit models in recent years. This is because, unlike typical ordered logit models, it is possible to create models such as ones where, after relaxing the parallel lines assumption (proportional odds

Table 4.1 Results of generalized ordered logit model analysis

Model		N	Log-likelihood	df	Significance	vs,	AIC	BIC
M1	C τ	6,493	−10083.8	11	–		20189.5	20264.1
M2	C τ τ*C	6,493	−9935.1	30	0.0000	M1	19930.1	20133.5
M3	S C τ τ*C	6,493	−9905.2	31	0.0000	M2	19872.5	20082.6
M4	S C F τ τ*C	6,493	−9445.3	33	0.0000	M3	18956.7	19180.3
M5	S C F τ τ*C τ*F	6,493	−9428.2	41	0.0291	M4	18938.5	19216.4
M6	S C F τ τ*C C*F	6,493	−9436.6	43	0.5595	M4	18959.2	19250.7
M7	S C F τ τ*C S*F	6,493	−9432.4	35	0.0016	M4	18934.9	19172.1
M8	S C F τ τ*C S*F S_m*F_c*C_{20}	6,493	−9427.1	36	0.0202	M7	18926.1	19170.1

assumption) and setting the threshold differently for each generation, the father's level of education (hereafter FLE) also varies for each generation. For example, the height of the barrier to entry (threshold) to a given school may differ from one generation to the next. In that case, the effect of one's FLE on own opportunity to attend university may also differ from one generation to the next. A generalized ordered logit model is a highly convenient method of verifying such varied hypotheses.

As such, I will largely follow Fujihara and Ishida's (2016) method of analysis in performing the following verification,[6] with reference to Kondō and Furuta (2009, 2011), who have conducted this analysis using SSM survey data up to 2005.

Firstly, in the 2015 SSM survey data, I will verify tendency (1) by comparatively examining, under the assumption that the threshold varies for each generation, (a) models that do not consider FLE, (b) models that regard the influence of FLE on the opportunity to attend university as stable, and (c) models that regard that influence as variable.

Secondly, I will implement an additional model where the FLE effect for males in their twenties is different than that for other generations, and verify tendency (2) by comparatively examining the model's goodness of fit.

The results from several generalized ordered logit models that explain the (six-category) educational attainment index with FLE (F), age cohort (C), and sex (S) as explanatory variables are shown in Table 4.1 below. Three categories of FLE, six categories of ten-year cohorts, and two sexes were input as dummy variables. Model 1 in Table 4.1 is an ordinary ordered logit model whose only explanatory variable is the cohort. Model 2 relaxes the proportional odds assumption and adds $\tau \times C$ to introduce the condition of differing thresholds for each cohort. If we look at the change in AIC and BIC, that premise appears to be valid. Model 3 adds sex as an explanatory variable, which further improves the model. Model 4 adds FLE to Model 3 and confirms that, of course, it explains educational attainment well. In Model 4, FLE is under the proportional odds assumption and so its interaction with the cohort

[6] I used Stata's gologit2 command for the analyses and referred to Williams (2006) regarding its operation.

is not observed, which would make the model regard the FLE effect as rather stable; however, the addition of various interactions to the model (Models 5–8) is not seen to result in improvements.[7] This confirms that the FLE effect is largely expressed by Model 4, supporting the finding in (1) that it is basically stable.

Let us next verify whether or not there is a growing trend in the disparity seen in males in their twenties, by looking specifically at whether or not a set of dummy variables representing "male of the twenty-something cohort with a father who only completed compulsory education" (S_m*F_c*C_{20}) further improves the model (Model 8). This is intended to directly verify the trend seen earlier in the PR and SYS graphs (that the relative educational attainment has decreased for males in their twenties with a father who has only completed compulsory education). If this improves the model, it would serve as evidence that even simple indices such as SYS can capture the approximate tendencies of trends in disparity. Looking at Model 8 in Table 4.1, actually adding these interactions to a model does not effect a dramatic improvement over Model 4. In that sense, it is reasonable to consider the FLE effect basically stable; however, the values of AIC and BIC suggest that Model 8 has the best fit to the data of all the models tested in this study. That is to say, while care must be taken in how this is expressed, it can be seen that this *does not deny* the possibility that educational opportunity for males in their twenties is more strongly influenced by their social class, as represented by their parents' level of education.[8]

4.9 Conclusion and Issues

Through all of the preceding analyses, this paper has illustrated the following points:

1. There are various relative indices of educational attainment, but among the PSI, PR, and SYS indices examined in this study, SYS has the advantages of (a) expressing trends in educational opportunity clearly and in a way that makes the meaning of the numerical values themselves easily understandable, (b) being easily adapted to analyses for other research besides educational opportunity.

[7] Comparing the models using a likelihood-ratio test found a significant improvement in the models, with Model 4 < Model 7 < Model 8. However, the decrease in the AIC and BIC levels here is relatively small compared to cases where other influential variables (age cohort, sex, FLE) were added. This is taken to mean that even if there is a statistically significant effect, it is not huge. Neither is it significant in Model 6, which takes the interaction of cohort and FLE into account, compared to model 4. This supports the finding that the FLE effect is largely stable across generations.

[8] The same tendency has been confirmed by Fujihara (2018), which uses the same 2015 SSM survey data. On the other hand, according to the results of the author's additional analysis after Nakamura (2018), the interaction term between father JSEI and generation in the OLS regression analysis with SYS as the dependent variable was not statistically significant for men in their 20 s (Nakamura 2021). This suggests that the class disparity is not particularly strong among men in their 20 s. Taking these results together, it should be added that the trend of widening inequality among men in their 20 s still needs to be considered with caution.

2. Trends in educational opportunity obtained from the 2015 SSM data using these relative indices of educational attainment exhibit largely stable changes, with an expanding tendency observed for males in the youngest age group.
3. Nearly identical results were obtained with regard to this tendency even in analyses using generalized ordered logit models; as such, it appears to be a robust effect in the 2015 SSM data. However, the trend among males in their 20 s needs to be closely examined by further research.
4. At the same time, the generalized ordered logit model analyses indicate a strong possibility that simple relative indices of educational attainment are sufficient to understand the gist of trends in educational opportunity and will not result in very large discrepancies.

This paper only looked at father's level of education as an index of inherited social class, but other indices of inherited social class should also be used to verify trends (for example, father's JSEI was used in Nakamura (2021)). Moreover, the question of whether or not applying the same method to past SSM data results in discrepancies in the basic trend description is another issue to be examined.

References

Amano, I. (1982). *Kyoiku to Senbatu (Education and Selection)*. Tokyo: Daiichi-Hoki. (in Japanese).

Amano, I. (1983). Kyoiku no Tiihyoji Kino ni tuite (About the Status-indicating Function of Education), Nihon Kyoiku Shakaigakkai *Kyoiku Shakaigaku Kenkyu* (the Japan Society of Educational Sociology (Ed.), *The Journal of Educational Sociology*), (pp. 44–49). Tokyo: Toyokan. (in Japanese).

Ando, B. (1979). Gakureki Shakai Kasetu no Kento (Examination for the Hypothesis of Academic Credentials' Effect). In: T. Kenichi (Ed.), *Nihon no Kaiso Kozo (Stratification Structure in Japan)*. Tokyo: University of Tokyo Press. (in Japanese).

Aramaki, S. (2000). Kyoiku Kikai no Kakusa ha Shukusho Shitaka? (Have disparities in educational opportunity narrowed?) In: H. Kondō, (Ed.), *Nihon no Kaiso Sisutemu3: Sengo Nihon no Kyoiku Shakai* (*Japan's Social Stratification System 3: Postwar Education in Japan)* (pp. 15–35). (in Japanese).

Boudon, R. (1973). *L'inégalité des chances : La mobilité sociale dans les sociétés industrielles*. A Colin.

Breen, R., & Goldthorpe, J. H. (1997). Explatining educational differentials: Towards a formal rational action theory. *Rationality and Society, 9*(3), 275–305.

Breen, R., Luijkx, R., Müller, W., & Pollak, R. (2009). Non-persistent inequality in educational attainment: Evidence from eight European countries. *American Journal of Sociology, 114*, 1475–1521.

Bourdieu, P., & Passeron, J. C. (1970). *La Reproduction : éléments pour une théorie du système d'enseignement*. Éditions de Minuit.

Bowles, S., & Gintis, H. (1976). *Schooling in capitalist America : Educational reform and the contradictions of economic life*. Basic Books.

Bukodi, E., & Goldthorpe, J. H. (2013). Decomposing 'social origins': The effects of parents' class, status, and education on the educational attainment of their children. *European Sociological Review, 29*(5), 1024–1039.

Fujihara, S., & Ishida, H. (2016). The absolute and relative values of education and the inequality of educational opportunity: Trends in access to education in postwar Japan. *Research in Social Stratification and Mobility, 43*, 25–37.

Fujihara, S., & Ishida, H. (2017). Social fluidity and education in Japan: What are the impacts of educational expansion on social fluidity? (unpublished paper at RC28, 2017).

Fujihara, S. (2018). An ordered logistic regression model for educational stratification: Applications to trend and comparative analyses. (unpublished paper).

Fujihara, S. (2019). Socio-economic standing and social status in contemporary Japan: Scale constructions and their applications. *European Sociological Review, 2020*, 1–14.

Fujita, H. (1979). Shakaiteki Tiikeiseikatei niokeru Kyoiku no Yakuwari (The role of education in the process of social status formation). In: K. Tominaga (Ed.), *Nihon no Kaiso Kozo (The Class Structure of Japan)*. University of Tokyo Press (pp. 329–361). (in Japanese).

Havighurst, R. T. (1961). Education and social mobility in four societies. In: A. H. Halsey, J. Floud, & C. A. Anderson (Eds.), *Education, Economy and Society* (pp.105–120). New York: The Free Press of Glencoe.

Hirasawa, K. (2011). Daigaku no Gakkoreki wo kamishita Kyoiku/Shokugyo Tassei Bunseki (An analysis of educational and occupational attainment that considers subjects' alma mater). In: H. Ishida, H. Kondo, & K. Nakao (Eds.), *Gendai no Kaiso Shakai 2: Kaiso to Ido no Kozo (Contemporary Stratified Society 2: The Structures of Stratification and Mobility)*. Tokyo: University of Tokyo Press (pp. 155–170). (in Japanese).

Imada, T. (1979). Shakaiteki Fubyodo to Kikai Kozo no Susei Bunseki (Trend analysis of social inequality and opportunity structure). In: K. Tominaga (Ed.), *Nihon no Kaiso Kozo (The Class Structure of Japan)*. University of Tokyo Press (pp. 88–132). (in Japanese).

Kondō, H., & Furuta, K. (2009). Kyoiku Tassei no Shakaikeizaiteki Kakusa (Socioeconomic disparities in educational attainment)." Nihon Shakai Gakkai (The Japan Sociological Society). In: Shakaigaku Hyoron (Ed.), *(Japanese Sociological Review) 59*(4), 682–698. (in Japanese).

Kondō, H., & Furuta, K. (2011). Kyoiku Tassei niokeru Kaisosa no Chokiteki Susei (Class differences and long-term trends in educational attainment). In: H. Ishida, H. Kondo, & K. Nakao, (Eds.), *Gendai no Kaiso Shakai 2: Kaiso to Ido no Kozo (Contemporary Stratified Society 2: The Structures of Stratification and Mobility)* (pp. 89–105). Tokyo: University of Tokyo Press. (in Japanese).

Nakamura, T. (2018). Soutaiteki Gakureki Shihyo to Kyoiku Kikai no Susei Bunseki (Relative Indices of Educational Attainment and Trend Analysis of Inequality of Educational Opportunity:Using the 2015SSM Survey Data) Suri Shakaigakkai(Japanese Association for Mathematical Sociology) (Ed.), *Riron to Hoho (Sociological Theory and Methods)* (Vol. 33, No. 2, pp. 247–259). (in Japanese).

Nakamura, T. (2021). Kyoiku Kikai Kakusa no Susei(Trends in Inequality of Educational Opportunity). In: T. Nakamura, S. Miwa, & H. Ishida, (Eds.), Jinsei Shoki no Kaiso Kozo. Tokyo Daigaku Shuppankai. (*The Structure of Social Stratification in the Early-stage of Life (The Structure of Stratification in the Aged Society with Low Fertility 1)*) (pp. 21–35) Tokyo: University of Tokyo Press. (in Japanese).

Nakanishi, Y. (2000). Gakko Ranku to Shakai Ido (School Rank and Social Mobility), Kondo, Hiroyuki ed. *Nihon no Kaiso Sistemu 3: Sengo Nihon no Kyoiku Shakai (Stratified System in Japan 3: Educational Credentials in the Postwar Stratification System)* (pp. 37–56). Tokyo: University of Tokyo Press. (in Japanese).

Nakazawa, W. (2017). Persistent inequality in educational attainment in Japan: Between decreasing youth population and increasing private cost for education. In: *Paper Presented at Summer Meeting of International Sociological Association, Research Committee* 28 (Columbia University in New York).

Ojima, F. (1990). Kyoiku Kikai no Susei Bunseki (Trend analysis of educational opportunity). In: J. Kikuchi (Ed.), *Gendai Nihon no Kaiso Kozo 3: Kyoiku to Shakai Ido (The Class Structure of Contemporary Japan 3: Education and Social Mobility)* (pp. 25–55) Tokyo: University of Tokyo Press. (in Japanese).

Ozaki, M. (1967). *Nihon Shushoku-Shi (The History of Employment in Japan)*. Tokyo: Bungei-Shunju. (in Japanese).
Schröder, H., & Ganzeboom, H. B. G. (2014). Measuring and modelling level of education in European societies. *European Sociological Review, 30*(1), 119–136.
Shavit, Y., & Blossfeld, H. P., (Eds). (1993). *Persistent Inequality: Changing Educational Attainment In Thirteen Countries*. Westview Press.
Shavit, Y., & Park, H. (2016). Introduction to the special issue: Education as a positional good. *Research in Social Stratification and Mobility, 43*, 1–3.
Shirahase, S. (2018). 2015 nen Shakai Kaiso to Shakai Ido ni kansuru Zenkoku Chosa (SSM Chosa) Jissi no Gaiyo (Overview of the 2015 *Nationwide Survey on Social Stratification and Social Mobility* (SSM Survey)). http://www.l.u-tokyo.ac.jp/2015SSM-PJ/2015ssmjisshigaiyo.pdf. (in Japanese).
Tam, T. T. (2007). A paradoxical latent structure of educational inequality: Cognitive ability and family background across diverse societies. In: *Paper to be presented at the RC28 Spring meeting*.
Tam, T. T. (2013). Analyzing education as a positional good: Categorical regression without arbitrary identification. In: *2013 Conference of the European Consortium for Sociological Research*.
Treiman, D. J., & Terrell, K. (1975). The process of status attainment in the United States and Great Britain. *American Journal of Sociology 81*(3), 563–583.
Trow, M. (1974). *The Problems in the Transition from Elite to Mass Higher Education* (OECD, pp. 51–101). OECD Publications.
Williams, R. A. (2006). Generalized ordered logit/partial proportional odds models for ordinal dependent variables. *The Stata Journal, 6*(1), 58–82.

Takayasu Nakamura is a professor of the division of social sciences in education in Graduate School of Education at The University of Tokyo, Japan. He is also one of the directors of The Japan Society of Educational Sociology and The Japanese Association for Social Research for now. His major is the sociology of education and he is interested especially in education and selection systems in contemporary society, including entrance examination systems, educational opportunity, meritocracy, etc. He suggested the idea of "reflexivity of meritocracy" in his book "*Boso suru Noryoku Shugi*" ("*Runaway Meritocracy*," in Japanese), which was based on Anthony Giddens' high-modernity theory. His achievements in English are on his Researchgate page.

Chapter 5
Long-Term Trends in Long-Term Employment in Japan

Tsutomu Watanabe

Abstract The purpose of this chapter is to describe the changes in the characteristics of the occupational history in Japan and the changes in the Japanese labor market from the 1920s to the 2010s. In this chapter, we take advantage of the uniqueness of the SSM survey and use long-term occupational history data to clarify the characteristics of the occupational history of men who entered the workforce from the 1920s to the 1990s. Those who entered employment from the 1920s to the 1940s were more likely to have long-term employment at large companies than at small companies, despite being affected by war and given that long-term employment was not necessarily common (approximately 20%) (support for 1920s theory). In contrast, from the promotion perspective, the superiority of long-term employment was not particularly high, and it could not be confirmed whether Japanese-style employment practices were actually in place. Due to the impact of the Asia–Pacific war, the work history of workers who entered employment around this period became unstable, and there was no superiority attached to long-term employment. Following this, job turnover declined, and employment became stable after the 1950s. During such times, there has been an increase in the number of long-term employees along with a reduction in the differences in the stability of work history among employees, leading to leveling. At the same time, the establishment of Japanese-style employment practices would clarify the superiority of long-term employees. The job turnover rate remained low even after the end of the period of high economic growth, although the rate has been gradually increasing since the 1980s. Therefore, the number of long-term employees who entered employment since the latter half of the 1970s is also decreasing. Superiority in terms of promotion in the case of long-term employment was also lost. While it is argued that long-term employment has been declining since the 2000s, the conclusion of this chapter is that its germination began with employees who entered employment around 1980.

T. Watanabe (✉)
Kwansei Gakuin University, 14-43 Koyoen-Nishiyamacho, Nishinomiya City, Hyogo Prefecture 662-0017, Japan
e-mail: t-nabe@kwansei.ac.jp

S. Shirahase (ed.), *Social Stratification in an Aging Society with Low Fertility*, Economy and Social Inclusion, https://doi.org/10.1007/978-981-19-3647-0_5

5.1 Introduction

The purpose of this chapter is to describe the changes in the characteristics of the occupational history in Japan and the changes in the Japanese labor market from the 1920s to the 2010s.

In social stratification research, intragenerational mobility, that is, changes in one's economic and occupational status due to one's occupational history, is an important theme. For example, a classic study in social stratification research is Blau and Duncan's (1967) analysis of the process of status attainment. This study connects intergenerational and intragenerational migration. After this study, in the 1970s and 1980s, there was an increase in research on job changes and career processes (Rosenfeld, 1992). Since then, there has been considerable research on occupational history, not only on social stratification but also across a wide range of fields, including the sociology of occupation and organization, industrial sociology, labor economics, occupational psychology, and career psychology (Kallberg & Mouw, 2018).

Kallberg and Mouw (2018) point to three studies as possible future developments in occupational history research. The first is a study of the patterns and mechanisms of occupational and organizational career lines. The second is a study to show how the pattern of intragenerational mobility is related to occupational structure and class structure. The third is a comparative and historical study to understand the impact of economic, political, and social institutions and policies.

The need for similar research in the study of occupational history can also be pointed out in Japan. However, due to data limitations in Japanese occupational history studies, it has been difficult to conduct the above three studies. To analyze occupational history, it is necessary to collect occupational history data through either a panel survey or a retrospective survey. However, in Japan, the use of panel surveys spread only after the 2000s, and research on analyzing career lines and patterns has not been widespread. It has also been difficult to study historical changes in occupational history.

In the current research situation in Japan, one of the few datasets available for the historical study of occupational history is from the Japanese Social Stratification and Social Mobility (SSM) survey. SSM survey data have two important features that are not found in many other social surveys. The first feature is that it is a continuous survey spanning 60 years, with surveys conducted every 10 years from 1955 to 2015 (a total of seven times). Hence, by using the SSM survey data, it is possible to conduct a historical study of social stratification in Japan. Second, the SSM survey is characterized by the inclusion of information on occupational history. The SSM survey retrospectively collects information on occupational history. In other words, the SSM survey includes job history data from 1896 to 2015 for men, and from 1928 to 2015 for women. Using these data, it will be possible to analyze career lines and career patterns and to identify the characteristics of Japanese occupational history over the long term.

Therefore, in this chapter, we take advantage of the uniqueness of the SSM survey and use long-term occupational history data to clarify the characteristics of the occupational history of men who entered the workforce from the 1920s to the 1990s. The occupational history of women is not treated here because of the complex influence of factors such as life events and life course as well as the labor market. As an analytical strategy, I will focus on the stability of professional history. Stability is a very important feature of Japanese occupational history and is determined by the frequency of changes in occupations and employers. An occupational history with few changes in occupation or employer is stable. In contrast, an occupational history with many changes in occupation and employer is unstable.

One of the major influences on the stability of occupational history in Japan is the country's unique employment practices, which can be characterized in three broad groups: lifetime employment, seniority-based system, and company unions. In such employment practices, interfirm mobility is reduced, and occupational history is more stable. Moreover, in Japan, the degree of stability of occupational history is likely to be deeply related to the inequality of social status and income.

Therefore, in this study, to clarify the characteristics of the changes in employment history in Japan, I will consider the stability of employment history as the degree of the job changes, and in particular, I will analyze long-term employment. Long-term employment is the most stable career pattern. In addition, as will be discussed later, the most remarkable characteristic of the Japanese career pattern is long-term employment.[1] Therefore, by focusing on long-term employment, it is possible to clarify the characteristics of occupational history, or intragenerational mobility, in Japan.

To summarize the purpose of the analysis in this chapter, the objectives of this study are as follows: Of the three studies identified by Kallberg and Mouw (2018), we will analyze long-term employment as a career pattern (the first study), and by clarifying the long-term trends of occupational history (the third study), we will examine the changes in the labor market (the second study).

On the one hand, the scarcity of SSM survey data was mentioned earlier, but on the other hand, these data have drawbacks. The first is the reliability of the data. Because the data are retrospective, the job history may be inaccurate due to memory errors, memory loss, or memory rewriting. Such data are less reliable than panel survey data. The second is the number of data points. If we merge the data from 1955 to 2015, we have data for 18,005 cases. However, the data are scattered because the subjects entered the workforce between 1896 and 2015, and splitting the sample into each year would result in a smaller sample size.

Given these two shortcomings, it is difficult to analyze in detail the impact of economic changes and events in a particular year. Therefore, the purpose of this chapter is not to focus on the effects of minor economic changes, as is common in economics, but to clarify the long-term trends of institutional and market changes.

[1] It has been pointed out that long-term employment practices were not always common in Japan (Levine 1983, Cheng and Kallberg 1996).

5.2 Historical Trends of the Japanese Labor Market

Employment for life, seniority system, and company unions are commonly held as characteristics of the Japanese employment system, and considerable research has been conducted regarding its origin and characteristics (Abegglen, 1958; Dore, 1973; Jacoby, 1979; Vogel, 1979).

Among such characteristics, when trying to analyze the Japanese labor market from the 1920s onward from the perspective of the stability of occupational history, long-term employment practice[2] is particularly important.

There are two questions related to long-term employment. First is the origin of the long-term employment, i.e., when and how the long-term employment practice was established in Japan. Second is the maintenance of long-term employment, i.e., whether the long-term employment practice was continued stably or collapsed after their establishment and, if it collapsed, when that occurred. Answering these questions is an important issue for illustrating the long-term changes in the Japanese occupational history and labor market.

Before answering these questions, I will summarize the conventional research on the history of the Japanese labor market.

There is little research on the history of Japanese occupational history in research on Japan's social class structure, and most of the extant research deals with labor economics. In particular, the research on labor economic history has focused on employment policy, the wage system, labor-management relations, the labor market, etc. We will take a brief look at the changes in the Japanese labor market based on the knowledge of labor economics (Moriguchi & Ono, 2006).

The conventional research on the history of the Japanese labor market reflects several aspects. First, incentives for workers for continued service were explored mainly in the large heavy industrial companies in the 1920s, when regular recruitment or an apprentice system, pay raises, etc., were introduced (Gordon, 1985). These changes were based on managerial logic (Hyodo, 1971), and diplomaism began to spread with the introduction of regular recruitment (Sugayama, 2011). There is a theory that the system of employment for life was established in the 1920s [Theory established in 1920s] (Hazama, 1964, Levine, 1983, Koike, 2012). The dual structure of modernized, large-scale rational capitalism management and traditional, mid-scale, family- and community-type management also evolved during this period (Odaka, 1984).

In the 1940s, the era of the Asia–Pacific war, the personnel management policy of large companies that had been common until the 1930s was followed under national military control, and the standardization of personnel policy made progress. Such progress mandated the mediation of an employment agency, the apprentice system,

---

[2] Long-term employment and employment for life are different concepts. Employment for life is a concept wherein new graduate (collective) recruitment is added to the long-term employment (Kambayashi and Kato 2017). This chapter focuses on employment for life since its focus is on workers who continue to work in the same company right after graduation, but it is referred to as long-term employment because work history until the retirement age is not followed.

regular pay raises, etc., in the recruitment of new graduates. Therefore, it is also said that the system of employment for life was established in wartime [Asia–Pacific wartime establishment theory] (Magota, 1965, Noguchi 2010). Although job change and dismissal were prohibited, there were, reportedly, many job changes due to labor shortages (Nakamura, 1993). The elimination of differences between white-collar and blue-collar jobs also existed as an idea that has been linked to the postwar removal of such differences, but it is said that these difference continued to exist at that time (Magota, 1965).

After the war, the population increased rapidly with the increase in repatriation from overseas, such as China or Southeast Asia. This increase generated excessive labor in agriculture. However, as the economy was recovering, there was also a shift from agroforestry to non-agroforestry, particularly to the manufacturing and construction industries (Nakamura, 1993). With the change in labor laws, the difference between workers (blue-collar) and employees (white-collar) was eliminated. Since it became common for typical workers to immediately find work after graduating from 1950 onward (Sugayama, 2011), it is also said that the system of employment for life was established during that period [1950s establishment theory] (Dore, 1973; Gordon, 1985; Nomura, 1994; Sugayama, 2011). The existence of a closed company labor market—in other words, a dual labor market—was revealed as a characteristic of the postwar labor market (Abegglen, 1958, Ujihara, 1966). Moreover, the practices or systems that initially evolved in the white-collar upper class gradually moved downward to the middle/lower class of white-collar workers and then to blue-collar workers (Sugayama, 2011). The so-called white-collarization of blue-collar workers progressed (Koike, 2005), and the system of employment for life began to spread with the creation of the labor and management conference system (Moriguchi & Ono, 2006).

During this time, small-group activities aimed at improving productivity were actively carried out in the workplace, and the completion of the Japanese-style personnel management model was promoted (Gordon, 1985). At the end of the 1960s, large companies established the collective recruitment of new graduates, systematic in-house training, regular salary hikes based on the professional qualification system, promotions, worker participation through small-group activities, employment security until retirement, labor-management consultation systems with companies, and established unification of white-collar and blue-collar management.

This Japanese employment practice, known as the Japanese model, was highly valued worldwide in the mid-1980s, but in the 1990s, it became less favored due to the country's worst recession, which began in the 1940s. As the competition became more intense, the relationship between economic trends and employment volume became stronger, and companies hired a large number of nonregular workers. However, even in the 1990s, long-term employment practices remained strong (Chuma, 1998).

In addition, in the 2000s, companies maintained regular and long-term employment and did not break long-term employment practices for main employees (Kato, 2001, Shimozutani & Yokoyama, 2009, Suzuki, 2010, Ono, 2010, Yu, 2010, Kambayashi & Kato, 2016, 2017). The increase in nonregular employment resulted in a decrease in self-employment (Kambayashi & Kato, 2016). The Japanese model, which still exists and is the core of most Japanese companies, is a system that applies to male full-time employees. On the one hand, the Japanese model is said to be resilient, yet, on the other hand, it is known that long-term employment practices have declined since the 2000s (Hamaaki et al., 2012; Kawaguchi & Ueno, 2013; Takahashi, 1997), and no definitive answer about the benefits of this practice has been obtained.

These findings are used as a framework for the following analysis, and in this chapter, we will confirm the establishment of long-term employment and the presence or absence of subsequent collapse from the work history data provided by the SSM survey.

First, this chapter determines the subject of analysis, which consists of male workers who are employed for the first time. This chapter pays attention to the system and practice of the long-term employment of employees, so agriculture and self-employment are excluded from the analysis. However, those who were employed for the first time but changed jobs to agriculture or self-employment are included in the analysis.

The occupational history to be analyzed is 20 years from the first job. It is possible to target a longer period, but the greater the number of years included in the study, the fewer samples exist for analysis. The first-time employment age of persons having a work history of 20 years or more ranges between 15 and 25 years in 95% or more of cases. In other words, the 20-year work history in the SSM survey data covers work history for workers aged, approximately, between 35 and 45 years. Given that most Japanese employees change jobs by the age of 30, most also have a stable work history between the ages of 35 and 45, and this period is long enough to clarify the characteristics of their work history.[3]

The information contained in the work history data of the SSM survey includes employee status, job description, employer (industry, scale), and job title, but since this chapter focuses on long-term employment, it focuses on changes in employer. We will only deal with job changes and job titles.[4]

[3] The data to be analyzed is person-year data. Therefore, one occupation and one employer are assigned per year. In the case of changes to multiple occupations and employer during the year, the data is based on the last occupation and the last work destination of each year.

[4] The change between regular and nonregular employment is an important factor in discussing the stability of the work history. However, this chapter does not deal with nonregular employment because there is a real change in nonregular work history from the 1920s to the 2010s, and nonregular workers can only be handled in the 1950s due to problems with the available questionnaires.

5.3 Long-Term Changes in Occupational History

5.3.1 Characteristics of Occupational History Data in SSM Surveys

Regarding the characteristics of work history data in available in SSM survey data, the number of male samples from 1955 to 2015 is 18,005. Of these, 10,074 were samples with more than 20 years of professional experience, and 6,819 were employed for the first time. In this chapter, these 6,819 samples are the target of analysis.

Figure 5.1 shows the yearwise distribution of these 6,819 samples by educational background, first-time industry, first-time occupation, and first-time company scale. Specifically, changes in the ratio of higher education, manufacturing, white-collar, and large enterprises were examined (5-year moving average).

Three characteristics of historical changes are reflected in Fig. 5.1. The first is the change in the labor market during the Asia–Pacific war. The percentage of large companies increased rapidly, and the percentage of manufacturing industries also increased. However, the manufacturing industries have been decreasing consistently since then. Second is the major change in Japanese society during the period of rapid economic growth. In particular, white-collarization and the popularization of higher education progressed. Third is the stagnation from the mid-1970s onward. The white-collarization and popularization of higher education continued to be stagnant in this period.

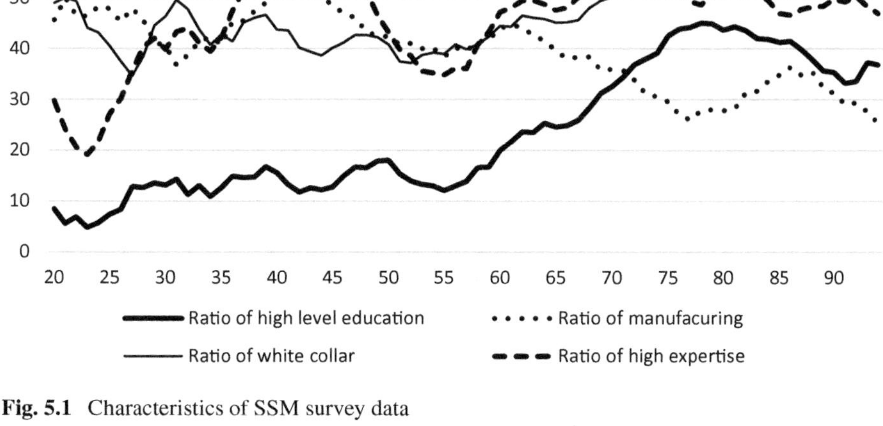

Fig. 5.1 Characteristics of SSM survey data

5.3.2 Stability of Occupational History

Next, we will first examine the changes in job turnover over time and then the changes in stability of occupational history over time to understand the changes in the stability of occupational history from the 1920s to the 2010s.

We will first describe the changes in job turnover with time. This analysis reveals the trend of labor market changes over time through the job turnover trends in each period of occupational history.

Figure 5.2 shows the changes in job turnover in chronological order from the first job until the 20th year (5-year moving average). The years after graduation are grouped into 5-year categories, and job turnover is calculated for four periods: years 1–5, years 6–10, years 11–15, and years 16–20.

As shown in Fig. 5.2, job turnover decreases as the years after graduation increase in any period. In other words, this result confirms that job change is active for young employees in the Japanese labor market, with the exception that during the Asia–Pacific wartime, there is almost no difference in job change across the years after graduation. Therefore, the job turnover coinciding with the Asia–Pacific wartime indicates the labor market turmoil of this period.

Next, the characteristics of changes in job turnover over time can be summarized in four points. First, the job turnover in the 1920s and the 1930s, i.e., before the Asia–Pacific wartime, was relatively low. The job turnover is higher than it was after the war, except for years 1–5 after graduation, but it is not extremely high. For example, for years 6–10, average job turnover in the 1920s and the 1970s is 9.2% and 6.7%,

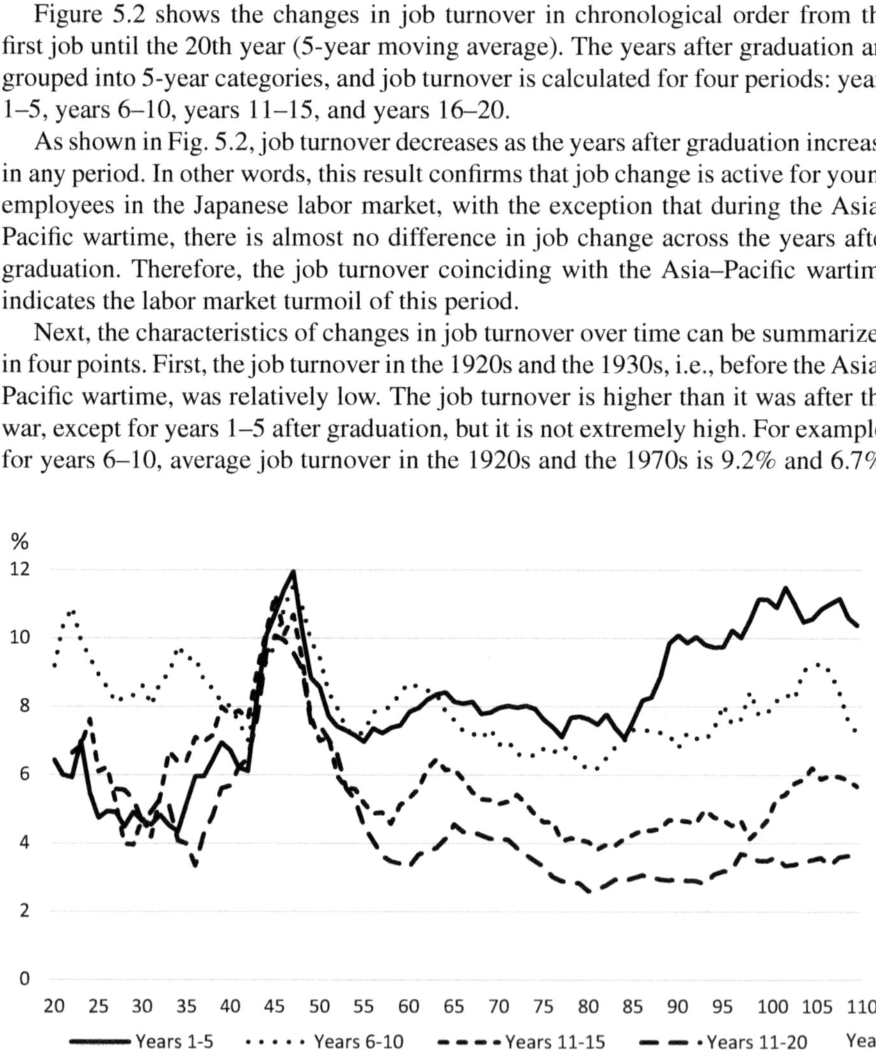

Fig. 5.2 Job turnover

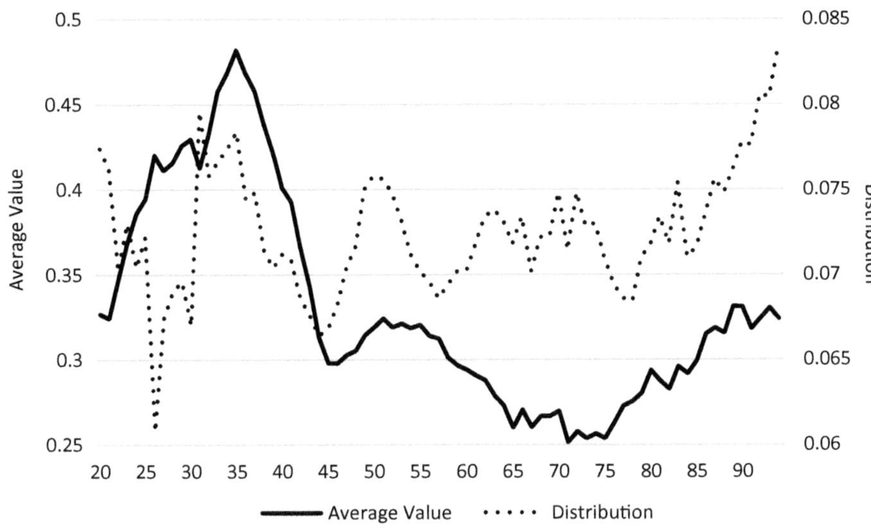

Fig. 5.3 Diversity of occupational history

respectively, with a difference of just 2.5%. This result is different from those of existing research (Gordon, 1985, Hyodo, 1971).[5]

A second reason for these results is that job turnover was extremely high during the Asia–Pacific war of 1937–46, regardless of the number of years after employment. The difference over time is also small. The average job turnover from 1943, when the Asia–Pacific war situation worsened, to 1950, when Korean special procurements started, was 10.0% for years 1–5, 10.0% for years 6–10, 9.4% for years 11–15, and 8.6% for years 16–20. The difference is less than 2%, and it is lowest for the period from the 1920s to the 2010s, which indicates that job changes between companies occurred more often in the labor market during the war (Nakamura, 1993). Such changes are considered to be due to the economic disturbance during the Asia–Pacific war and consequent labor shortages.

The third reason is that job turnover stabilized to a low rate in the 1970s despite an increase in job turnover in any period from the 1950s to the 1960s. In particular, the job turnover from the sixth year onward decreases significantly and consistently from the 1960s onward. Although employees had changed jobs every few years after taking their first job before this era, they began to follow a stable career path at this time, demonstrating the penetration of Japanese employment practices.

The fourth reason is that job turnover gradually began to increase from approximately 1980. Regardless of the number of years after employment, job turnover after employment is high in any period after this. Specifically, from the mid-1980s, job turnover increased significantly until the fifth year after employment (7.7% for the

[5] The first possible reason for the difference could be that the past information was simplified for the retrospective survey. The second could be the possibility of a range of samples different from the existing research.

1970s, 8.0% for the 1980s, 10.1% for the 1990s, and 10.9% for the 2000s), and the instability of initial work history increased.

From the above information, changes in job turnover can be divided into three periods: the 1920s to the 1940s (first period), during which employment instability increased; the 1950s to the mid-1980s (second period), which saw stable employment; and the late 1980s onward (third period), which saw a resumption of employment instability.

Next, we will describe the change in the stability of occupational history. Each employee has at least 20 years of work experience. This 20-year work history is combined into one unit, and its characteristics are quantified based on stability. Specifically, a diversity index is used as an index for the stability of work history. The diversity index D is defined by the following equation. As understood from the defining equation, the value of the diversity index of work history changes with the number of places of employment after job change and the number of years of experience at the respective employer. For example, if a person continues to work for 20 years at the same place of employment, then the diversity index D will be 0, and if a person has worked at a different place of employment every year during the 20-year period, then the diversity index will be 0.95. In other words, the lower the value of D is, the more stable the occupational history.

$$\mathrm{D} = 1 - \sum_{i=1}^{n} p_i^2$$

p_i Percentage of number of years for which a person worked at a place of employment 'i' out of total number of years of work history.
n Number of places of employment, i.e., number of job changes (n = 20 when the occupational history is 20 years).

The change in the distribution of the diversity index over time obtained in this way is studied through the average value and distribution. The change in distribution and average value by employment year is shown in Fig. 5.2 (5-year moving average).[6] For example, the average value of 1950 indicates the average stability of work history for 20 years, from the beginning of employment in 1950–1969.

The overview of the changes in the stability of work history over time can be understood through the average value. The unequal change in the stability of work history over time can be understood from the distribution.

The discussion divides the duration of employment into three periods based on changes in the distribution value and average value. This period division largely corresponds to the earlier division for the change in job turnover.

The first period is the years up to 1945. Instability continues in this period since the average value increased significantly from the 1920s to 1935. However, subsequently,

[6] Only the number of people employed until 1996 are considered since work history for 20 years is considered.

the diversity of occupational history moves toward stabilization. The average value again swings backward around 1945. In contrast, distribution decreases in the 1920s and increases thereafter. This value is stable because it is likely that few people among those employed were sent to military service in the 1920s, but the work history of many people among those employed from the 1930s onward was discontinued due to conscription or impressment, leading to instability. Furthermore, there is a possibility that the hierarchical difference (Watanabe, 2020) in conscription or impressment increased the value of distribution. However, distribution subsequently continues to decrease until approximately 1945.

The second period is from the late 1940s to the mid-1970s. The average value increases slightly in the 1950s but subsequently decreases fairly consistently. The distribution increases temporarily from the late 1940s but again decreases from 1950s onward. Although distribution continues to fluctuate slightly, it remains largely stable at a low value until the mid-1970s. The career of all the employees employed in this period was stable. Equalization also continued since the distribution also continued to stabilize, to some extent, and thus, this period can be considered one of stabilization and equalization.

The third period is from the mid-1970s onward. The average value as well as distribution value continue to increase in this period. The level of instability in the career of employees who were employed during this period continues to increase gradually. Instability continues as a characteristic of all the workers. Since the value of distribution has increased, occupational history has diversified.

The change in the longest number of working years at one place of employment in the 20-year work history after entering the first job further illustrates the background of change in career instability (Fig. 5.4). For example, years 1–10 in the figure represent the percentage of people whose highest number of working years at one place of employment in the 20-year work history is 1–10 years. The year 20 group refers to the percentage of people who have never changed their place of employment (hereinafter referred to as long-term employees).

The percentage of long-term employees decreases in 1920s but continues to increase from 1930s. However, it reaches peak in mid 1970s and continues to decrease thereafter. On the other hand, the percentage of people who have worked at the same place of employment only for a short duration of 1 to 10 years increases significantly from 1920 to 1930s and continues to decrease from 1940s onward. It changes at the same rate from 1940s onward but continues to increase after mid-1970s. From this trend, it can be guessed that the cause of instability of work history is increase and decrease in the long-term employees and increase and decrease in the short-term employees.

We tried to obtain the average change in the diversity index excluding the long-term employees. The diversity index of all the employees from 1967 to 1976 is 0.263. It becomes 0.287 for 1977–86 and 0.328 for 1987–96. On the other hand, diversity index excluding the long-term employees is 0.464 for 1967–76, 0.460 from 1977–86, and 0.494 from 1987–96. From this change, it can be considered that the increase in the instability of work history from late 1970s is due to the decrease in the long-term

Fig. 5.4 Maximum number of years of work experience at one place of employment

employees and instability of work history other than the long-term employees i.e., short-term employees continue to increase from 1987 onward.

From the above information, decrease in the long-term employees can be considered one of the major causes of increase in instability of workers from 1970s onward. Therefore, we will track the qualitative shift focusing on the long-term employees in the following sections.

The following sections will specifically illustrate two questions.

First, who was likely to become long-term employee depending on the period? We will illustrate the types of attributes of workers likely to become long-term employees in the three periods that became evident, particularly from the analysis so far, i.e., from the 1920s to the mid-1940s, from the late 1940s to the mid-1970s, and from the late 1970s onward.

Second, did the priorities of long-term employees within the company change with time? Did the priorities of long-term employment change or remain the same during the continued establishment of Japanese employment practices from the 1920s onward? Then, we will study whether the decrease in long-term employees from the late 1970s onward changed the priorities of long-term employment.

5.4 Trend of Long-Term Employment

5.4.1 *Who Will Become Long-Term Employee?*

This section describes the change in characteristics of long-term employees by analyzing by period what kind of people are likely to become long-term employees. The analysis focuses on the first job because the situation at the time of first employment is considered to exert the greatest influence on whether one can continue working in the same company for a long time, according to the characteristics of long-term employment practice in Japan.

The employment practices peculiar to Japan also exert a major influence on long-term employment, as explained in Sect. 5.2. Specifically, there are three characteristics of the company and occupation related to the presence of long-term employment practices.

First is company scale. It is easier to adopt long-term employment practices in large companies than in small to medium-sized companies. Second is occupation. It is thought that long-term employment began with white-collar workers and then gradually spread to blue-collar workers. In other words, the employment of white-collar workers lies at the core of the employment practice, and blue-collar workers lie outside this practice. Therefore, there is a possibility that the system of long-term employment is more strongly maintained by white-collar workers than by blue-collar workers. Third is industry. Since the system of employment for life spread from the manufacturing industry, centered around heavy industry as discussed in Sect. 5.2, a system of long-term employment was more likely to be adopted in the manufacturing industry than in other industries.

In addition to these three factors, general human capital can be considered a factor that influences long-term employment. Higher education offers a high amount of general human capital. Therefore, since the company does not want to lose highly educated employees, long-term employment is easy to achieve. From this information, this section analyzes whether the size of first company, industry, occupation, and education influences long-term employment by period.

The specific analysis will employ binomial logistic regression analysis, considering the presence of long-term employment as the dependent variable.

Long-term employment, which is a dependent variable, is considered 1 for people who have never changed jobs in the 20 years after taking their first job and is considered 0 otherwise.

The size of first company, industry of first job, occupation of first job, and education are the independent variables. The size of first company is classified into two categories: (1) 1–299 employees (small to medium-sized company) and (2) more than 300 employees/public office (large company); small to medium-sized companies are considered the standard. The presence of the dual structure of the labor market will be ascertained from the influence of the size of first company. The industry of first job is classified into four categories: manufacturing, construction/transportation, wholesale and retail, and other industry; the manufacturing industry is considered the standard. The occupation of first job is classified into four categories: white-collar (professional, managerial level, clerical job), grey-collar (sales), upper-class blue-collar (skilled work), and lower-class blue-collar (semi/less-skilled work); upper-class blue-collar is considered the standard. Education is considered a continuous variable, and a value of 3 is assigned to higher education, 2 to secondary education, and 1 to elementary education. The categories of employment period are as follows: before 1936, 1937–46, 1947–56, 1957–66, 1967–76, 1977–86, and 1987–96.

Table 5.1 shows the results of analysis.[7]

For education, only 1957–66 and 1967–76 are statistically significant. The difference in the ratio of long-term employment based on education began to increase around this time. In particular, the long-term employment ratio increased for secondary and higher education but decreased for elementary education. However, since the long-term employment ratio decreased even for secondary and higher education after 1977, the statistical significance of this result is considered as having been eliminated.

Regarding company scale, long-term employment is more likely in larger companies in almost all periods. Since the impact on those employed before the war can also be confirmed, it is understood that the long-term employment system was formed prewar, to a certain extent, in large companies. During the wartime period of 1937–46, statistical significance was not present, and long-term employment practice was not functioning amid the wartime turmoil. The percentage of long-term employees changed over time (refer to Fig. 5.4), but, in contrast, the difference between the large companies and small to medium-sized companies remained the same.

Regarding the impact of occupation, before the war and from the postwar period until 1976, white-collar workers were more likely to opt for long-term employment than upper-class blue-collar workers. In other words, white-collar employment was an important condition for working in stable, long-term employment. The results are consistent with the conclusion of Cheng and Kallberg (1997) that the gap between white-collar and blue-collar workers continued to exist even after the war. However, after 1977, white-collar superiority can no longer be seen. While there were times when it was easy for gray-collar workers to obtain long-term employment, this is not true across generations. In addition, there is no difference in long-term employment among blue-collar workers, and possession of skillset is unrelated to long-term employment.

According to Sect. 5.2, existing studies have shown that the differences between white-collar and blue-collar employees have ceased to exist since 1950. However, in the case of long-term employment in Japan's labor market, the analysis of SSM Survey data shows that the differences between white-collar and blue-collar employment continued to exist consistently for new hires until the mid-1970s. Moreover, occupation has not created any impact since 1977. From these results, it can be

[7] This analysis analyzes regular and nonregular employment. We also conducted the analysis only for regular employment for employees after 1957, but the result was the same.

Table 5.1 Binomial logistic regression analysis of long-term employment (by employment period)

	– 1936	1937–46	1947–56	1957–66	1967–76	1977–86	1987–96
Education	−0.125	−0.122	0.069	0.293**	0.431**	0.224	0.284
Ref. upper blue							
White	1.278**	0.343	0.782**	0.643**	0.498*	0.404	0.467
Grey	0.730	−0.513	0.706*	0.277	0.529*	0.26	−0.628
Lower blue	0.595	−0.302	0.247	0.025	0.334	0.269	0.185
Large company	1.304**	0.163	1.229**	1.145**	1.399**	1.361**	1.330**
Ref. manufacturing							
Construction/transportation	0.814*	0.950**	0.023	−0.152	0.032	0.011	−0.493
Wholesale and retail	−0.282	0.053	−0.600*	−0.389*	−0.659**	−0.649*	−0.518
Other industry	−1.118	0.597*	−0.11	0.003	0.574**	−0.175	−0.003
AIC	116.049	158.973	176.311	257.962	247.369	220.831	168.823
BIC	152.411	200.061	221.668	307.138	293.195	264.745	206.950
NagelkerkeR2	0.173	0.079	0.191	0.210	0.267	0.182	0.235
N	420	710	1141	1744	1202	972	511

** $p < 0.01$, * $p < 0.05$

inferred that white-collar superiority has ceased to exist, and the long-term employment of white-collar workers has been changing in the case of new hires since 1977.

With regard to industries, the construction and transportation industries were more likely to offer long-term employment than the manufacturing industry both before and during the war. The long-term employment rate of the manufacturing industry was low from the prewar to the postwar era, which could indicate the existence of so-called migrant workers (Gordon, 1985); thus, the cause for this low rate cannot be identified. Postwar, long-term employment is even less likely in wholesale and retail trading when compared to the manufacturing industry, which could be a manifestation of the postwar introduction of employment for life by the manufacturing industry. However, the influence of industry is not seen in the 1987–96 era. The decline in long-term employees suggests that there are no more industries that can maintain long-term employment practices.

5.4.2 Changes in Japan's Corporate Labor Market

This section will examine the changes with respect to the predominance of long-term employees. In the corporate labor market of Japan, the superiority of long-term employees can be sourced to firm-specific human capital. Long-term employees should have a higher income and be promoted more easily when compared to other types, since they possess more firm-specific human capital.

As analyzed earlier, the number of long-term employees fluctuates across generations, and the facts also change. Such fluctuations in the number of long-term employees and variation in facts appear to have changed the position of long-term employees within companies and given rise to changes in Japanese-style employment practices.

Here, we pay attention to promotions in particular and study whether the superiority of long-term employees changes across generations. In particular, we examine whether the superiority of long-term employees increased or decreased in the following periods: the prewar to postwar period, which saw an increase in the number of long-term employees, and the period from the latter half of the 1970s onward, which saw a decline in the number of long-term employees.

Two hypotheses can be considered with regard to the relationship between the superiority and the increase/decrease in long-term employees.

The first hypothesis is that an increase in the number of long-term employees leads to a decline in their scarcity and a decrease in their superiority. In a firm with only long-term employees, everyone would have firm-specific human capital, and long-term employment as such thus does not hold any particular superiority within the firm. In contrast, a decrease in the number of long-term employees increases their scarcity. If there are few long-term employees within a firm, then more preferential treatment should be given to the long-term employees possessing firm-specific human capital.

The second hypothesis is that an increase in the number of long-term employees is representative of the establishment of Japanese employment practices, whereas a decrease represents its collapse. If that is the case, when there is an increase in long-term employees, there will be an increasing emphasis on firm-specific human capital and thereby an increase in the superiority of such employees, while the same will decrease when there is a decrease in long-term employees.

The analysis employs a multinomial logit analysis, with the job title in the 20th year (20th-year job title) as the dependent variable, for each year of employment. This analysis is conducted to confirm whether an employee with a 20th-year job title is a long-term employee. This analysis includes persons who have held job titles at some point up to the 19th year and have continued to work in the same company since. Therefore, holding a job title can also be considered as leading to long-term employment, and it is not possible to identify the causality of whether long-term employment has resulted in holding a job title or whether job title has led to long-term employment. However, this analysis serves to clarify whether long-term employees would hold a job title 20 years later.

The dependent variable is the 20th-year job title. There are three categories: no job title (standard), Manager/Assistant Manager, and Section Head/Department Head. President is excluded from the analysis.[8]

Explanatory variables refer to the presence or absence of the following: educational background (high, moderate, or low level of education), first job occupation (white-collar (specialization/management/clerical work), grey-collar (sales), higher-level blue-collar (skilled [reference]), lower-level blue-collar (semi/unskilled), size of first job company (large companies, small and medium-sized companies [reference]), first job industry (manufacturing industry [reference], construction/transportation industry, wholesale/retail industry, others), long-term employment (employed at the same company for 20 years).

Figures 5.5 and 5.6 indicate the time-series change in the odds ratio obtained from coefficient B of long-term employment based on the analysis results (it also indicates a 95% confidence interval). Figure 5.5 represents the odds ratio for Manager/Assistant Manager, and Fig. 5.6 gives the odds ratio for Section Head/Department Head.

First, for promotion to Manager/Assistant Manager, as shown in Fig. 5.5, long-term employment was not advantageous for new hires until 1946, after which it became advantageous for several decades before beginning to diminish again in 1987, after which the advantage for new hires disappeared.

In the case of promotion to Section Head/Department Head shown in Fig. 5.6, the trend is similar to that of Manager/Assistant Manager shown in Fig. 5.5. The odds ratio is low for new hires up to 1946 but has been increasing since then. However, the statistical significance is applicable only to the periods from 1957–66 and from

[8] Although the analysis was also carried out including the President, the case was not the same as considering job titles up to Department Head, and therefore, it was difficult to analyze the impact of long-term employment since the former includes entrepreneurship. This aspect calls for a separate study.

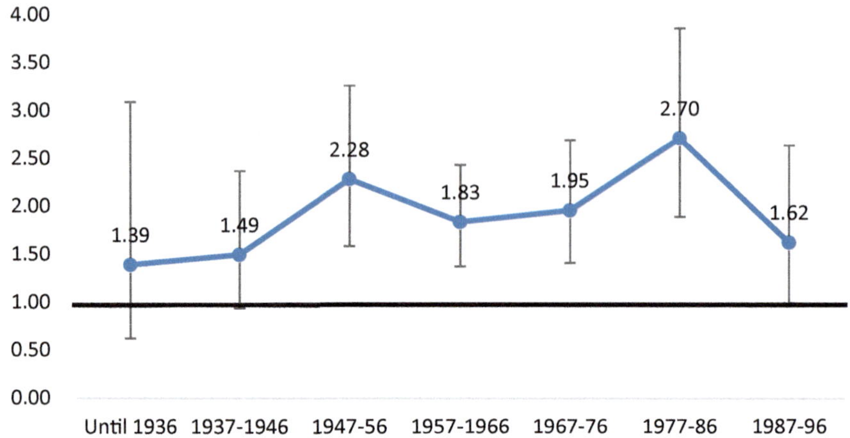

Fig. 5.5 Promotion to manager/assistant manager

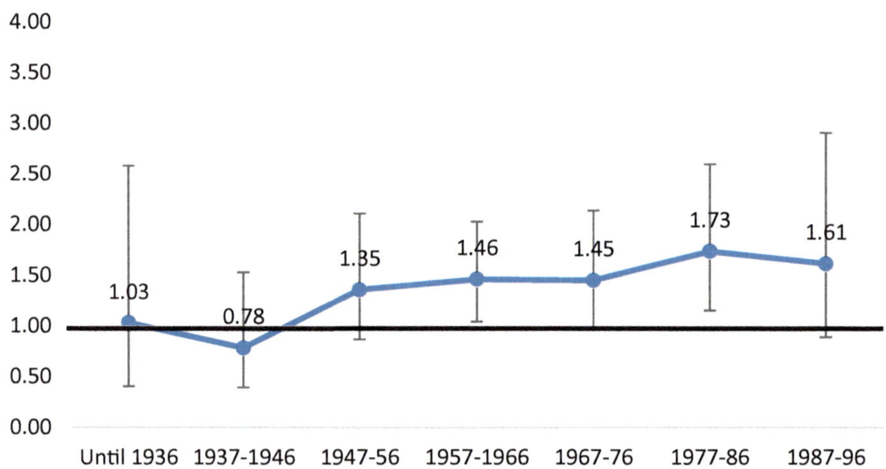

Fig. 5.6 Promotion to section head/department head

1977–86, and long-term employment is not greatly advantageous. In addition, the odds ratio decreases from 1987 and is no longer significant.

These time-series changes can be summarized into three characteristics. First, the superiority of long-term employment had no effect until the end of the war in 1946. Second, the superiority of long-term employment was seen for new hires from the end of the war to just before the bubble economy in 1986. However, the superiority of long-term employment has diminished since 1987 following the bubble economy period.

Table 5.2 Effect of long-term employment on promotion and effect of promotion on long-term employment

	Effect on promotion				Effect of promotion			
	Assistant manager		Section head		Assistant manager		Section head	
−36	0.431	**	0.822		−1.665	**	−0.460	
37–46	0.709		0.413		−0.096		−0.773	
47–56	1.077		0.796		0.655	**	0.000	
57–66	1.194		1.813	*	0.446	**	0.561	*
67–76	1.387	**	1.571		0.694	**	0.278	
77–86	1.299	*	1.845	*	0.686	**	0.583	*
87–96	1.300		1.167		0.403		0.286	

** $p < 0.01$, * $p < 0.05$

Comparing this result with the previous hypothesis reveals that it is suitable with the second hypothesis. That is, when there is an increase in long-term employees, their superiority increases, and their superiority decreases when there is a decrease in long-term employees. This result shows that, first, Japanese employment practices were established from the prewar to the postwar period of rapid economic growth, and therefore, firm-specific human capital was valued and preferential treatment for long-term employees progressed gradually. Second, Japanese employment practices have gradually begun to collapse since the latter half of the 1970s, indicating that the preferential treatment for long-term employees is being lost (Table 5.2).[9]

Furthermore, binary logistic regression analysis was used to analyze whether promotion encouraged long-term employment. The dependent variable is the presence or absence of long-term employment, and the independent variable is the presence or absence of promotion as follows: promotion to assistant manager (no promotion [standard], promotion up to the fifth year, promotion from the sixth year onwards) and promotion to section head (no promotion [standard], promotion up to the 15th year, promotion from the 16th year onwards). Control variables are the same as those for the previous analysis. The results show only promotion from the sixth year onwards (Assistant Manager) and from the 16th year onwards (Section Head).

These results are similar to those shown in Figs. 5.3 and 5.4 with regard to the ease of promotion and the ease of working in the same company after promotion. Specifically, the period of high economic growth witnessed the impact of long-term employment on promotion as well as the impact of promotion on long-term employment. However, such effects ceased to exist for new hires after 1987.

[9] Two additional analyses were carried out. The first was an analysis using the discrete time logit model from person-year data to analyze whether continuing to work for the same company would be advantageous for promotion. Employees working for six years or more were targeted for Assistant Manager, and employees working for 11 years or more were targeted for Section Head. The dependent variable is promotion to Assistant Manager or promotion to Section Head, and the independent variable is whether those promoted were still employed at their first company. Control variables are the same as those for previous analysis.

5.5 Conclusion

In this chapter, with a main focus on the characteristics of new hires from the 1920s to the 1990s, we have clearly explained the occupational history for 20 years from the time of employment in the first job and the trends of the changes that took place.

Those who entered employment from the 1920s to the 1940s were more likely to have long-term employment at large companies than at small companies, despite being affected by war and given that long-term employment was not necessarily common (approximately 20%) (support for 1920s theory).In contrast, from the promotion perspective, the superiority of long-term employment was not particularly high, and it could not be confirmed whether Japanese-style employment practices were actually in place.

Due to the impact of the Asia–Pacific war, there was a rapid increase in job changes in the period from the war to the postwar chaos. The work history of workers who entered employment around this period became unstable, and there was no superiority attached to long-term employment. Following this, job turnover declined, and employment became unstable after the 1950s. During such times, there has been an increase in the number of long-term employees along with a reduction in the differences in the stability of work history among employees, leading to leveling. At the same time, the establishment of Japanese-style employment practices would clarify the superiority of long-term employees. In other words, long-term employment practices did not occur in the 1950s but were established in that period.

The job turnover rate remained low even after the end of the period of high economic growth, although the rate has been gradually increasing since the 1980s. Therefore, the number of long-term employees who entered employment since the latter half of the 1970s is also decreasing. Until that point, white-collar workers working in specialization, management, clerical work, etc., were more likely to be in long-term employment; however, later, such superiority disappeared, and the differences between white-collar and blue-collar workers ceased to exist. Superiority in terms of promotion in the case of long-term employment was also lost. While it is argued that long-term employment has been declining since the 2000s, the conclusion of this chapter is that its germination began with employees who entered employment around 1980. This claim is based on a characteristic that can only be observed by analyzing the entire work history and is a point that has not been substantially discussed so far.

However, limitations include that this chapter examined only 20 years of work experience and considered only those who continue to work as long-term employees, which could exert an impact on the conclusion of this chapter. It will be necessary to consider other aspects of this issue in future.

References

Abegglen, J. C. (1958). *The Japanese Factory: Aspects of Its Social Organization*. Free Press.

Blau, P. M., & Duncan, O. D. (1967). *The American Occupational Structure*. Wiley.

Cheng, M. M., & Kallberg, A. L. (1996). Labor market structures in Japan: An analysis of organizational and occupational mobility patterns. *Social Forces, 4*, 1235–1260.

Cheng, M. M., & Kallberg, A. L. (1997). How permanent was permanent employment?: Patterns of organizational mobility in Japan, 1916–1975. *Work and Occupations, 24*(1), 12–32.

Chuma, H. (1998). Is Japan's Long-Term Employment System Changing?, Isao Ohashi and Toshiaki Tachibanaki eds, International Labour Markets, Incentives and Employment, Macmillan Press.

Dore, R. (1973). *British Factory – Japanese Factory: The Origins of National Diversity in Industrial Relations*. University of California Press.

Gordon, A. (1985). *The Evolution of Labor Relations in Japan: Heavy Industry, 1853–1955*. Harvard University Press.

Hamaaki, J., Hori, M., Maeda, S., & Murata, K. (2012). Changes in the Japanese employment system in the two lost decades. *ILR Review, 65*(4), 810–846.

Hazama, H. (1964). *Nihon Roumu Kanrishi Kenkyuu [A Study of the History of Japanese Labor Management]*. Daiamondo Sha

Hyodo, T. (1971). Nihon niokeru Roushi-Kankei no Tenkai (The Development of Labor-Management Relations in Japan). Tokyo: Tokyo Daigaku Shuppankai.

Jacoby, S. (1979). The origins of internal labor markets in Japan. *Industrial Relations, 18*, 184–196.

Kambayashi, R., & Takao, K. (2016). Good Jobs and Bad Jobs in Japan: 1982–2007. Centeron-Japanese Economy and Business (CJEB) Working Paper No. 348, Columbia University.

Kambayashi, R., & Kato, T. (2017). Long-term employment and job security over the past 25 years: A comparative study of Japan and The United States. *ILR Review, 70*(2), 359–394.

Kato, T. (2001). The end of lifetime employment in Japan?: Evidence from national surveys and field research. *Journal of the Japanese and International Economies, 15*, 489–514.

Kalleberg, A. L., & Mouw, T. (2018). Occupations, organizations, and intragenerational career mobility. *Annual Review of Sociology, 44*, 283–303.

Kawaguchi, D., & Ueno, Y. (2013). Declining long-term employment in Japan. *Journal of the Japanese and International Economies, 28*, 19–36.

Koike, K. (2005). *Shigoto no Keizaigaku [Economics of Labor]*. Toyo Keizai Shinpo Sha.

Koike, K. (2012). *Kouhinshitu Nihon no Kigen [Origin of high quality Japanese products]*. Hihon Keizai Shinbun Shuppan.

Levine, S. B. (1983). Careers and mobility in Japan's labor markets. In: D. W. Plath (Ed.), *Work and Lifecourse in Japan* (pp. 18–33). State University of New York Press.

Magota, R. (1965). Senji Roudou-ron eno Gimon (A Question of Wartime Labor Theory). *Nohon Roudo Kenkyu Zasshi (Japanese Journal of Labor Rsearch), 75*, 11–23.

Moriguchi, C., & Ono, H. (2006). Japanese lifetime employment: A Century's perspective. Magnus Blomstrom and Summer La Croix eds. *Institutional Change in Japan* (pp. 152–176). Taylor & Francis.

Nakamura, T. (1993). *Nihon Keizai: Seicho to Kouzo* (*Japanese Economy: Growth and Structure*). Tokyo: Tokyo Daigaku Shuppankai.

Nomura, M. (1994). *Shuushin Koyou* (*Lifetime Enployment*). Tokyo: Iwanami Shoten.

Odaka, K. (1984). Rodo-Shijo Bunseki: Niju-Kozo no Nihonteki Tenkai (Labor Market Analysis: Japanese Development of Dual Structures). Tokyo: Iwanami Shoten.

Ono, H. (2010). Lifetime Employment in Japan: Concepts and Measurements. *Journal of the Japanese and International Economies, 24*, 1–27.

Rosenfeld, R. A. (1992). Job mobility and career processes. *Annual Review of Sociology, 18*, 39–61.

Shimizutani, S., & Yokoyama, I. (2009). Has Japan's long-term employment practice survived?: Developments since the 1990s. *Industrial and Labor Relations Review, 62*(3), 313–326.

Sugayama, S. (2011). "*Shuusha*" *Shakai no Tanjo* (*The Evolution of Employment Relations and Labor Market Institutions in Japan*). Nagoya: Nagoya Daigaku Shuppankai.

Suzuki, H. (2010). Employment relations in Japan: Recent changes under global competition and recession. *Journal of Industrial Relations, 52*(3), 387–401.

Takahashi, Y. (1997). The Labor Market and Lifetime Employment in Japan. *Economic Industrial Democracy, 18*, 55–66.

Ujihara, S. (1966) *Nihon Roudou Mondai Kennkyu* (*Research on Labor Issues in Japan*). Tokyo: Tokyo Daigaku Shuppankai.

Vogel, E. F. (1979). *Japan as Nunber One: Lessons for America.* Harvard University Press.

Watanabe, T. (2020). Senso to Shakaiteki-Fubyoudo (War and Social Inequality). Kyoto: Nineruba Shobo.

Yu, W.-H. (2010). 2010, Enduring an economic crisis: The effect of macroeconomic shocks on intragenerational mobility in Japan. *Social Science Research, 39*, 1088–1107.

Tsutomu Watanabe is Professor of Sociology at the Scool of Sociology, Kwansei Gakuin University, He received his Ph.D. in literature from Tohoku University. He conducted his research at Tohoku University as teaching associate, held positions of Associate Professor of Sociology at Shinshu University. Dr. Watanabe's research interests include social stratification and job career, war and economic history.His publicaitons are "Analysis of Labor Markets in Postwar Japan: the Viewpoint of Job Mobility" (with Yoshimichi Sato) (International of Journal of Sociology 30(2): 3-33,2000) and "International Comparison on the Occurrence of Social Movement" (Journal of Bussiness Research 60(7): 806-812, 2007).

Chapter 6
Intragenerational Mobility Between Regular and Non-regular Employment Sectors in Japan: From the Viewpoint of the Theory of Mobility Regime

Yoshimichi Sato

Abstract This chapter examines intragenerational mobility between the regular and non-regular employment sectors in Japan by analyzing the dataset of the 2015 Social Stratification and Social Mobility National Survey from the viewpoint of the theory of mobility regime. The Japanese mobility regime comprises Japanese employment practices, the Japanese welfare-employment regime, and the male-single-breadwinner model. This regime places male regular workers at the core of the labor market while pushing female non-regular workers to its periphery, and suppresses job turnover. However, it is believed that globalization, the shift to a service industry, and neoliberal labor policies have weakened the regime. From these theoretical perspectives, I analyzed the job histories of the survey's respondents by using discrete-time logit models while selecting for gender. The main finding of the analysis is that the prevailing regime is changing, but not necessarily weakening. Movement from regular to non-regular employment sector is more likely to occur at the time of this study than it has been historically, while movement from non-regular to regular employment is less likely.

6.1 Non-Regular Workers in Japan and the Theory of Mobility Regime

Attention is often brought to the deteriorating situation of non-regular workers in contemporary Japan. Wages for these workers are much lower, their job security is worse, and their social security benefits are less than those of their counterparts in

This chapter is based on a working paper of the 2015 SSM project titled "Intragenerational Mobility between the Regular and Non-regular Employment Sectors in Japan: From the Viewpoint of the Theory of Mobility Regime" by Yoshimichi Sato. This research was supported by JSPS KAKENHI Grant Numbers JP 25000001, 15H03405, and 16K13406. I thank the 2015 SSM Survey Project members for their productive comments.

Y. Sato (✉)
Kyoto University of Advanced Science/Tohoku University, Kyoto, Japan
e-mail: sato.yoshimichi@kuas.ac.jp

S. Shirahase (ed.), *Social Stratification in an Aging Society with Low Fertility*, Economy and Social Inclusion, https://doi.org/10.1007/978-981-19-3647-0_6

the regular employment sector. The hourly wage of regular workers is about two times higher than that of non-regular workers (Cabinet Office of Government of Japan, 2017: 95, Fig. 2-1-3). Almost all regular workers have employment insurance and receive an employee pension, whereas for non-regular workers, this percentage stands at 65% and 51%, respectively (Kim, 2015). From an international perspective, non-regular workers share common features with workers in precarious situations in other advanced industrial countries (cf. Campbell & Price, 2016), but the difficulty of becoming a regular worker is exceptionally high in Japan. The odds ratio of mobility between regular and non-regular workers, using the Labor Force Survey conducted by the Statistics Bureau of the Ministry of Internal Affairs and Communications, is shown in Fig. 6.1. The ratio for male workers is 5.05, and that for female workers is 5.06 as of 2018. This implies that the odds of getting a regular job for male (female) workers who were regular workers in the previous year are 5.05 (5.06) times higher than the odds for those who were non-regular workers during the same period. The figure also shows that the trend is rather stable. This is evidence that the mobility barrier between the non-regular and regular employment sectors is very high and persistent in Japan. Other scholars have also reported the significance of this mobility barrier (Genda, 2008).

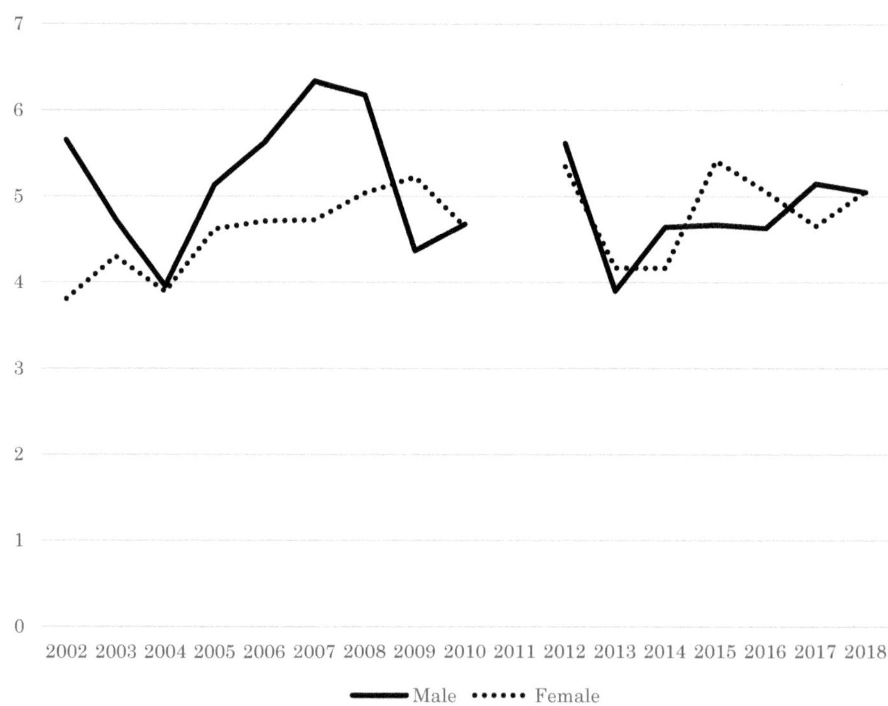

Fig. 6.1 Odds ratio of getting regular jobs. *Source* Created by the author using Labor Force Survey data

Why is this mobility barrier so high and persistent? I argue that applying the theory of mobility regime as proposed by Diprete (2002) to the study of the Japanese labor market will aid in answering this question. The crux of my argument asserts that intragenerational mobility is not an independently arising phenomenon. Rather, this type of mobility occurs based on the institutional arrangements of the labor market and the general conventions of society. Thus, different institutional arrangements result in different patterns of intragenerational mobility, which explains, for example, the lower job turnover rate in Japan as compared to that in the United States (this is explained in detail later).

I assume that the Japanese employment practices, the Japanese welfare-employment regime, and the male-single-breadwinner model are the institutional arrangements that affect intragenerational mobility. Based on observations of Japanese factories, Abbeglen (1958) proposed that the Japanese employment practices comprise the long-term employment practice, seniority-based wage scheme, and company unions. The first two components suppress job changes because of the following mechanism: If an employee leaves a company and obtains employment at another company, their seniority does not transfer. It then becomes probable that this employee's wages will decline. Since employees expect this to occur, they are less likely to seek new employment. The third component (i.e., company unions) excludes non-regular workers; only regular workers are qualified as union members. There is a historical reason for this exclusion. Before World War II, there existed in Japan segregation by status between white- and blue-collar workers. The former enjoyed stable monthly salary and generous benefits provided by their company, while the latter's economic and working conditions were significantly worse-off. In other words, there were two status groups in the same company. Thus, after World War II, labor unions attempted to democratize their companies by demolishing the segregation by status, and succeeded in introducing the institutional arrangements whereby white- and blue-collar workers were treated equally as members of the same company. However, the "members" were regular workers; non-regular workers were excluded from these unions. This practice of exclusion has existed and partially contributed to the construction of the barrier preventing non-regular employees from seeking regular employment.

The theory of welfare-employment regime assumes that society secures the livelihood of its members through welfare and employment, and that the balance between welfare and employment varies across societies (Esping-Andersen, 1990; Imai, 2011). Imai (2011) points out that the salient feature of the Japanese welfare-employment regime is "welfare through employment." This implies that companies provide their employees with welfare packages. For example, companies cover half of their employees' pension and health insurance premiums. Furthermore, some companies provide their employees with housing. One caveat should be mentioned, however. These ample welfare packages are usually reserved for regular employees; companies do not typically offer them to non-regular employees. Because of this difference in labor cost between regular and non-regular employees, companies tend to replace regular employees with non-regular employees if possible. This practice

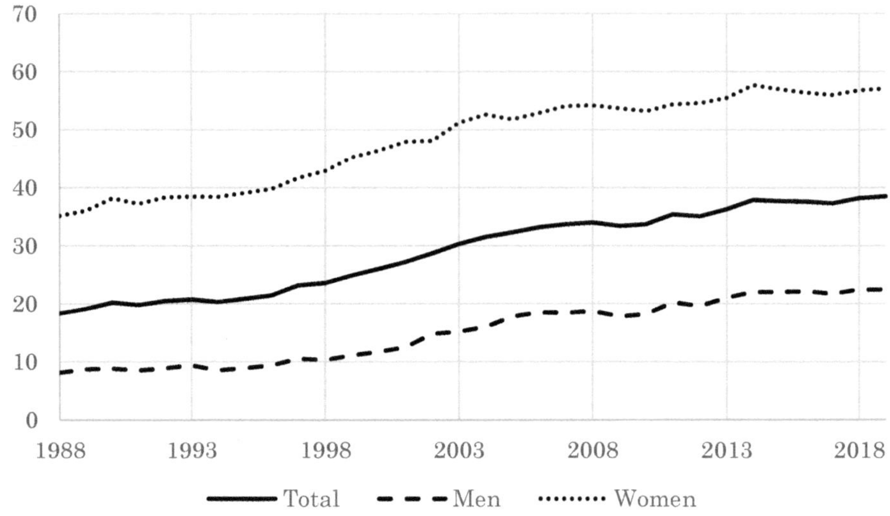

Fig. 6.2 Percentage of non-regular workers. *Source* Created by the author using Labor Force Survey data

has contributed to an increase in the proportion of non-regular workers in contemporary Japan. As shown in Fig. 6.2, the percentage of non-regular workers has been increasing not only among women but also among men, who have been major participants in the Japanese employment practices.

The male-single-breadwinner model reinforces the Japanese employment practice in the labor market, and vice versa. Male regular employees show their loyalty to companies by working long hours and accepting company transfers in exchange for regular employment status and ample welfare packages. However, it would be difficult for these employees to maintain such loyalty without the help of an at-home domestic partner. That is, at-home partners perform most of the household chores, and tend to be housewives or part-time workers to secure sufficient time for homemaking. This sexual division of labor has increased the share of female non-regular workers in the labor market, most of whom are married women.

The reviewed features of the Japanese mobility regime can thus far be summarized as pointing to a regime that places male regular workers at the core of the labor market, pushes female non-regular workers to the periphery of the market, and suppresses job turnover. This regime was strong and influential during Japan's period of high economic growth (1955–1973), but has weakened recently.

Globalization, a shift in the industrial structure from heavy to service industry, and neoliberal labor policies are major factors that have weakened the Japanese mobility regime. Globalization has increased the opportunity cost for companies adhering to the Japanese employment practices. Through such adherence, these companies lose the opportunity to find a better labor force at a cheaper cost outside Japan. The shift to the service industry has increased the share of non-regular workers who are not protected by labor unions. Neoliberal labor policies have also contributed to increases in flexibility in the labor market and, eventually, in the proportion of non-regular workers. For example, the Temporary Dispatching Work Law enacted in 1986 involves a series of revisions that have led to an increase in the number of dispatched workers, which is a type of non-regular employment (Imai, 2011).

These changes have made the labor market more flexible, but have not affected all segments of labor market. Regular workers at large firms and in the public sector are still protected by Japanese employment practices. By contrast, non-regular workers at the periphery of the labor market are experiencing increased flexibility. Sato (2010) called this situation "the coexistence of stability and increasing flexibility." This coexistence, however, makes it difficult for non-regular workers to transition to the regular employment sector.

6.2 Hypotheses

As pointed out in the previous section, the core of the labor market is still intact, while flexibility is increasing at the periphery. Male regular workers at large firms and in the public sector are at the market's core (Nomura, 1994), while female workers, those at small and mid-sized firms, and non-regular workers are concentrated at the periphery. Therefore, I focus on gender and firm size to derive hypotheses on intragenerational mobility between the regular and non-regular employment sectors.

Furthermore, distinct time periods should be considered in such a study because, as abovementioned, the Japanese mobility regime has weakened over time. Thus, I use four time periods in this study: The high economic growth period (1955–1973), the slow economic growth period after the oil crises (1974–1984), the bubble economy period (1985–1991), and the post-bubble economy period (1992–2015). It is commonly accepted that the Japanese mobility regime with Japanese employment practices, Japanese welfare-employment regime, and the male-single-breadwinner model as the main components was established during the high economic growth period (Brinton, 1993). Since then, the regime is thought to have weakened. Therefore, I use the high economic growth period as the reference point for the statistical analysis in Sect. 6.4.

6.2.1 Hypotheses on Intragenerational Mobility from Regular to Non-regular Employment

Regarding mobility from regular to non-regular employment sectors, I propose two competing hypotheses on the effects of firm size, and two additional competing hypotheses on the effects of time period.

Hypothesis 1-1: Male regular workers at large firms and in the public sector are less likely to become non-regular workers than their counterparts at small and mid-sized firms. By contrast, the probability of a female regular worker becoming a non-regular worker is not affected by firm size.

This hypothesis is derived from the abovementioned difference between the core and the periphery of the Japanese labor market. Male regular employees at the market's core are still protected by the Japanese employment practices, while their counterparts at the periphery are not. This leads to the difference in probability of becoming a non-regular worker between regular workers at large firms and in the public sector and those at small and mid-sized firms. By contrast, female workers are placed at the market's periphery regardless of firm size. Thus, there is no difference in the probability of becoming a non-regular worker among female regular workers.

Hypothesis 1-2: Female regular workers at large firms and in the public sector are less likely to become non-regular workers than their counterparts at small and mid-sized firms. By contrast, the probability of a male regular worker becoming a non-regular worker is not affected by firm size.

This hypothesis is the opposite of Hypothesis 1–1, and is derived from the strength of the Japanese mobility regime. That is, the regime is so strong that even male regular workers at small and mid-sized firms are under its influence. Therefore, there is no difference in the probability of becoming a non-regular worker among male regular workers. Furthermore, if the regime is strong, it might also cover female regular workers at large firms or in the public sector, which would lower the probability of their becoming non-regular workers.

The next two hypotheses are about the effect of time periods.

Hypothesis 2-1: The probability of a male regular worker becoming a non-regular worker increased during the post-bubble economy period, but the status of female regular workers is not affected by time periods.

This hypothesis is derived from the same mechanism as that of Hypothesis 1-1. The Japanese mobility regime that has protected male regular workers has weakened. This occurred most significantly during the post-bubble economy period. Thus, these workers were more likely to become non-regular workers during this period than previously. In contrast, female regular workers have not been protected by the mobility regime at any time period. Thus, their status is not affected by time periods.

Hypothesis 2-2: The probability of a female regular worker becoming a non-regular worker increased during the post-bubble economy period, but the status of male regular workers is not affected by time periods.

This hypothesis is derived from the same mechanism as that of Hypothesis 1-2. Male regular workers have been protected by the Japanese mobility regime at each time period, while female regular workers, who are at the periphery of the labor market, are affected by the increasing flexibility that began to occur during the post-bubble economy period.

6.2.2 *Hypotheses on Intragenerational Mobility from Non-regular to Regular Employment*

I propose three hypotheses on intragenerational mobility from the non-regular to the regular employment sector based on the theory of the Japanese mobility regime.

Hypothesis 3: The probability of becoming a regular worker for both male and female non-regular workers is not affected by firm size.

"Being non-regular worker" is a form of social status in Japan (cf. Arita, 2016). This implies that non-regular workers are placed at the market's periphery regardless of their gender or the size of their firm. Thus, the probability of becoming a regular worker is not affected by firm size.

Hypothesis 4: The probability of becoming a regular worker for both male and female non-regular workers decreases when firm size increases.

While Hypothesis 3 concerns the size of workers' current firms, Hypothesis 4 pertains to the entry barrier. It is more difficult for non-regular workers to enter large firms or the public sector as regular workers midway during their careers than it is to enter small and mid-sized firms. This is because most of the large firms and the public sector are still under the strong influence of the Japanese mobility regime. Therefore, the entry barrier to these areas is higher than it is at small and mid-sized firms.

Hypothesis 5: The probability of becoming a regular worker for both male and female non-regular workers increased more significantly during the post-bubble economy period than previously.

As abovementioned, it is believed that the Japanese mobility regime weakened during the post-bubble economy period, while the labor market became more flexible. Thus, it is possible that non-regular workers found it easier to obtain regular jobs during this period than previously.

6.3 Data and Methods

I used the dataset from the 2015 Social Stratification and Social Mobility National Survey (hereafter, the 2015 SSM Survey) to examine the empirical validity of this study's hypotheses.[1] The 2015 SSM Survey was conducted using nationwide representative samples in Japan. The samples were from individuals between 20 and 79 years of age. There were 7817 respondents, and the response rate was 50.1%.

The dataset from the survey contains the job histories of respondents, which can be used for my analysis of intragenerational mobility between the regular and non-regular employment sectors. Information on job history was contained in a wide-type

---

[1] I thank the 2015 SSM Survey Management Committee for allowing me to use the SSM data.

data format; I converted it to long-type data format so that discrete-time logit models could be applied.[2] I focused on job histories from before respondents became 55 years of age to avoid the effects of mandatory retirement.

I analyzed the job histories of men and women separately because their positions are segregated in the labor market. Two dependent variables were used in the models: hazard probability of moving from the regular to non-regular employment sector, and that of moving from the non-regular to regular employment sector.[3] An event is defined as mobility from regular to non-regular employment, or vice versa.

Four independent variables were used to examine the hypotheses: the duration time as the baseline hazard function, firm size at $t-1$, firm size at t, and time period. Duration time was measured by the interval of time (in years) that had passed since a respondent entered a job, and was converted to dummy variables expressing each year in logit models. Firm size was measured by the number of employees in the firm. Firm size at $t-1$, which indicates the size of firms' workers currently employed, was used to examine Hypothesis 3. Firm size at t, which indicates the number of workers entering firms, was used to examine Hypothesis 4. Time period was divided into abovementioned four periods with the high economic growth period as the reference category.

The risk sets for analysis are defined as follows. In the analysis of mobility from regular to non-regular employment, an individual enters the risk set when they become a regular worker. An event then occurs if they become a non-regular worker. Otherwise, the data are judged as right-censored. In the analysis of mobility from non-regular to regular employment, an individual enters the risk set when they become a non-regular worker. Then, if they become a regular worker, an event occurs; otherwise, the data are judged as right-censored.

6.4 Results

6.4.1 Intragenerational Mobility from the Regular to Non-Regular Employment Sector

Descriptive statistics are summarized in Table 6.1.

Table 6.2 shows the results of five discrete-time logit models for males. If the coefficient for a variable is larger than 1, the variable has a positive effect on the hazard rate of moving from the regular to the non-regular employment sector; if the coefficient is less than 1, the variable's effect is negative. Model 1 uses only dummy variables for duration time as the baseline hazard function. Coefficients for dummy

---

[2] I thank Tokio Yasuda of Kansai University for providing the 2015 SSM Survey Project members with an SPSS syntax for converting the data. I also referred to Mugiyama (2016) to create the long-type data for analysis.

[3] The mobility from being unemployed to becoming a non-regular worker to regular worker is also an important research topic. See Moriyama (2018) for a detailed analysis of this mobility.

Table 6.1 Descriptive statistics (mobility from regular to non-regular employment)

	Observations	%
Event		
No	119,907	99.21
Yes	959	0.79
Total	120,866	100
Gender		
Male	76,812	63.55
Female	44,054	36.45
Total	120,866	100
Firm size at $t - 1$		
1–99	42,974	37.01
100–999	28,249	24.33
1000 >= or public sector	44,891	38.66
Total	116,114	100
Period		
High economic growth period	20,241	16.75
Slow economic growth period	23,472	19.42
Bubble economy period	19,057	15.77
Post-bubble economy period	58,096	48.07
Total	120,866	100

Duration of time after entering the regular employment

Observations	Mean	Sd	Min	Max
120,866	13.364	9.751	1	40

variables are omitted in Table 6.2 to save space. In Model 2, firm size at $t - 1$ as an independent variable is added to Model 1, while Model 3 adds time period to Model 1. Model 4 uses both firm size at $t - 1$ and time period as independent variables. In Model 5, the jobs-to-applicants ratio is added to Model 4. This is a control variable to determine whether the effect of time period exists after controlling for economic situations in the labor market.

The effect of firm size at $t - 1$ is clear in Model 5. The coefficients for mid-sized and large firms, and the public sector are less than 1, and they become smaller as the firm size increases. This implies that, as firm size increases, male regular workers are less likely to move to the non-regular employment sector. The coefficient for the post-bubble economy period is the largest among those for time periods in Model 5. This means that mobility from regular to non-regular sector is more likely to occur in this period than in other periods.

Table 6.3 shows the results of the same five discrete-time logit models for females. Similar results are observed for Model 5.

Table 6.2 Discrete-time logit models for males (Mobility from regular to non-regular employment)

	Model 1		Model 2		Model 3		Model 4		Model 5	
	Odds ratio	Robust SE	Odds ratio	Robust SE	Odds ratio	Robust SE	Odds ratio	Robust SE	Odds ratio	Robust SE
Constant	0.017***	0.012***	0.022	0.016	0.004***	0.003	0.006***	0.005	0.004***	0.003
Duration time	(omitted)		(omitted)		(omitted)		(omitted)		(omitted)	
Firm size at $t-1$										
1–99			Ref				Ref		Ref	
100–999			0.719**	0.103			0.672***	0.097	0.668***	0.096
1000 >= or public sector			0.292***	0.048			0.299***	0.049	0.298***	0.049
Period										
High economic growth period					Ref		Ref		Ref	
Slow economic growth period					1.748**	0.433	1.808**	0.448	2.076***	0.556
Bubble economy period					1.563	0.435	1.585*	0.442	1.580	0.440
Post-bubble economy period					3.968***	0.829	3.888***	0.810	4.366***	0.996
Jobs-to-applicants ratio									1.519	0.395
# of observations	69,270		69,270		69,270		69,270		69,270	
# of samples	3168		3168		3168		3168		3168	
Log pseudolikelihood	−1724.146		−1690.568		−1688.212		−1656.680		−1655.367	
Pseudo R^2	0.048		0.067		0.068		0.086		0.086	

***$p < 0.01$, **$p < 0.05$, *$p < 0.1$

Table 6.3 Discrete-time logit models for females (Mobility from regular to non-regular employment)

	Model 1		Model 2		Model 3		Model 4		Model 5	
	Odds ratio	Robust SE	Odds ratio	Robust SE	Odds ratio	Robust SE	Odds ratio	Robust SE	Odds ratio	Robust SE
Constant	0.011***	0.011	0.014***	0.015	0.003***	0.003	0.005***	0.005	0.004***	0.004
Duration time	(omitted)		(omitted)		(omitted)		(omitted)		(omitted)	
Firm size at $t-1$										
1–99			Ref				Ref		Ref	
100–999			0.824**	0.080			0.760***	0.075	0.759***	0.075
1000 >= or public sector			0.471***	0.051			0.473***	0.052	0.473***	0.052
Period										
High economic growth period					Ref		Ref		Ref	
Slow economic growth period					1.484**	0.257	1.520**	0.264	1.601***	0.286
Bubble economy period					2.515***	0.420	2.580***	0.431	2.572***	0.430
Post-bubble economy period					3.358***	0.490	3.365***	0.492	3.514***	0.530
Jobs-to-applicants ratio									1.180	0.194

(continued)

Table 6.3 (continued)

	Model 1		Model 2		Model 3		Model 4		Model 5	
	Odds ratio	Robust SE	Odds ratio	Robust SE	Odds ratio	Robust SE	Odds ratio	Robust SE	Odds ratio	Robust SE
# of observations	37,098		37,098		37,098		37,098		37,098	
# of samples	3354		3354		3354		3354		3354	
Log pseudolikelihood	−3070.2015		−3042.2635		−3014.6402		−2987.5671		−2987.0875	
Pseudo R^2	0.020		0.028		0.037		0.046		0.046	

$^{***}p < 0.01$, $^{**}p < 0.05$, $^{*}p < 0.1$

The results shown in Tables 6.2 and 6.3 imply that Hypotheses 1–1 and 1–2 are partially supported. Both male and female regular workers at large firms and in the public sector are less likely to become non-regular workers than their counterparts at small and mid-sized firms. By comparing the values of coefficients for large firms and the public sector in Tables 6.2 and 6.3 (0.298 and 0.473, respectively), female regular workers are more likely to become non-regular workers than their male counterparts. However, I believe that these results show the strength of the Japanese mobility regime.

The results in Tables 6.2 and 6.3 also show that Hypotheses 2–1 and 2–2 are partially supported. Both male and female regular workers were more likely to become non-regular workers during the post-bubble economy period than previously. This implies that the effects of globalization, the shift to service industry, and neoliberal labor policies on the Japanese mobility regime are stronger than the expectations set forth in the hypotheses.

Although it has become weaker, the Japanese mobility regime still functions as a mobility barrier. As mentioned above, the coefficients for mid-sized firms, large firms, and public sector are less than 1, and they become smaller as firm size becomes larger. Thus, the proposed "coexistence of stability and increasing flexibility" by Sato (2010) is verified by this analysis.

6.4.2 Intragenerational Mobility from Non-Regular to Regular Employment Sector

Descriptive statistics are summarized in Table 6.4.

Table 6.5 shows the results of six discrete-time logit models for males. In Table 6.5, Models 1–5 are the same as those in Table 6.2 with the exception of the dependent variable, which is the hazard probability of non-regular workers becoming regular workers. Model 6 uses firm size at t instead of firm size at $t-1$ to examine Hypothesis 4.[4]

Model 5 in Table 6.5 shows that firm size at $t-1$ does not affect the hazard probability of becoming a regular worker, and that the probability became lower during the post-bubble economy period. Model 6 also shows similar patterns.

Table 6.6 shows the results of the same six discrete-time logit models for females. Model 5 shows that female non-regular workers at mid-sized firms at $t-1$ are more likely to become regular workers than their counterparts at small and large firms, while Model 6 shows that they are also more likely to become regular workers at mid-sized firms at t than their counterparts at small and large firms at t. Models 5 and 6 show that female non-regular workers are less likely to become regular workers during any period following the high economic growth period.

[4] Firm size at t and firm size at $t-1$ were not included in the model simultaneously because of multicollinearity.

Table 6.4 Descriptive statistics (Mobility from non-regular to regular employment)

	Observations	%
Event		
No	29,444	97.06
Yes	892	2.94
Total	30,336	100
Gender		
Male	5560	18.33
Female	24,776	81.67
Total	30,336	100
Firm size at $t-1$		
1–99	14,249	55.25
100–999	5002	19.4
1000 > = or public sector	6539	25.35
Total	25,790	100
Firm size at t		
1–99	13,998	55.17
100–999	5014	19.76
1000 >= or public sector	6361	25.07
Total	25,373	100
Period		
High economic growth period	1796	5.92
Slow economic growth period	3455	11.39
Bubble economy period	3828	12.62
Post-bubble economy period	21,257	70.07
Total	30,336	100

Duration of time after entering the non-regular employment

Observations	Mean	Sd	Min	Max
30,336	7.905	6.390	1	40

The results in Tables 6.5 and 6.6 imply that Hypotheses 3 and 4 are only valid for male non-regular workers. Female non-regular workers at mid-sized firms in the labor market have more opportunities to become regular workers. The theory of the Japanese mobility regime assumed a significant difference between small/mid-sized firms and large firms/public sector. However, the study of the mechanisms that produce mobility for female workers between mid-sized firms is an interesting future research topic.

Furthermore, Hypothesis 5 was not supported. Contrary to the hypothesis, mobility from non-regular to regular employment sector became difficult during

Table 6.5 Discrete-time logit models for males (Mobility from non-regular to regular employment)

	Model 1		Model 2		Model 3		Model 4		Model 5		Model 6	
	Odds ratio	Robust SE	Odds ratio	Robust SE	Odds ratio	Robust SE	Odds ratio	Robust SE	Odds ratio	Robust SE	Odds ratio	Robust SE
Constant	0.077**	0.080	0.080**	0.083	0.099**	0.106	0.101**	0.108	0.131*	0.141	0.131*	0.141
Duration time	(omitted)		(omitted)		(omitted)		(omitted)		(omitted)			
Firm size at $t-1$												
1–99			Ref				Ref		Ref			
100–999			0.841	0.139			0.871	0.145	0.880	0.146		
1000 >= or public sector			0.977	0.139			1.012	0.148	1.007	0.147		
Firm size at t												
1–99											Ref	
100–999											1.102	0.203
1000 >= or public sector											0.963	0.163
Period												
High economic growth period					Ref		Ref		Ref		Ref	
Slow economic growth period					0.768	0.159	0.774	0.161	0.716	0.154	0.700*	0.150
Bubble economy period					0.968	0.219	0.973	0.221	0.991	0.225	0.984	0.223
Post-bubble economy period					0.726**	0.118	0.733*	0.122	0.693**	0.117	0.679**	0.116

(continued)

Table 6.5 (continued)

	Model 1		Model 2		Model 3		Model 4		Model 5		Model 6	
	Odds ratio	Robust SE	Odds ratio	Robust SE	Odds ratio	Robust SE	Odds ratio	Robust SE	Odds ratio	Robust SE	Odds ratio	Robust SE
Jobs-to-applicants ratio									0.752	0.189	0.734	0.187
# of observations	3471		3471		3471		3471		3471		3471	
# of samples	587		587		587		587		587		587	
Log pseudolikelihood	−1025.857		−1025.278		−1023.382		−1022.969		−1022.242		−1022.287	
Pseudo R^2	0.041		0.042		0.044		0.044		0.045		0.045	

$***p < 0.01$, $**p < 0.05$, $*p < 0.1$

Table 6.6 Discrete-time logit models females (Mobility from non-regular to regular employment)

	Model 1		Model 2		Model 3		Model 4		Model 5		Model 6	
	Odds ratio	Robust SE	Odds ratio	Robust SE	Odds ratio	Robust SE	Odds ratio	Robust SE	Odds ratio	Robust SE	Odds ratio	Robust SE
Constant	0.041***	0.029	0.038***	0.028	0.074***	0.055	0.071***	0.052	0.085***	0.065	0.089***	0.068
Duration time		(omitted)	(omitted)		(omitted)		(omitted)		(omitted)			
Firm size at $t-1$												
1–99			Ref				Ref		Ref			
100–999			1.206	0.149			1.250*	0.156	1.253*	0.157		
1000 >= or public sector			1.051	0.124			1.071	0.127	1.071	0.127		
Firm size at t												
1–99											Ref	
100–999											1.304**	0.170
1000 >= or public sector											0.778*	0.104
Period												
High economic growth period					Ref		Ref		Ref		Ref	
Slow economic growth period					0.585**	0.127	0.575**	0.125	0.539***	0.122	0.537***	0.121
Bubble economy period					0.491***	0.108	0.478***	0.106	0.479***	0.106	0.476***	0.106
Post-bubble economy period					0.563***	0.099	0.543***	0.097	0.516***	0.096	0.523***	0.098

(continued)

Table 6.6 (continued)

	Model 1		Model 2		Model 3		Model 4		Model 5		Model 6	
	Odds ratio	Robust SE	Odds ratio	Robust SE	Odds ratio	Robust SE	Odds ratio	Robust SE	Odds ratio	Robust SE	Odds ratio	Robust SE
Jobs-to-applicants ratio									0.834	0.171	0.832	0.171
# of observations	17,045		17,045		17,045		17,045		17,045		17,045	
# of samples	2021		2021		2021		2021		2021		2021	
Log pseudolikelihood	−1985.173		−1984.061		−1979.878		−1978.324		−1977.934		−1973.255	
Pseudo R^2	0.023		0.024		0.026		0.027		0.027		0.029	

***$p < 0.01$, **$p < 0.05$, *$p < 0.1$

the post-bubble economy period. This is also evidence that the Japanese mobility regime is still strong and influential.

6.5 Conclusions and Discussion

This study shows that the Japanese mobility regime still protects regular workers at large firms and in the public sector. It was assumed that only male regular workers were part of this regime, but the results of the discrete-time logit models show that female regular workers are also under its influence. In this sense, the regime is stronger than I expected.

Meanwhile, the regime is changing, but is not necessarily weakening. Mobility from regular to non-regular employment sector was more likely to occur during the post-bubble economy period, while that from non-regular to regular employment sector was less likely. A possible social mechanism of this asymmetric mobility is that firms have become more selective in the competitive global market and offer job security only to regular workers they really need. Exploring other possible social mechanisms that created this asymmetric change would lead to a more detailed analysis of the Japanese mobility regime, and would also make a substantive contribution to the advancement of the theory of mobility regime.

Furthermore, three topics should be addressed in future research. First, as mentioned in Footnote 3, the effects of unemployment on mobility should be considered. Second, there rarely occurs mobility from regular to non-regular employment sector, or vice versa (see Tables 6.1 and 6.4). Thus, methods that properly deal with this issue should be introduced to the analysis (King & Zeng, 2001). Third, although mobility between the regular and non-regular employment sectors rarely occurs, some workers experience this more often than others. To properly deal with the differences between these types of workers, multilevel modeling should be considered (Teachman, 2011).

References

Abbeglen, J. C. (1958). *The Japanese factory: Aspects of its social organization.* Free Press.

Arita, S. (2016). *The sociology of reward inequality among employment positions: A comparison of non-standard employment and social stratification in Japan and Korea.* University of Tokyo Press (in Japanese).

Brinton, M. C. (1993). *Women and the economic miracle: Gender and work in postwar Japan.* University of California Press.

Cabinet Office of Government of Japan. (2017). *Annual report of economy and finance, 2017.* Retrieved Jan 9, 2021, from https://www5.cao.go.jp/j-j/wp/wp-je17/index_pdf.html (in Japanese).

Campbell, I., & Price, R. (2016). Precarious work and precarious workers: Toward an improved conceptualisation. *The Economic and Labour Relations Review, 27,* 314–332.

Diprete, T. A. (2002). Life course risks, mobility regimes, and mobility consequences: A comparison of Sweden, Germany, and The United States. *American Journal of Sociology, 108,* 267–309.

Esping-Andersen, G. (1990). *The three worlds of welfare capitalism.* Polity Press.

Genda, Y. (2008). Transition into regular employment among separating non-regular employees. *Japanese Journal of Labour Studies, 580,* 61–77. (in Japanese)

Imai, J. (2011). *The transformation of Japanese employment relations: Reform without labor.* Palgrave MacMillan.

Kim, M.-J. (2015). Are employer contributions to social insurance increasing non-regular employment? *Japanese Journal of Labour Studies, 659,* 27–46. (in Japanese)

King, G., & Zeng, L. (2001). Logistic regression in rare events data. *Political Analysis, 9,* 137–163

Moriyama, T. (2018). Does the effect of non-regular employment as a "Stepping Stone" also exist in Japan? In *The 2015 SSM survey project working paper*. (in Japanese)

Mugiyama, R. (2016). Data processing and model selection for event history analysis. Retrieved Oct 9, 2017, from http://ryotamugiyama.com/wp-content/uploads/2016/01/%E3%82%A4%E3%83%98%E3%82%99%E3%83%B3%E3%83%88%E3%83%92%E3%82%B9%E3%83%88%E3%83%AA%E3%83%BC%E5%88%86%E6%9E%90%E3%81%AE%E3%81%9F%E3%82%81%E3%81%AE%E3%83%86%E3%82%99%E3%83%BC%E3%82%BF%E5%8A%A0%E5%B7%A5%E3%81%A8%E3%83%A2%E3%83%86%E3%82%99%E3%83%AB%E9%81%B8%E6%8A%9E.pdf. (in Japanese)

Nomura, M. (1994). *Life-long employment*. Iwanami-shoten. (in Japanese)

Sato, Y. (2010). Stability and increasing fluidity in the contemporary Japanese social stratification system. *Contemporary Japan, 22,* 7–21.

Teachman, J. (2011). Modeling repeatable events using discrete-time data: Predicting marital dissolution. *Journal of Marriage and Family, 73,* 525–540.

Yoshimichi Sato is jointly appointed by Faculty of Humanities, Kyoto University of Advanced Science and Graduate School of Arts and Letters, Tohoku University as professor of sociology and behavioral science. He was a visiting scholar at Department of Sociology of University of Chicago and Cornell University to conduct research on rational choice theory and agent-based modeling. He studies social inequality between regular and non-regular workers, social capital, and social change with the tools of statistical models, game theory, and agent-based modeling. His major publications include *Social Exclusion: Perspectives from France and Japan, Japan's New Inequality: Intersection of Employment Reforms and Welfare Arrangements, Deciphering Stratification and Inequality: Japan and Beyond, and Intentional Social Change: A Rational Choice Theory*, all of which were published by Trans Pacific Press.

Chapter 7
Gap in Attitudes Toward Higher Education Between Graduates and Non-graduates: Growing Educational Disparity in Younger Cohorts

Toru Kikkawa

Abstract In this chapter, I examine the relationship between adults' educational background and their attitudes toward higher education. As the period of the post-expansion phase continues, parents' educational level is catching up with children's level. Consequently, second-generation college and university graduates are gradually becoming more common in younger cohorts. Using SSM2005 and SSM2015, I demonstrate that recent college and university graduates exhibit a positive attitude toward the attainment of higher education. I establish that this phenomenon is generated by the increasing number of second-generation graduates. These results imply that the difference of attitude toward higher education exists between graduates and non-graduates may also be enhanced through the increase in second-generation graduates. The gap in attitudes of adults' presents a psychological basis for actual inequality of educational opportunity in the next generation. Thus, the possibility exists that exclusive reproduction of college or university education could become a social problem.

7.1 Emersion of Educational Disparity

7.1.1 Latent Transformation of Adults' Educational Composition in the Post-expansion Phase

Education plays a pivotal role in intergenerational mobility. Persistent inequality of educational opportunity is an important issue in both sociology of education and studies of stratification and mobility (Blossfeld & Shavit, 1993). In the former field, education tends to be closely associated with *the school as institution* because the main concern regards the state of public education. Researchers in the latter field

T. Kikkawa (✉)
Osaka University, Suita, Japan
e-mail: kikkawa@hus.osaka-u.ac.jp

S. Shirahase (ed.), *Social Stratification in an Aging Society with Low Fertility*, Economy and Social Inclusion, https://doi.org/10.1007/978-981-19-3647-0_7

tend to see education in terms of individual's *educational attainment*. The educational career in pre-adulthood demonstrates crucial effects on the adult's later career, economic status, family formation, life course, lifestyle, and a variety of attitudes. Also, it influences the environment and conditions of how one raises children. Then, this becomes the social background for educational attainment among the next generation. In consequence, exclusive intergenerational reproduction with respect to higher education is achieved. Studies of stratification and mobility investigated comprehensive influences of one's educational attainment on intergenerational mobility as well as on one's life in adulthood. In this chapter, I examine the field of social stratification.

As in other industrialized societies, the essential structure of educational opportunity was concealed behind the outsize impact of educational expansion that was taking place until the late twentieth century in Japan. People became more educated than their parents, and the average educational level rose in the younger generations. This was widely known and was taken to be positive. Within the ongoing currents of industrialization, the study of stratification and mobility carefully examined the latent structures of the inequality of educational opportunities (Hara & Seiyama, 2005; Ishida, 1993, 2007; Ishida & Miwa, 2008).

Today's Japan moved on to a new phase. The total enrollment in college or university in the eighteen-years-olds in Japan (the age of high school graduation) achieved universal access, or more than 50% (Trow, 1970, 2010), and it has kept this level, with slight growth, for 15 years and more. In 2021, the university enrollment rate was 54.9% (Ministry of Education, Culture, Sports, Science, and Technology, 2021).

The educational composition of adults reflects the long-lasting, stable situation. Figure 7.1 presents the survey respondents' education by birth year (sorted in age order).[1] The data used in the figure are drawn from SSM2015. Here, attained education is categorized into compulsory (junior high school), secondary (high school and post-secondary special vocational school), and college or university (junior college, bachelor's level, and further).[2] The left half of the graph indicates that the proportions of college or university graduates and non-graduates (compulsory and secondary) are roughly equal for those born after the late 1950s. This reflects the known historical sequence, whereby high school enrollment reached a ceiling of full completion, followed by a leveling off of college or university enrollment in the 1970s.[3] Thus, overall, the later the year of one's birth is, the higher one's educational level, but this is no longer a remarkable trend ($\gamma = 0.107$, significant at the 1% level). At a glance, the achievement of simple educational expansion seems to be nothing more than a historical fact.

Despite this apparent trend of leveling off, the influence of educational expansion is still not entirely gone. Viewing individuals in terms of their parental background, it is clear that Japanese society continues to transform toward *maturation*. Figure 7.2 indicates the relationship between respondent's birth year and father's education.[4] Again, the data are from SSM2015. Father's educational expansion proceeds with about a 25-year delay. Figure 7.2 virtually follows the sequence of the right half of Fig. 7.1 and moves back beyond the right end. Thus, it still reflects the expansion phase, and the negative correlation between respondent's birth year and father's education is $\gamma = 0.325$ (significant at the 1% level).

Fig. 7.1 Educational composition of respondents by birth year

Fig. 7.2 Educational composition of father by respondents' birth year

A symptom can be noted here. For respondents born after 1985, the youngest cohort in the data, not only their own but their parent's background reaches the post-expansion plateau phase. For respondents born around 1989 (aged around 25 during the survey period), father's education reaches compulsory education for 8.8%, secondary for 48.5%, and college or university for 42.9%; the figures for respondents themselves are 0.9%, 46.8%, and 52.3%, respectively. For both, high school enrollment is almost perfect, and tertiary enrollment is close to fifty-fifty. In consequence, the amount of structurally enforced intergenerational mobility is smaller than that of elder cohorts. This is the beginning of the true termination of educational expansion. Although this remains only an indication at this point, the state of parent–child parallel repetition appears to be complete over ten years for young adults. This will undoubtedly continue in succeeding generations; such that Japanese society reaches the phase of a fully mature highly educated society (Kikkawa, 2004). The question is whether educational opportunity in this phase will be equalized or remain unequal. This issue prompts recall of the proposition of Treiman (1970: 221) about the consequence of industrialization: "the more industrialized a society, the smaller the influence of parental status on educational attainment."

7.1.2 Increasing Second-Generation Graduates

Following this concern, I examine the current state of parent–child association with respect to educational attainment.[5] In Fig. 7.3, I present father's and respondent's education together to identify four patterns of intergenerational mobility: *first-generation graduates, second-generation graduates, non-graduate stayers*, and *downshifters*. For *first-generation graduates*, the father is a non-graduate, and the respondent is a graduate. These are cases of upward intergenerational mobility. Where both father and respondent are graduates, we have *second-generation graduates*. For the cases where neither father nor respondent did not complete college or university, we have *non-graduate stayers*, where lower educational status is retained. Finally, where the father is a graduate and the respondent is not, we have *downshifters*. All data are from SSM2015.

The composition of these intergeneration mobility patterns is presented by 10-year birth cohorts. A gradual sequence is seen. The proportion of graduates increases in concert with the trend of educational expansion, as is seen above: college or university graduates are only 15.3% in the 1935–44 cohort, but graduates and non-graduates are each about half in the youngest cohort, 1985–94. A proportional transformation within graduates is also seen (Table 7.1). First-generation graduates are predominant, with a rate of more than seven to three in the two older cohorts. Second-generation graduates exhibit a greater proportion in younger cohorts: the relative proportion of second generations within college or university graduates is 0.313 for the 1955–64 cohort, 0.419 for the 1965–74 cohort, 0.470 for the 1975–84 cohort, and rising to 0.560 for the youngest cohort, 1985–94. At present, more than half of young college or university graduates come from a parental background where the father

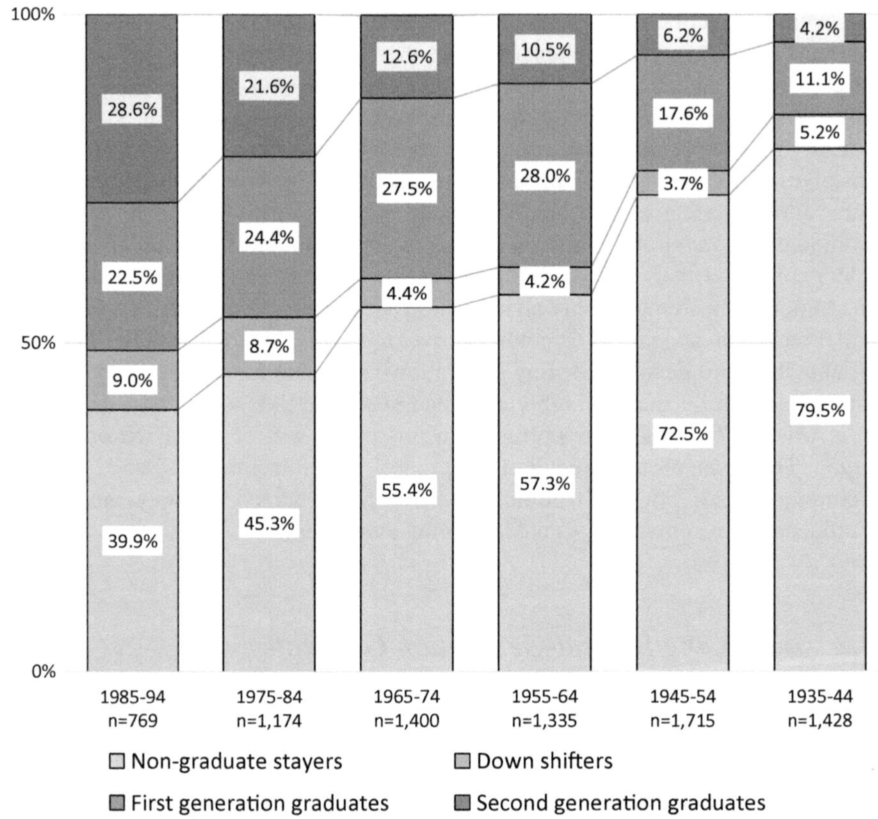

Fig. 7.3 Patterns of intergeneratinal mobility of education by cohort

Table 7.1 Composition of college/university graduates

Birth year cohort	Relative proportion of second generations within graduates	Odds ratio of second-generation/first-generation
1935–44	0.275	3.390
1945–54	0.261	4.150
1955–64	0.313	3.389
1965–74	0.419	3.876
1975–84	0.470	3.448
1985–94	0.560	4.391

and possibly the mother received college or university education. We should also note second-generation graduates forms the second-largest pattern of intergenerational educational mobility in the youngest cohort overall (28.6%).

Predicting that the volume of second-generation graduates would grow would be reasonable, due to the observation of the growth of the father's educational level. In addition, the increase of second-generation graduates results from the inequal arrangement of respondent-father association to some extent. The odds ratios of second-generation to first-generation graduates are given with respect to cohorts in Table 7.1. The overall tendency is immediately clear. The respondent's opportunity of college or university enrollment is far above complete equality (1.000), and it is not equalized. Moreover, it is noteworthy that the youngest cohort, 1985–94, exhibits the highest odds ratio (4.391). It means that the advantage that second-generation graduates demonstrate for entering college or university is more than four times as large as that of first-generation graduates who come from a non-graduate parental background. Ishida (2007) demonstrates that the opportunity to obtain post-secondary education in Japan is not equal, even after the post-expansion phase. Also, Table 7.1 implies a recent turn toward exclusion with respect to the father's education.

Why has opportunity of college or university enrollment not equalized even as society is moving forward in a post-expansion phase? Many considerations came from economics (Becker 1991, Blau, 1999; Dahl and Lochner 2012; Kaushal et al., 2011) and stratification studies in sociology (Arum et al., 2007; Blossfeld & Shavit, 1993; Hout, 1989; Mare, 1981). Among these, I focus on the subjective factor. Regarding this concern, it is noteworthy that Breen and Goldthorpe (1997) theorized the mechanism of relative risk aversion (RAA). Following rational choice theory, they predict that working-class parent–child pairs tend to obtain less education than middle-class parent–child pairs because they retrieve no utility from doing so in terms of promoting their future social status. In other words, when children reach a certain threshold level of education, which the parent–child pairs consider brings them to the same social status as that of the parents, the cost of pursuing further education outweigh the utility of doing so. The threshold level differs by socio-economic background. Note that Breen and Goldthorpe (1997) describe father's occupation, not educational status.

Bringing this line of thought to the Japanese reality, where higher education is highly respected, Kikkawa (2006) argues that familial socio-economic status is involved with educational attainment of parents more closely than with occupational status of parents. That is to say, if a parent is a high school graduate, both parent and child regard graduation from high school to be a necessary threshold for maintaining status. That is, the child does not expect to enter college or move beyond it. However, if the parent is a college or university graduate, both the parent and child strongly expect to complete college or university education and make the effort to enroll the child to avoid downward mobility. This is the reasoning behind the downward educational mobility aversion proposed by Kikkawa (2006, 2009, 2018). This is an analogy to RRA, but undecided future risk does not require consideration but instead to downshifting directly. Here, I focus on the gap between college or university graduates and non-graduates. This is because it divides the Japanese adult population into halves vertically. Other studies also examine the graduate/non-graduate gap for its relevance for or effect on educational orientation (Fujihara 2012; Matsuoka 2019a; Sunaga, 2020).

Regarding educational background, I propose another consideration: second-generation graduates can be thought to be more highly motivated toward college or university education of the next generation than first-generation graduates are. Although both tend to require college or university education to maintain status, second-generation graduates expect to complete college education to a greater degree to prevent the failure to maintain the succession of their status from the previous generation. In other words, the assumption concerning the particularity of second-generation graduates indicates that parental education, practically father's educational attainment, exhibits an effect on the respondent's educational orientation. Statistically, the second-generation effect can be decomposed into the effect of respondent's college or university graduation, the effect of father's college or university graduation, and the interaction effects of those two.[6] So long as tertiary education access is restricted, the difference within graduates is not the issue. However, along with the increase in college or university graduates and successive catch up of parental education, the compositional replacement from the first generation to the second within college or university graduate makes progress. If the latter tend to be more motivated to seek higher education, college or university graduates overall may demonstrate expectations for the child's college or university education that are stronger than ever. If so, we can predict that the generational reproduction of education will become more exclusive in coming phases. All in all, the long-lasting post-expansion phase is changing the composition within the set of college or university graduates; this change then brings about a solidification with respect to the gap between graduates and non-graduates, or exclusion from tertiary education. We can verify this proposition using the latest survey data.

7.2 Attitude Toward Higher Education

7.2.1 Psychological Basis for Intergenerational Mobility

In previous works on inequality in educational opportunity, a thoroughgoing assumption has been that *higher education is desirable for everyone.* Researchers tend to believe that almost all parents expect university or college education for their children if economic and geographical questions do not limit it. Kariya (1995) describes Japanese society before the 1980s as the "mass education society," where this principle, as a widely spread collective premise, drives the guidance for children's scholastic activities in school. However, education cannot expand endlessly. It is not realistic to suppose a future of complete access to university education such that almost all adolescents remain in school through their early twenties. Some proportion of them must leave school as non-graduates. The question is how strong the expectation of college or university education is. Survey data demonstrate that a certain proportion of adults and adolescents do not follow such desirability in every social segment. In addition, the apparent tendency the higher the parent's socio-economic status is, the more strongly the parent and child expect higher education is widely known. This inclination of attitude differentiates the educational strategy for children. Accordingly, an inequality of educational opportunity may arise (Aramaki, 2019b; Matsuoka, 2017). Thus, the educational orientation can be considered to be the psychological basis for intergenerational mobility (of education).

Educational orientation is treated as several sub items because of the variety of research subjects and that diversity of survey question. In examining students' and parents' intention towards advanced educational stage, educational orientation can be regarded in terms of educational aspirations (Sewell et al., 1970). Fujihara (2009) distinguishes educational expectation from educational aspirations. Aramaki (2019b) interprets the educational orientation of one's parents as the educational intention for a specific child. In surveys of the overall adult population, such as the one used here, the question investigates attitude toward higher education in general. The SSM surveys utilize one item prompting the respondents to give the degree of their agreement with the statement "children should be given the highest possible level of education." I term the value produced attitude toward higher education.[7] Although educational orientation is commonly examined in Japanese sociology, similar work has not been widely undertaken in other societies, except for the well-known Wisconsin model (Sewell et al., 1970) and its successors. Studies of public opinion on the topic have largely been limited to Japan.[8] This is probably because Japanese society exhibits a strong concern with educational credentialism as a collective mentality, which led to industrialization and social equalization.

7.2.2 Previous Studies and Research Questions

Regarding social factors and their role in forming attitudes, previous studies elucidated an analytical framework. Using the results of SSM1995, the first survey to introduce the question of attitude toward higher education, Nakamura (2000) examines the relationship between this attitude and age, education, occupation, and other social attitudes. He remarks the reduction of this attitude in the younger cohort, although the data do not allow him to assess aging or cohort effects. Using a panel dataset, Fujihara (2015) demonstrates changes in socio-economic status in an individual respondent influences the state of this attitude. Kikkawa (2000, 2012, 2015) introduces multivariate analysis to nationwide data from 1995, 2005, and 2010. These studies point out the theoretical and substantial relevance of examining the outstanding effects of education on attitude toward higher education, in addition to the effects of age or cohort (greater with age). At the same time, he indicates occupation (upper white-collar position) and household income (higher) result in small but significant effects in the OLS regression analysis, controlling other elements.

Fujihara (2011, 2018) examines the robustness of the effect of higher education and higher status on the attitude more precisely.

Moreover, Aramaki (2019b) argues that the educational level of relatives and of the consulting network improves parent's intention toward higher education. Sewell et al. (1970) demonstrate the importance of significant others on the educational aspiration of high school students. They also demonstrate the positive effects of perceived parental encouragement to attend college on student's educational aspirations. The causal paths structure is termed the Wisconsin model. Studies using this model stress the influence of parents or relatives on respondent's attitudes toward higher education. Studies that refer to familial educational background support to my assumption that second-generation graduates whose fathers (and possibly mothers) are college or university graduates tend to exhibit positive attitudes toward higher education. All in all, intergenerational reflexive systems of subjectivity (i.e., educational orientation) and objectivity (i.e., educational attainment for the next generation) likely function in cert.

Matsuoka (2019a, b) stresses neighborhood effects in addition to the robust effects of the parental graduate/non-graduate gap. Matsuoka and Maeda (2015) demonstrate that the educational level of neighbor exhibits an effect on the attitude. Finally, most previous studies examine gender differences to determine that males respond even positively. However, the difference is not remarkable.

My first research question is *Who values higher education more?* Education and age or generation are essential attributes that should be closely examined. In relation to education, I pay close attention to not only graduate/non-graduate gap among the respondents but also intergenerational mobility patterns. With respect to temporal differences, I can identify age-based and cohort-based tendencies by using data from different survey periods. However, the validity of this operation is restricted because only two available survey years exist. In addition, I examine whether the graduate/non-graduate gap in attitudes is expanding or decreasing by age, period, and cohort.

The second research question is *If the graduate/non-graduate gap in attitudes is expanding over time, what is behind the change?* Here, I focus on compositional transformations within recent young college or university graduates as a clue for understanding the newly emerging phenomena. This answer allows me to discuss the intergenerational reproduction of education based on subjective–objective reflexivity.

7.3 Analysis

7.3.1 Data and Descriptive Features

I use data from SSM2005 and SSM2015. The items I use retain a comparable design within them, which allows the two surveys to be merged to a single dataset. The respondents to be analyzed are men and women aged 20–69 years.[9] The data enable me to examine recent temporal changes in working-age adults with respect to a variety of social attributions and attitudes.

The dependent variable is attitude toward higher education.[10] The attitudes are obtained from agreement or disagreement with this sentence: children should be given the highest possible level of education, as noted above. I treat this as a dichotomous variable for agree or disagree. The original answer categories are "agree," "somewhat agree," "somewhat disagree," and "disagree." The first two are joined to create agree, and the latter two are joined to create disagree.

In the 2015 data, 63.3% of respondents agree, and 61.4% do in 2005. It is surprising that more than one-third of respondents express themselves against that children should achieve "the highest possible level of education" in both periods. I consider that respondents might regard the words "the highest possible education" as practically implying college or university education. My reasoning here is as follows. In SSP2015, carried out at the same time as SSM2015, a question that contained the expression "higher than college education" was presented in place of "the highest possible level of education," and the response frequencies do not differ between two surveys; the proportion of agreement, which is 63.3% in SSM2015, is 63.4% in SSP2015 (Kikkawa, 2019). Therefore, I interpret that the variable represents respondent's intention to obtain college or university education for the respondent's child if the respondent presented with it. In this aspect, the variable represents not just a public opinion but a motivation for a specific level of educational attainment. According to the recent actual enrollment in tertiary education, where the latest share of junior college enrollment is only 4.0%, whereas that of university is 54.9%, the level practically denote university or more.

When it comes to the degree of temporal change, the observed difference over the ten years is only 1.9% points, although it is statistically significant (at the 5% level). The NHK Broadcasting Culture Research Institute reports 86.4% of their respondents expect an education beyond college for their boys and 84.9% for their girls in a survey conducted in 2018, compared to the respective figures of 83.6% and 82.3% from 2008. Though the rates are even higher than those of SSM surveys because of the differences in survey design and sentences of the questions, the increase over the ten years is 1.5% points for boys and 2.6 for girls (Aramaki, 2019a). The observed size of the temporal change is small in general, so it cannot be taken as a critical issue for our analyses.

7.3.2 Peculiarity of Young College or University Graduates

The principal concern here is to examine differences in age and generation and the influence of educational background. Figure 7.4 presents attitudes toward higher education (proportion of agreement) among college or university graduates and non-graduates in 2005 and 2015, divided into ten-year age groups. The tendencies in 2005 and 2015 are roughly identical; young respondents, particularly aged 20–29 years, tend to disagree with the idea; the slopes gradually become gentle with age; and

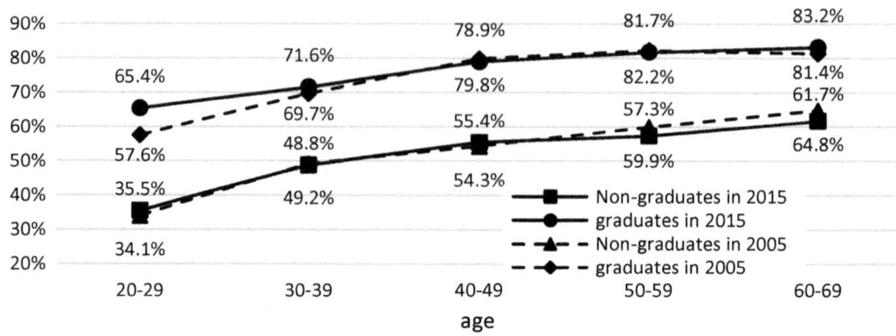

Fig. 7.4 Gap in attitudes toward higher education between graduates and non-graduates in 2005 and 2015

college or university graduates exhibit acceptances that are constantly higher than that of non-graduates, with about 20%-points differences. Concerning aging, the proportion of positive answers in the same cohort improves during young-to-middle age in both graduates and non-graduates: the answers for the 1975–84 cohort gain about 14% points of agreement with ages from their 20s to their 30s; the answers for the 1965–74 cohort gain about 6–9% points of agreement and by about 1–3% points for cohorts in late middle age. Because the trajectories are similar across all subgroups, a curved linear aging effect is suggested. Life stage events like marriage, child rearing, completion of children's educational attainment, and others may cause this change. However, this dataset does not allow further deduction. Detailed examination must remain as a task for the future.

Recognizing the above, a peculiar tendency strikes the eye in relation to the trajectories of the graphs. Graduates aged 20–29 years in 2015, corresponding to the 1985–94 cohort, marks 65.4% of agreement of 7.8% points higher than the value of the equivalent age group in 2005. The suggestion here is that the newly joined college or university graduates stay within a particular condition. Other studies also report that young college or university graduates demonstrate outstanding characteristics in terms of their social attitudes. In a comparative analysis of 1995 and 2015 data, Hazama (2017) indicates that recent young college or university graduates agree more with the opinion "I should make effort for the future rather than enjoy present time," while young non-graduates remain at the same level over the entire 20 years. Matsutani (2019) reports that young male college or university graduates in 2015 are more supportive of the Liberal Democratic Party, the party in power, than those in 1990s.

Why do recent college or university graduates show such steady traits? My assumption is as follows: in terms of parental education, the composition of college or university graduates is gradually changing; second-generation college or university graduates are particularly increasing in the segment, as seen above; this change may lead to the development of positive attitudes toward higher education as well

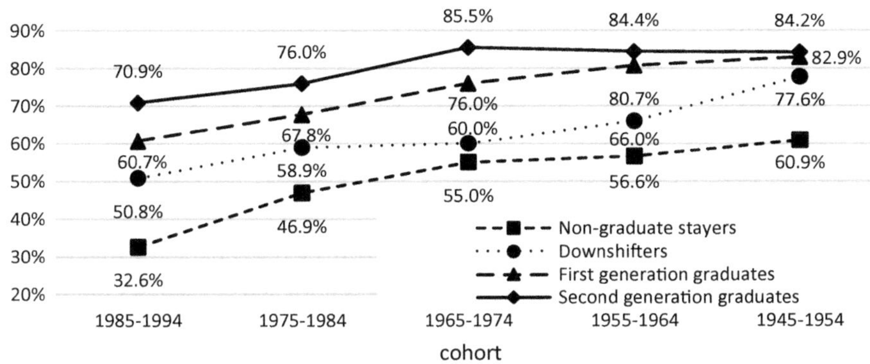

Fig. 7.5 Attitudes toward higher education by segment in 2015

as other aspects of social attitudes. Studies of higher education management demonstrated that second-generation students are more adaptive and take more advantage of college or university education than first-generation students (Froggé and Woods 2018; Gofen, 2017; London, 1989; Stephens et al., 2012).[11]

When it comes to differences of attitude regarding parental education, Hazama and Tanioka (2015) argue that second-generation graduates are more likely to identify themselves as upper middle class rather than lower middle class, in terms of subjective social stratification, relative to first-generation graduates. Aramaki (2019b) finds that mother's educational intention improves when the educational attainment of her siblings and spouse are high. This fact implies an influence of parental education because an individual's educational attainment is closely associated with that of the family. This suggests that second-generation graduates should demonstrate a more positive attitude toward higher education.

To confirm this assumption, Fig. 7.5 demonstrates the proportion of the positive responses in relation to the four patterns of intergenerational mobility of education by cohort in SSM2015. It seems clear that second-generation graduates born after 1965 are about 10% points higher than first-generation graduates. The fact leads me to assume that the observed peculiarity of young college or university graduates in recent data comes from the proportional gain (Fig. 7.3) of second-generation graduates, who tend to demonstrate more positive attitudes about college or university education. Downshifters coming from highly educated parental backgrounds also constantly express higher educational values than non-graduate stayers. This fact indicates that the effect of father's education to the attitude is not restricted to college or university graduates. Rather, it is found in the entire population. However, the characteristics of downshifters are substantially less important than those of second-generation graduates, as the relative proportion of downshifters are generally as small as less than 10% in each cohort. Hereafter, I selectively refer to the tendencies of second-generation graduates.

7.3.3 Multivariate Analysis (Logistic Regression)

To confirm the pro-education tendency of recent young college or university graduates, I carry out a logistic regression analysis to determine the effects of the following independent variables: (1) survey year, (2) gender, (3) marital status, (4) size of residential area,[12] (5) occupational status [arbitrated EGP class categories (Erikson & Goldthorpe, 1992)], and (6) income[13] (yearly individual income including tax), in addition to (7) education and (8) cohort. Moreover, the model contains variables that indicate interaction effects among survey period, cohort, and education (Table 7.2).

Model 1 indicates the following: respondents in 2015 tend to answer less positively than those in 2005; males tend to agree more than females; those who are married tend to answer positively; the size of the residential area exhibits positive effects on the attitude; self-employed, manual workers, agricultural workers, and unemployed tend to answer negatively in comparison with upper white-collar workers; and income exhibits a positive effect on the attitude. In addition, two main effects are observed: college/university graduates tend to agree more than non-graduates; and younger cohorts tend to answer less positively than older ones.

Examining the interaction effects among survey year, education, and generation, the three-way interaction of 2015, graduated, and in their twenties, on which I gave a remark above, shows a positive effect on the attitudes with 5% significance, while all other effects are non-significant. This demonstrates a peculiarity of recent young graduates that is not explained by differences among survey year, education, and cohort. In other words, the attitudes of all other segments do not contain any particular tendencies that are not predicted by three main effects.

In model 2, I test the assumption that the positive tendency of recent young graduates is generated by the compositional feature that second-generation graduates are dominant in this segment. For the purpose, I introduce father's education (graduate or non-graduate) into the lineup of independent variables. This operation controls proportional bias of father's education in each segment.

For the result, father's education shows positive effects on attitude, and model fit is improved. Together with this fact, the peculiar effects seen in 2015, graduate, and in their twenties in model 1 diminishes and is non-significant. This consequence demonstrates that compositional change in educational background, namely the improvement in father's educational level, makes recent young graduates more strongly motivated toward college or university education enrollment.

7.4 Conclusion

Treiman (1970) considers that the more industrialized a society becomes, the smaller the influence of parental status on educational attainment. This proposition is rooted in ongoing industrialization. Blossfeld and Shavit (1993) emphasize the persistent socio-economic inequality of educational opportunity throughout industrialization

Table 7.2 Logistic regression analyis on attitudes toward higher education

n = 11,819	Model 1				Model 2			
	B	sig	SE	Exp. (B)	B	sig	SE	Exp. (B)
Intercept	0.314		0.103		0.301		0.103	
Survey year (2015)	−0.258	**	0.095	0.773	−0.256	**	0.095	0.774
Gender (male)	0.193	**	0.055	1.213	0.202	**	0.055	1.224
Marital status (married)	0.227	**	0.055	1.255	0.227	**	0.055	1.254
Size of residential area (ref. towns and villages)								
Metropolis	0.327	**	0.077	1.386	0.297	**	0.078	1.346
Cities larger than 200,000	0.165	*	0.074	1.179	0.144		0.074	1.155
Cities larger than 100,000	0.220	**	0.078	1.246	0.210	**	0.079	1.233
Small cities	0.151	*	0.073	1.163	0.144	*	0.073	1.155
Occupational status (ref. upper white I + II)								
Lower whilte (III)	0.037		0.089	1.037	0.030		0.089	1.030
Self-employed (I + Vab)	0.151	*	0.081	1.163	0.163	*	0.081	1.177
Skilled Manmual (V + VI)	−0.276	**	0.095	0.759	−0.272	**	0.095	0.762
Non-skilled Mannual (IVc)	−0.457	**	0.092	0.633	−0.440	**	0.092	0.644
Agricultual (VIIab)	−0.309	**	0.078	0.734	−0.293	**	0.078	0.746
Unemployed	−0.297	*	0.137	0.743	−0.285	*	0.138	0.752

(continued)

Table 7.2 (continued)

n = 11,819	Model 1				Model 2			
	B	sig	SE	Exp. (B)	B	sig	SE	Exp. (B)
Education (college/univ. graduate)	0.662	**	0.246	1.938	0.580	*	0.247	1.787
Age group (ref. 60–69)								
20–29	−1.221	**	0.169	0.295	−1.259	**	0.170	0.284
30–39	−0.647	**	0.126	0.524	−0.671	**	0.126	0.511
40–49	−0.540	**	0.119	0.583	−0.548	**	0.119	0.578
50–59	−0.301	**	0.109	0.740	−0.306	**	0.109	0.737
Income (1 = 1,000,000 yen)	0.048	**	0.012	1.049	0.049	**	0.012	1.049
Interaction of period, education and age (ref. 2005*non-graduate*60–69)								
Garaduate*20–29	0.046		0.332	1.047	0.051		0.333	1.052
Graduate*30–39	−0.228		0.296	0.796	−0.230		0.297	0.795
Graduate*40–49	0.313		0.304	1.367	0.347		0.304	1.414
Graduate*50–59	0.321		0.320	1.379	0.359		0.321	1.432
Non-graduate*20–29	0.303		0.219	1.353	0.286		0.219	1.331
Non-graduate*30–39	0.178		0.162	1.195	0.156		0.162	1.168
Non-graduate*40–49	0.236		0.152	1.266	0.230		0.152	1.258
Non-graduate*50–59	0.113		0.145	1.119	0.107		0.145	1.113
2015*graduate*20–29	0.715	*	0.344	2.044	0.663		0.344	1.940
2015*graduate*30–39	0.263		0.316	1.301	0.229		0.316	1.257

(continued)

Table 7.2 (continued)

n = 11,819	Model 1				Model 2			
	B	sig	SE	Exp. (B)	B	sig	SE	Exp. (B)
2015*graduate*40–49	0.478		0.317	1.612	0.484		0.317	1.623
2015*graduate*50–59	0.385		0.317	1.470	0.406		0.317	1.501
2015*graduate*60–69	0.251		0.290	1.285	0.264		0.291	1.302
Father's education (college/univ. graduate)					0.367	**	0.071	1.444
Improvement of −2 log likelyhood χ^2			742.088**				769.134**	
d.f			32				33	
Cox and Snell's pseudo R^2			0.078				0.081	
Nagelkerke's pseudo R^2			0.107				0.110	

**$p < 0.01$, *$p < 0.05$

and the following post-industrialized phase. Most of subsequent studies, including those conducted in Japan by Ishida (2007) and Ishida and Miwa (2008), support the assumption. That is, the opportunity to pursue higher education consistently depends on one's social background.

With respect to societal educational orientation in Japan, Kariya (1995) describes an equally standardized state as the "mass education society." Along with the procession of the post-industrialized phase, he changes his view to insist that a vertical division of educational orientation arises. He calls this the "incentive divide" instead of the "mass education society" (Kariya, 2001) During this period, the idea of the gap society in Japan begins to be widely discussed. Few studies have demonstrated a systematic association of the consequence of post-industrialization, in particular post-educational expansion, and the enhancement of social division.

This chapter focuses on more recent characteristics of Japanese society, where the post-expansion phase of education continues over one parent–child generation. The descriptive analysis demonstrates that educational attainment among parents is catching up to that of respondents in the younger cohort. As a result, second-generation graduates are increasing their presence. The assumption here is that improvement of educational level in parental generation enhances the educational gap in attitudes toward higher education.

The assumption is basically proven true and a systematic reasoning is proposed. Focusing on the formation process of attitudes toward higher education, multivariate causal analyses of data from Japan in 2005 and 2015 shows the following. First, a robust effect of respondent's educational attainment on attitudes toward higher education is found. No doubt exists that a person who graduated from college or university tends to demonstrate a positive attitude toward higher education, whereas non-graduates tend not to. This suggests a motivation for educational descendant aversion, which is proposed as a pertinent reasoning (Kikkawa, 2006), is appearing. The graduate/non-graduate gap in educational orientation can be regarded as an essential fact in educational inequality. Second, the attitude differs according to age; the younger segments are not positive at first, then they generally exhibit more positive attitudes, along with life stage transition. The trajectory is similarly observed in the data from 2005 and 2015. However, we cannot expect a diminishing of the graduate/non-graduate gap along aging, as the effect covers both in sequence. Thirds, the peculiar fact exists that recent young college or university graduates show a significantly positive attitude toward higher education. A detailed analysis demonstrates that the peculiarity is produced by compositional feature of the segment, as it contains a larger proportion of second-generation graduates.

Thus, a symptom of social inequality emerges on the surface of society as a phenomenon that the differences in attitudes toward higher education between graduates and non-graduates increase in the younger cohorts. It is noteworthy this does not arise from decline in attitudes of non-graduates, but from improvement of pro-educational attitudes of college or university graduates. The structure behind this is that the long-lasting post-expansion phase is changing the composition within the set of college or university graduates, the gradual increase of the presence of second-generation graduates who tend to have pro-educational attitudes. The gap in attitudes between graduates and non-graduates then functions as a psychological basis for inequality of educational opportunity for the next generation. This change brings about a solidification with respect to the gap between graduates and non-graduates, or exclusion of non-graduates from tertiary education.

A certain span of continuation of exclusive reproduction of higher education in post-expansion phase ends up enhancement of attitude gap which encourages sequential repetition of unequal educational attainment. An indication of such a subjective–objective reflexive system of inequality can be seen in recent young college or university graduates.

Notes

1. Three-year moving averages are presented in Figs. 7.1 and 7.2. The data are from SSM2015. I analyze men and women aged 20–69 years old, namely respondents born in 1935–1994.
2. School dropout ratio is generally very law at any stage in Japan. I do not tell the difference between graduation and leaving school in the analysis. Most of previous works using SSM datasets also do the same way. Hereafter, I regard those who reported to be enrolled each school level as graduates.
3. Ishida (2007) describes the institutional features and history of postsecondary education in Japan. Although I classify special vocational school attendants into *non-graduates* in this chapter, he includes special vocational school in postsecondary education. He interprets that "the development of Japanese post-secondary education was not liner. Postwar development can be divided into four stages: an initial period of preparation for take-off (before 1960), the first stage of expansion (1960–75), a period of stability and stagnation (1976–85), and the second stage of expansion (after 1986)" (Ishida, 2007: 73). It should be noted that the years he refers represent not that of high school graduation. In the data used in this chapter, the range of respondents does not cover initial period of preparation for take-off. In addition, the data I use do not indicate a remarkable improvement of college or university enrollment in a period of second stage expansion. The trajectory of educational expansion with respect to college or university follows two-fold sequence, rather to follow the four period that he describes. And strictly speaking, college or university enrollments start expanding slightly in recent years.
4. I use father's education as an index of parental educational background. Concerning to SSM2015, more than 95% of respondent's fathers who graduated from tertiary education are university graduates. This is because short cycle tertiary education is not popular for male in Japan. In the case when I use mother's education instead, the graph shows a tendency roughly like Fig. 7.2. Because of educational assortative mating, two indices of parental education are closely associated.
5. Results are not very different when I use mother's education or parental higher education in place of father's education. When I analyze male and female separately, results are also not very different.

6. The interaction effect of respondent's education and father's education is not significant when I introduce it to the analysis in Table 7.2, though the results is not shown. This implies intergenerational mobility effects (Sobel, 1981) on the attitudes in terms of education is not remarkable. In other words, father's college or university education drives downshifters as well as second-generation graduates toward positive direction. Even though, effect of father's education cannot be crucial for non-graduates because relative proportion of downshifters is small. I focus on the characteristics of second-generation graduates in the chapter.
7. The sentence is specified to college education in SSP2015, another nationwide survey: "children should be given education higher than college." The Survey on Japanese Value Orientation conducted by NHK Broadcasting Culture Research Institute keep using the question asking "how far respondent would like to have their child's education advance, if he/she had one?".
8. See the detailed review by Matsuoka (2019b).
9. The designed sample of SSM2005 ranges 20–69 years old, while SSM2015 covers respondents aged 20–79 years old.
10. In SSM surveys, the question was inquired three times since 1995. SSM1995 is not comparable to SSM2005 and SSM2015 in terms of survey mode. SSM1995 was carried out as a face-to-face interview, though other two surveys used self-administrated questionnaire. Therefore, I do not examine SSM1995 in this study.
11. For this reason, institutions to support first-generation college students have been established in the United States.
12. Matsuoka (2019a, b) and Matsuoka and Maeda (2015) exhibit the significance of social capital and social network within residential neighborhood. I introduced size of residential area in individual level. Regional differences are partially controlled by this in the analysis. However, it has a limitation in examining the effect of neighborhood on attitudes toward higher education.
13. I do not introduce household income in the analysis, as there contains many missing in the response of it particularly in younger cohorts. The effect of household income is not significant if I introduce it. The result is not shown.

References

Aramaki, H. (2019a). 45 nen de nihonjin ha dou kawattaka (1): Dai jikkai 'nihonjin no ishiki' chosa kara (How the Japanese have changed over 45 years [Part I]: From *the 10th Survey on Japanese Value Orientations*) in *Hōsō kenkyū to chōsa (The NHK Monthly Report on Broadcast Research), 59*(5), 2–37.

Aramaki, S. (2019b). *Kyōiku kakusa no kakureta haikei: Oya no pāsonaru nettowāku to gakureki shikou (Unrevealed background of educational gap: Personal network of parents and the educational orientation.* Keiso Shobo.

Arum, R., Gamoran, A., & Shavit, Y. (2007). More inclusiton than diversion: expansion, differenciation, and market structure in higher education. In Y. Shavit, R. Arum, & A. Gamoran (Eds.), *Stratification in higher education: A comparative study* (pp. 1–35). Stanford University Press.

Becker, G. S. (1991). *A treatise on the family*. Harvard University Press.

Blau, D. M. (1999). The effect of income on child development. *The Review of Economics and Statistics, 81*(2), 261–276.

Blossfeld, H.-P., & Shavit, Y. (1993). Persisting barriers: Changes in educational stratification in 13 countries. In Y. Shavit & H.-P. Blossfeld (Eds.), *Persistent inequality: Changing educational attainment in thirteen countries* (pp. 1–23). Westview Press.

Breen, R., & Goldthorpe, J. H. (1997). Explaining educational differentials: Towards a formal rational action theory. *Rationality and society, 9*(3), 275–305.

Dahl, G. B., & Lochner, L. (2012). The impact of family income on child achievement: Evidence from the earned income tax credit. *The American Economic Review, 102*(5), 1927–1956.

Erikson, R., & Goldthorpe, J. H. (1992). *The constant flux: A study of class mobility in industrial societies*. Oxford University Press.

Froggé, G. M., & Woods, K. H. (2018). Characteristics and tendencies of first and second-generation university students. In *College quarterly, 21*(2), 1–21.

Fujihara, S. (2009). Gendai kōkōsei to hahaoya no kyōiku kitai: Sogo izon moderu wo mochiita oyako dōji bunseki (Educational expectations of Japanese senior high school students and mothers: Simultaneous analysis of student-mother dyadic data with interdependence model). In *Riron to hōhō (Sociological theory and methods), 24*(2), 283–299.

Fujihara, S. (2011). Breen and Goldthorpe no sōtai teki risuku kaihi kasetsu no kenshō: Chichioya no kodomo ni taisuru shokugyō kyōiku kitai wo mochiita keiryo bunseki (Empirical test of breen and Goldthorpe's relative risk aversion hypothesis in the Japanese society: Data analysis of a father's occupational and educational expectations for his child). *Shakai Gaku Hyōron (Japanese Sociological Review), 62–1*, 18–35.

Fujihara, S. (2012). "Kōkō sentaku ni okeru soutaiteki risuku kaihisetsu to gakureki kakō kaihisetsu no kensyō (Empirical tests of the relative risk aversion hypothesis and the downward educational mobility aversion hypothesis regarding choice of high school in Japan)" in *Kyōku shakaigaku kenkyū (The Journal of Educational Sociology) 91*, 29–49.

Fujihara, S. (2015). Kyōiku ishiki no kojinkan no sai to kojinnai no henka: 'Hatarakikata to raihusutairu no henka ni kansuru zenkoku chōsa' (JLPS) deta wo mochiita bunseki (Differences among individuals and changes within individuals in terms of their attitudes toward education: Analysis using data of Japanese life course panel survey (JLPS). *Shakai to Chōsa (advances in Social Research), 15*, 40–47.

Fujihara, S. (2018). Oya no kyōiku ishiki no ruikei to kodomo ni taisuru kyōiku kitai: Senzai kurasu moderu ni yoru apurōchi (Typification of educational orientation of parents and educational expectation toward children). In T. Nakamura, K. Hirasawa, S. Aramaki, & W. Nakazawa (Eds.), *Kyōiku to Shakaikaisou: ESSM zenkoku chōsa kara mita gakureki gakko kakusa (Education and social stratification: Analysis based on the ESSM2013 survey in Japan)* (pp. 149–167). University of Tokyo Press.

Gofen, A. (2017). Family capital: How first-generation higher education students break the intergenerational cycle. *Family Relations, 58–1*, 104–120.

Hara, J., & Seiyama, K. (2005). *Inequality amid affluence: Social stratification in Japan*. Trans Pacific Press.

Hazama, R. (2017). Genzai-shikō ga jakunenso no otonashisa ni ataeru eikyō: Seiji inin shiki to kakusa kōtei ishiki ni chūmoku shite (The effect of present-orientation on Japanese youth's quietness: Focusing on political delegation and neoliberal perception of inequality). *Soshioroji (sociology), 62*(1), 79–95.

Hazama, R., & Tanioka, K. (2015). Kaisō kizokui shiki no kitei yōin toshite no shakai idō: Shukanteki shakai idō ga toraeru hutatsu no keiro (Social mobility as determinants of subjective status identification: Subjective social mobility captures two paths). *Nenpō ningen kagaku (Annals of Human Sciences) 36*, 1–17.

Hout, M. (1989). *Following in father's footsteps: Social mobility in Ireland*. Harvard University Press.
Ishida, H. (1993). *Social mobility in contemporary Japan, Stanford*. Stanford University Press.
Ishida, H. (2007). Japan: Educational expansion and inequality in access to higher education. In Y. Shavit, R. Arum, & A. Gamoran (Eds.), *Stratification in higher education: A comparative study* (pp. 63–86). Stanford University Press.
Ishida, H., & Miwa, S. (2008). Trends in intergenerational class mobility and education in Japan. In H. Ishida (Ed.), *Social stratification and social mobility in late-industrializing countries* (pp. 1–48). The 2005 SSM Research Committee.
Kariya, T. (1995). *Taisyū kyōiku shakai no yukue (The future of mass edcation society)*. Chūo Kōron Sha.
Kariya, T. (2001). *Kaisoka nihon to kyōiku Kiki (Stratified Japanese society and the crisis in education)*. Yushindo.
Kaushal, N., Magnuson, K., & Waldfogel, J. (2011). How is family income related to investments in children's learning? In G. J. Duncan & R. J. Murnane (Eds.), *Whither opportunity? Rising inequality, schools, and children's life chances* (pp. 187–205). Russell Sage Foundation.
Kikkawa, T. (2000). Taishū kyōiku shakai no nakano kaisō ishiki (Social attitudes related to stratification in the mass education society). In H. Kondo (Ed.), *Sengo nihon no kyōiku shakai (Educational credentials in the postwar stratification system), Nihon no kaisō shisutemu 3 (Japanese stratification system Vol. 3)* (pp. 175–195). University of Tokyo Press.
Kikkawa, T. (2004). Effect of educational expansion on educational inequality in post-industrialized societies: A cross-cultural comparison of Japan and the United States of America. *International Journal of Japanese Sociology, 13*, 100–119.
Kikkawa, T. (2006). *Gakureki to kakusa/fubyōdō Seijuku suru nihongata gakurekishakai (Education and social inequality: Contemporary educational credentialism in Japan)*. University of Tokyo Press.
Kikkawa, T. (2009). *Gakureki bundan shakai (Society of educational disparity)*. Chikuma Shobo.
Kikkawa, T. (2012). Jinzai ikuse katsuyō no kiban to shite no gakureki ishiki no jitsuzo (The state of the attitude toward higher education as the fundamental of development and utilization of human resources). In Y. Higuchi & Policy Research Institute of the Ministry of Finance (Eds.), *Gurōbaru shakai no jinzai ikusei katsuyō: Shugaku kara shugyō e no ikō kadai (Development and utilization of human resources in the globalized society: From school enrollment to job employment)* (pp. 211–232). Keiso shobo.
Kikkawa, T. (2015). Kaisō ishiki no gakurekisa wo kangaeru: shakai ishiki no sai umekomi (Examining the educational gap of social attitudes related to stratification) In N. Sudo (Ed.), *Shakai-ishiki kara mita nihon (New dimension of social identification and consciousness)* (pp. 229–255). Yuhikau.
Kikkawa, T. (2018). *Nihon no bundan: Kirihanasareru hidaisotsu wakamonotathi (Social division in Japan: Separation of young non-graduates)*. Kobunsya.
Kikkawa, T. (2019). Hidaisotsu wakamono no daigaku banare: Gakureki bundan no sofutowea (Disinterest in college education seen in young non-graduate: A form of 'Softwere' of educational disparity). In T. Kikkawa & R. Hazama (Eds.), *Bundan shakai toWakamono no ima (Divided society and the youth of today)* (pp. 179–197). Osaka University Press.
London, H. (1989). Breaking away: A study of first-generation college students and their families. *American Journal of Education, 97*(2), 93–103.
Mare, R. D. (1981). Change and stability in educational stratification. *American Sociological Review, 46*, 72–87.
Matsuoka, R. (2017). Inequality of effort in an egalitarian education system. *Asia Pacific Education Review, 18*, 347–359.
Matsuoka, R. (2019a). *Kyōiku kakusa (Educational gap)*. Chikuma Syobo.
Matsuoka, R. (2019b). The vanishing mass education society. *Social Science Japan Journal, 22*(1), 65–84.

Matsuoka, R., & Maeda, T. (2015). Attitudes toward education as influenced by neighborhood socio-economic characteristics: An application of multilevel structural equation modeling. *Behaviormetrika, 42*(1), 19–35.

Matsutani, M. (2019). Wakamono ha naze Jimintō wo shijisuru noka (Why young people support LDP?). In T. Kikkawa & R. Hazama (Eds.), *Bundan shakai to wakamono no ima (Divided society and the youth of today)* (pp. 92–120). Osaka University Press.

Ministry of Education, Culture, Sports, Science and Technology, Japan. (2021). Retrieved Dec 29, 2021, from https://www.mext.go.jp/en/index.htm.

Nakamura, T. (2000). Kōgakureki shikō no sūsei: Sedai no henka ni chūmoku shite (Trend of preference for high education: Focusing on generational change). In H. Kondo (Ed.), *Sengo Nihon no kyōiku shakai (Educational credentials in the postwar stratification system), Nihon No Kaisō Shisutemu 3 (Japanese stratification system Vol. 3)* (pp. 151–173). University of Tokyo Press.

Sewell, W. H., Haller, A. O., & Ohlendorf, G. W. (1970). The Educational and early occupational status attainment process: Replication and revision. *American Sociological Review, 35*(6), 1014–1027.

Sobel, M. E. (1981). Diagonal mobility models: A substantively motivated class of designs for the analysis of mobility effects. *American Sociological Review, 46*(6), 893–906.

Stephens, N. M., Townsend, S. S. M., Markus, H. R., & Taylor Phillips, L. (2012). A cultural mismatch: Independent cultural norms produce greater increases in cortisol and more negative emotions among first-generation college students. *Journal of Experimental Social Psychology, 48*, 1389–1393.

Sunaga, T. (2020). Hidaisotsu oya naibu no kyōiku asupirēshon no kanetsu/reikyaku: 'gakureki fuman ni yoru genteiteki-kanetsu' mekanizumu, (Differences in parents' educational aspirations among non-graduates: The mechanism of restricted activation caused by dissatisfaction with one's educational qualification). *Kyōiku Shakaigaku Kenkyū (The Journal of Educational Sociology), 105*, 93–114.

Treiman, D. J. (1970). Industrialization and social stratification. In E. O. Lawman (Ed.), *Social stratification: Research and theory for the 1970s* (pp. 207–234). Bobbs-Merrill.

Trow, M. (1970). Reflections on the transition from mass to universal higher education. In S. R. Graubard & G. A. Ballotti (Eds.), *The Embattled University* (pp. 1–42). George Braziller.

Trow, M. (2010). *Twentieth-century higher education: Elite to mass to universal*. Johns Hopkins University Press.

Toru Kikkawa is a professor of sociology in the Graduate School of Human Sciences at Osaka University. He got his Ph.D. from Osaka University in 1994. He includes quantitative sociology, social research methodology, sociology of education, social psychology, and social stratification studies among his areas of research, and has a special interest in contemporary Japanese society. He is the author of *Social mentality in contemporary Japan: Quantitative social consciousness studies* (Osaka University Press, 2016). He also published; Carola Hommerich and, Toru Kikkawea, 2019, "Movement behind the scenes: The quiet transformation of status identification in Japan," *Social Science Japan Journal, 22-1*, 11–24. Sho Fujihara, Toru Kikkawa and Carmi Schooler, 2018, "Work made us what we are: Complexity of work, self-directedness of orientation, and intellectual flexibility of older US and Japanese men," *Research in Social Stratification and Mobility, 54*, 36–45.

Chapter 8
Effects of Regional Inequality on Political Attitudes: Social Capital and Support for Redistribution and Free Competition

Naoki Sudo

Abstract In this study, I investigate the effects of regional inequality on support for social policies and explore the relationships between support for social policies and social capital. To do so, I analyzed the data from two Japanese surveys, the National Survey of Social Stratification and Social Mobility in 2015 and the 2015 Population Census by using factor analyses and multi-level ordered probit regression models. The results of the analyses revealed that regional disadvantages at the municipality level had positive effects on support for redistribution and negative effects on support for free competition, while regional disadvantage's effects on support for social policies did not depend on social capital at the municipality level. The results also showed that social capital at the municipality level was positively associated with regional inequality. This finding suggests that regional disadvantages generate social capital, but social capital does not have sufficient effects to offset negative consequences deduced from regional disadvantage.

8.1 Introduction

In this study, I focus on the relationships between regional inequality and political attitudes. Previous studies have clarified that social inequality can affect support for social policies (Finseraas, 2009; García-Sánchez et al., 2018; Schmidt-Catran, 2016). For example, pessimistic information about social mobility increases support for redistribution (Alesina et al., 2018; Linos & West, 2003; Smyth et al., 2010), and disparities in employment status stability are related to social policy preferences (Gingrich & Ansell, 2012). However, other studies have denied significant relationships between social inequality and support for social policies (Breznau & Hommerich, 2019; Dallinger, 2010; Lübker, 2007). Thus, the relationship between social inequality and support for social policies is rather complicated and remains an unresolved problem.

N. Sudo (✉)
Graduate School of Social Sciences, Hitotsubashi University, Kunitachi, Japan
e-mail: naoki.sudo@r.hit-u.ac.jp

S. Shirahase (ed.), *Social Stratification in an Aging Society with Low Fertility*, Economy and Social Inclusion, https://doi.org/10.1007/978-981-19-3647-0_8

Here, the complexity of relationships between social inequality and support for social policies may reflect multi-dimensionality and diverse political interests within a society. As an example, consider the relationships between increased immigration and support for social policies. Some studies have noted that increased immigration negatively affects support for welfare policies (Eger, 2010; Finseraas, 2012; Kymlicka, 2016). However, other studies have insisted that increased immigration does not directly lead to support for anti-welfare policies (Brady & Finnigan, 2014; Burgoon et al., 2012; Steele, 2016). Thus, increased immigration has no constant effect on support for social policies, and these depend on various social contexts (Kwon & Curran, 2016; Reeskens & van Oorschot, 2012).

Dimick et al. (2016) revealed that, even though wealthy people prefer wealth redistribution less than poor people, they still react to changes in social inequality as if they want to reduce social inequality. This suggests that people do not react to situations according only to self-interest. As people react to situations according to self-interest and common interest simultaneously, their policy preference formation process becomes more complex (Jæger, 2009; Sudo, 2020). Thus, to examine the formation process of their policy preferences correctly, effects of self-interest and common interest on support for social policies must be distinguished from each other. Here, I consider the effects of regional inequality on support for social policies. As regional disadvantages affect all residents living in a given region, regional inequality can be considered a common interest for them.

In addition to regional inequality, I also examine the effects of social capital on support for social policies. As social capital plays a key role of achieving common interests in a community, the negative influences of regional inequality on support for social policies may be reduced via effects of social capital. According to Putnam, social capital is composed of generalized trust, norm of reciprocity, and social network (Putnam, 2000; Putnam et al., 1994). In other words, there is a possibility that social trust and solidarity derived from social capital can stimulate activities of regional associations and, as a result, compensate for regional disadvantage (Mitani & Hiramatsu, 2020). This social capital may be classified as a bonding type of social capital that reinforces social ties between residents within a community, rather than a bridging type of social capital that reinforces social ties between different communities (Beyerlein & Hipp, 2005; Ruef & Kwon, 2016; Teney & Hanquinet, 2012).

Here, social capital is assumed to be part of public goods for residents of a community. If residents view social capital as public goods compensating for regional disadvantages, the social capital that they perceive will weaken the effects of regional inequality on support for social policies. Namely, social capital might weaken support for redistribution and strengthen support for free competition through the mitigating effects of regional disadvantage on social policies. As a result, a negative effect of social capital on support for redistribution and a positive effect of social capital on support for free competition are expected in the social survey data analyses. As an example, members of religious groups tend to oppose income redistribution by the state (Stegmueller et al., 2012).

On the other hand, social capital-derived solidarity might also reinforce sympathy among residents in the community (Jaime-Castillo & Marqués-Perales, 2019; Kymlicka, 2016). If the residents are sympathetic to social justice and social equality within their community, their social capital will influence the effect of regional inequality on support for social policies. In other words, social capital can strengthen support for redistribution and weaken support for free competition. As a result, a positive effect of social capital on support for redistribution and a negative effect of social capital on support for free competition are expected. Thus, I examine which prediction is more fitted to a real society: Does social capital weaken or strengthen the effects of regional disadvantage on support for social policies?

In order to explore the relationships between regional inequality, social capital, and political attitudes, I focus on Japanese society as a case study. Japan is well known as one of the most affluent nations and the most highly aging society in the world. According to the World Population Prospect (United Nations, Department of Economic and Social Affairs, 2019), Japan had the highest worldwide old-age dependency ratio (ratio of population aged over 65 per 100 population aged from 20 to 64) in 2015 at 46.2. This rate suggests that active generations in Japan bear an extremely high burden to sustain the social welfare system compared to the other nations. The World Population Prospect also recorded Japan's total fertility rate (children per woman) from 2010–2015 as 1.41, which is one of the lowest ranks globally. Although low fertility rates are common among affluent nations, this feature is most prominently observed in Japan. Therefore, the problem that the social welfare system's sustainability poses for Japan will become increasingly severe in the future.

Even though the Japanese population has been consistently declining since 2008, the Japanese government has not held favorable immigration policies. As a result, the 2015 ratio of the foreign residents in Japan was only 0.014 (Statistics Bureau, 2017b). However, this low ratio represents 1,752,368 foreign residents, according to the Population Census (Statistics Bureau, 2017a). Although foreign residents form a small portion of the population, their presence may have greater significance for Japanese people in the context of the rapidly gaining population and low fertility rate.

It should also be noted that the diffusion of aging populations varies across regions. In Japan, it is well known that there are large differences in industrial and demographic structures between urban and rural areas (Lützeler, 2017). Japan has three mega metropolitan areas: *Shuto-ken* (Tokyo and its neighboring areas), *Kinki-ken* (Kyoto City, Osaka City, Kobe City, and their neighboring areas), and *Chukyo-ken* (Nagoya and its neighboring areas). These urban areas are highly industrialized and are unaffected by population shrinkage; meanwhile rural areas have suffered sharp demographic shrinkage due to young residents moving to urban areas. It should be noted that while social inequalities in urban areas have widened over the past decades because of the economic pressures due to the neoliberal regime, which had been enforced by *Jimin-to* (Japanese conservative party), social inequalities in rural areas have not changed remarkably. As a result, inequalities between urban and rural areas at the prefecture level have not increased over the past decades. However, as Lützeler (2017) emphasized, inequalities between urban and rural areas at the municipality level have widened through social changes during the past decades, because the people living in the poor areas of mega cities such as Tokyo, Kyoto, Osaka, Kobe, and Nagoya have faced various hardships. Therefore, if social researchers focus on inequalities solely at the prefecture level, they may underestimate inequalities between urban and rural areas in Japan. To correctly understand regional inequality, focus should be on regional inequality at the municipality level, and not at the prefecture level, in this article. For example, the highest percentage of the population over the age of 65 compared with the whole population at the municipality level is 60.5%, while the lowest percentage is 12.7% (Statistics Bureau, 2017b). Additionally, population aging is significantly associated with other social factors such as economic growth, increasing immigration, levels of social capital, and fiscal power at the municipality level. Generally, as highly aged municipalities are economically disadvantaged, they are more likely to experience low economic growth and weak fiscal power. Conversely, as the less aged municipalities are economically advantaged, they are more likely to have strong economic power and be financially sound. As a result, paradoxically, the regions experiencing relatively moderate population aging have more immigrants because they offer strong economic attractions, whereas the regions experiencing relatively severe population aging have less immigration because of weak economic enticements. These factors are likely related to the political attitudes of these regions' residents.

From this inference, we would expect this regional inequality to generate political opposition between the advantaged and disadvantaged municipalities, which could affect Japanese policymaking because members of the National Diet in Japan are elected by the electoral district. This political opposition would likely disturb effective policies for a sound social welfare system. In sum, as population aging and low fertility rates have direct and indirect influences on the sustainability of the social welfare system, political attitudes of Japanese people could be affected by regional inequality derived from differing demographics. These factors make Japan one of the most expedient cases for exploring the relationships between regional inequality and political attitudes.

8.2 Hypotheses

In this study, I focus on support for redistribution and support for free competition in social policies, which are not necessarily incompatible. Certainly, support for redistribution and support for free competition are likely to be negatively associated with each other. People supporting redistribution are less likely to support free competition and, conversely, people supporting free competition are less likely to support redistribution. As previous studies (Koos & Sachweh, 2017; Nagayoshi & Sato, 2014; Sudo, 2020) have noted, however, an individual supporting free competition might simultaneously support redistribution. Thus, support for redistribution and support for free competition should be treated as distinct variables. Accordingly, support for redistribution and support for free competition are analyzed separately in this article.

First, I present hypotheses for relations between support for redistribution and regional inequality. Typically, people suffering from social inequality prefer to reduce such inequality (Becker, 2019; Kevins et al., 2018; Wilkinson & Pickett, 2010) and are expected to support policies reducing social inequality, such as redistributive policies (Alesina et al., 2018; Wietzke, 2016). Additionally, regional inequality is one of the most salient inequalities for residents in a community. Therefore, people living in disadvantaged communities are more likely to support redistribution because redistributive policies are expected to reduce regional inequality. Conversely, people living in advantaged communities are less likely to support redistribution (Brady & Bostic, 2015). Based on these inferences, Hypothesis 1 is formulated as follows:

Hypothesis 1. Compared to individuals living in advantaged communities, individuals living in disadvantaged communities are more likely to support redistribution.

On the other hand, how social capital influences support for redistribution seems to be unclear. If social capital mitigates the problems caused by regional disadvantage, which promotes support for redistribution, it might have negative influences on support for redistribution. However, if social capital reinforces social ties among residents within a community, it might have positive influences on support for redistribution (Borisova et al., 2018; van Oorschot & Arts, 2005). Furthermore, if positive and negative effects of social capital on support for redistribution are offset by each other, social capital will have weak effects on it (O'Connell, 2003). Accordingly, the hypotheses related to social capital and support for redistribution are formulated as follows:

Hypothesis 2a. Compared to individuals holding poor social capital at the community level, individuals holding rich social capital at the community level are less likely to support redistribution.

Hypothesis 2b. Compared to individuals holding poor social capital at the community level, individuals holding rich social capital at the community level are more likely to support redistribution.

By analyzing social survey data, I will confirm which hypothesis (Hypothesis 2a or 2b) is supported by empirical evidence.

Second, I present hypotheses regarding relations between support for free competition and regional inequality. Regional disadvantage might weaken a community's economic competitiveness. For residents in disadvantaged communities, thus, policies prioritizing free competition are undesirable because they might widen regional inequality. As a result, residents in disadvantaged communities tend not to support free competition, while residents in advantaged communities tend to support it (VanHeuvelen, 2017). Hypothesis 3 is therefore formulated as follows:

Hypothesis 3. Compared to individuals living in advantaged communities, individuals living in disadvantaged communities are less likely to support free competition.

As for support for redistribution, the relationships between social capital and support for free competition are unclear. Social capital may encourage entrepreneurship among community members and promote economic growth (S. W. Kwon et al.,

2013), in which case, social capital would have a positive effect on support for free competition. Thus, social capital mitigates the negative effects of regional disadvantage on support for free competition. On the other hand, if social capital grows solidarity among residents, such solidarity may foster residents' cooperative, rather than competitive, relationships. As a result, social capital might weaken support for free competition, in which case, social capital encourages the negative effects of regional disadvantage on support for free competition. Based on these inferences, Hypotheses 4a and 4b are formulated as follows:

> Hypothesis 4a. Compared to individuals holding poor social capital at the community level, individuals holding rich social capital at the community level are more likely to support free competition.

> Hypothesis 4b. Compared to individuals holding poor social capital at the community level, individuals holding rich social capital at the community level are less likely to support redistribution.

Similar to Hypotheses 2a and 2b, through the statistical analyses based on social survey data, I will confirm which hypothesis (Hypothesis 4a or 4b) has more validity.

If the hypotheses presented in this study are adequately examined, their results will show how regional inequality influences political attitudes of individuals. Furthermore, the results of the analyses will also clarify how these effects are mitigated or reinforced by social capital. In other words, regional inequality's effects on political attitudes are expected to be inconstant, depending on each region's social circumstance. To understand the role of common interest at the regional level on the formation process of support for social policies, social circumstances such as social capital at the level of region should be considered more carefully.

8.3 Data and Methods

8.3.1 Data

To examine the above hypotheses, I used two social survey data: the National Survey of Social Stratification and Social Mobility in 2015 (SSM 2015) (SSM Survey Management Committee, 2018), which is a nationwide representative social survey in Japan, and the 2015 Population Census (Statistics Bureau, 2017a). SSM 2015 data include respondents' residential information (i.e., which municipality they live in), while the Population Census has various information for each municipality in Japan (Statistics Bureau, 2017b). Using both datasets, I merged SSM 2015 data with data from the 2015 Population Census.

SSM 2015 was conducted from January to August 2015 using a multistage stratified random sampling method based on the Basic Resident Register that is administrated by each municipality. The survey method of SSM 2015 used a combination of interview and self-administrated questionnaire. Respondents' demographic and social-economic status were collected through a personal interview, and the information related to their social and political attitudes was collected by questionnaire. Additionally, the respondents' municipality were obtained from the Basic Resident Register (the sampling list).

The total number of respondents to SSM 2015 was 7816, and the response rate was 50.1%. However, some cases included missing values for variables that were used in the analyses of this study. When I analyzed the combined SSM 2015 and Population Census data, I excluded the cases with missing values from my analyses. As a result, the actual number of respondents used in the analyses was 6,888. Even though that response rate may seem low, SSM 2015 is considered one of the most reliable datasets for Japanese society given low response rate typical of academic social surveys in Japan. There were 631 municipalities used in this study's analyses.

8.3.2 Variables

Dependent Variables. The dependent variables in this study are "support for redistribution" and "support for free competition." In SSM 2015, support for redistribution was measured by using the following questions:

> *The following opinions concern how society should work. What do you think about each statement?*
>
> *Rather than protecting free-market competition, it is more important to eliminate differences among people.*

Then, respondents were asked to respond using one of five options (Agree, Somewhat agree, No opinion either way, Somewhat disagree, Disagree). Similarly, support for free competition was measured by using the following question:

> *To the extent that opportunities are equally available, we must accept the disparity in wealth that results from competition.*

As with support for redistribution, respondents were asked to indicate their response using one of five options. The two dependent variables were treated as an ordinal variable and coded as follows: Agree = 5, Somewhat agree = 4, No opinion either way = 3, Somewhat disagree = 2, Disagree = 1.

Independent Variables. As independent variables related to regional disadvantage at the municipality level, I used the percentage of the population that was over age 65, population density per 0.01 km^2, percentage of the population of foreigners, and the 2015 Fiscal Power Index. The Fiscal Power Index is published annually by the central government and indicates a degree of financial independence from the central government and assigns a value between 0 and 1 (MIC, 2020). Three other variables were estimated for each municipality by using the information acquired from the 2015 Population Census.

As independent variables related to subjective evaluation of social capital, I focused on generalized trust score, solidarity score, and reciprocity score. Respondents self-evaluated their scores using a five-point scale. Each score was measured by the following questions:

Most people can be trusted (generalized trust),

There is a good relationship among neighborhoods (solidarity),

If someone has trouble, neighborhoods will help them (reciprocity).

Additionally, as independent variables related to social activities as social capital, I focused on political activities score, civic activities score, volunteer activities score, and residents' association score. As with the subjective evaluation for of social capital scores, respondents self-reported using a five-point scale. Then, I calculated the scores' averages for each municipality and treated them as a variable at the municipality level.

Control Variables. In my analyses, I controlled for the effects of demographic characteristics on support for redistribution or free competition, including age, gender (man coded as 0, and woman coded as 1), and marital status (married = reference category, unmarried, and divorced/bereaved) in my analytical models as control variables.

Furthermore, I controlled for the effects of socioeconomic status on support for redistribution and free competition. According to previous studies (Busemeyer, 2013; Gonthier, 2017), education has significant effect on policy preferences. Therefore, I included educational level (higher education, middle education = reference category, and primary education) in my analytical models as a control variable. Similarly, previous studies have indicated that occupation (Arndt, 2018) and employment status (Levanon, 2018; MARGALIT, 2013; Naumann et al., 2016; Owens & Pedulla, 2014) have significant effects on policy preferences. Based on these studies, I also included occupation (upper white collar, lower white collar = reference group, and blue collar) and employment status (self-employed, regular employee = reference group, non-regular employee, no job, and job seeker) into my analytical models as control variables. Finally, as income is a well-known influence on policy preferences (Gidron & Mijs, 2019; Owens & Pedulla, 2014; Shin, 2018; Sumino, 2018), I included household income into my analytical models as a control variable.

8.3.3 Analytic Strategy

The variables at the municipality level were expected to be highly correlated with each other. Considering the possibility of multicollinearity, I avoided putting variables at the municipality level into my analytical model simultaneously. To solve the problem of multicollinearity, I implemented a factor analysis by using the population of residents over age 65, population density, the population of foreigners, and the 2015 Fiscal Power Index. Then, I calculated the regional disadvantage scores based on that factor analysis's scores. I also implemented another factor analysis based on generalized trust, solidarity, reciprocity, political activities, civic activities, volunteer activities, and residential association scores. Then, I calculated the social capital scores based on that factor analysis's scores.

Next, by using the regional disadvantage and social capital scores as independent variables, I implemented multilevel ordered probit models predicting support for redistribution or support for free competition. The multilevel ordered probit models used in this study represented by the following equation:

$$y_{ij}^{*} = \beta_{0j} + \beta_1\, Regional\ Disadvantage + \beta_2\, Social\ Capital + \varepsilon_{ij},$$

$$\beta_{0j} = \gamma_{00} + \mu_{0j},$$

where β is a regression coefficient and ε is the variance among individuals. γ is the overall intercept, and μ is the variance among municipalities. Furthermore, i is the respondent's identification number, and j is the municipality's identification number. y_{ij}, the observed ordinal variable, takes on values 1 through 5 according to the following scheme:

$$y_{ij}^{*} = k \leftrightarrow \kappa_{(k-1)} < y_{ij}^{*} \leq \kappa_k,$$

where $k = 1, \cdots, 5$, and $\kappa_0 = -\infty\ \kappa_5 = +\infty$.

Then, the coefficients β and the cutpoints $\kappa_1, \kappa_2, \ldots, \kappa_{k-1}$ were estimated. To estimate coefficients, cutpoints, and variances in the multilevel ordered logit models, R software and mixor package were used (Hedeker & Gibbons, 1996; R Core Team, 2018).

If the hypotheses presented above are correct, the coefficients of regional disadvantage score and social capital score on support for social policies will have a statistically significant value. Specifically, the coefficient of regional disadvantage score on support for redistribution is expected to have a statistically significant and positive value, while the coefficient of regional disadvantage score on support for free competition is expected to have a statistically significant and negative value. The coefficient of social capital score on support for redistribution is expected take a statistically significant and negative (or positive) value according to Hypothesis 2a (or Hypothesis 2b), and the coefficient of social capital score on support for free competition is expected to take a statistically significant and positive (or negative) value according to Hypothesis 4a (or Hypothesis 4b). Moreover, the statistical significance of these is expected to remain even after controlling for respondents' demographic characteristics and socioeconomic status.

8.4 Results

8.4.1 Descriptive Statistics

Table 8.1 shows the results of descriptive statistics for the variables at the individual level. The mean of support for redistribution (=3.31) is more than 3.0, which indicates that many respondents support redistribution policies. However, as the mean of support for free competition (=3.43) is above 3.0, they also support free competition policies. This suggests that support for redistribution and free competition may coexist within Japanese people.

It is worth noting that the variable of household income was missing many values to the extent that the exclusion of such cases would considerably reduce the effective number of cases in my analyses. To avoid this problem, I estimated the predicted values for the variable of household income based on Markov chain Monte Carlo (MCMC) methods and substituted the predicted values for the missing values for the variable of household income. Then, I used Rstan software to estimate the predicted values based on MCMC method (Stan Development Team, 2018).

Table 8.1 Descriptive statistics of variables at the individual level

Variable	N	Mean	SD	Min	Max
Support for redistribution	6888	3.31	1.06	1	5
Support for free competition	6888	3.43	1.12	1	5
Age	6888	52.75	16.11	20	80
Woman (=1)	6888	0.53	0.50	0	1
Higher education	6888	0.26	0.44	0	1
Middle education	6888	0.62	0.49	0	1
Primary education	6888	0.12	0.32	0	1
Married	6888	0.73	0.45	0	1
Unmarried	6888	0.17	0.37	0	1
Divorced/Bereaved	6888	0.11	0.31	0	1
Self-employed	6888	0.15	0.36	0	1
Regular employment	6888	0.31	0.46	0	1
Non-regular employment	6888	0.20	0.40	0	1
Upper white collar	6888	0.17	0.38	0	1
Lower white collar	6888	0.23	0.42	0	1
Blue collar	6888	0.27	0.44	0	1
No job	6888	0.31	0.46	0	1
Job seeker	6888	0.03	0.16	0	1
Household income (10,000JPN)	5014	597.04	433.83	0	7625

Table 8.2 Descriptive statistics of variables at the municipality level

Variables	Mean	SD	Min	Max
Population of over-65 s (%)	27.26	5.46	14.90	55.91
Population density (per 0.01 km^2)	39.49	45.17	0.36	223.80
Foreigners (%)	1.32	1.33	0.09	14.64
Fiscal power index	0.72	0.23	0.11	1.48
Average score of generalized trust	3.04	0.37	1.67	4.40
Average score of solidarity	3.63	0.39	1.67	5.00
Average score of reciprocity	3.55	0.40	1.67	4.80
Average score of political activities	1.90	0.40	1.00	4.00
Average score of civic activities	1.65	0.35	1.00	4.12
Average score of volunteer activities	2.07	0.39	1.00	3.60
Average score of residents' association	2.88	0.60	1.25	5.00
Number of municipalities is 631				

Table 8.2 provides the descriptive statistics for variables at the municipality level. For variables related to regional disadvantages (population aged over 65, population density, population of foreigners, and Fiscal Power Index), there are large variances between municipalities. This result indicates regional disadvantages among municipalities cannot be overlooked. For variables related to social capital, the averages of solidarity score and reciprocity score seem to be high because they are more than 3.0, while the averages of political activities and civic activities scores seem to be low because they are less than 2.0. Overall, the level of social activities seems to be weak compared to the level of social norm.

Here, it is necessary to examine how items related to social capital are correlated to each other at the municipality level. Table 8.3 shows the correlation matrix of variables related to social capital at the municipality level. This table shows that items related to social capital except for generalized trust have statistically significant and positive correlations with each other. Generalized trust has a statistically significant and positive correlation with solidarity and reciprocity, but it has no significant correlation with political or civic activities. These results reveal that social capital measured by these items tends to be a bonding type of social capital, rather than a bridging type of social capital. Thus, Table 8.3 shows that a bonding type of social capital at the municipality level in Japanese society can be observed by using social survey data.

8.4.2 *Factor Analyses*

Table 8.4 shows the results of the factor analysis for regional inequality with varimax rotation. One factor that was extracted from the items related to regional

Table 8.3 Correlation matrix of variables related to social capital

	1	2	3	4	5	6	7
1. Average score of generalized trust	1.000						
2. Average score of solidarity	0.381***	1.000					
3. Average score of reciprocity	0.247***	0.687***	1.000				
4. Average score of political activities	0.058	0.226***	0.171***	1.000			
5. Average score of civic activities	0.075	0.233***	0.258***	0.531***	1.000		
6. Average score of volunteer activities	0.085*	0.207***	0.303***	0.400***	0.569***	1.000	
7. Average score of residents' association	0.132**	0.391***	0.443***	0.373***	0.443***	0.401***	1.000

N = 631. ***$p < 0.001$, **$p < 0.01$, *$p < 0.05$ (two-tailed test)

Table 8.4 Results of factor analysis with varimax rotation for regional inequality

Item	Factor 1	Uniqueness
Population of over-65 s (%)	−0.781	0.390
Population density (per 0.01 km^2)	0.646	0.583
Foreigners (%)	0.471	0.778
Fiscal power index	0.881	0.224
Eigen value	2.472	
Proportion variance	0.506	

Note Bartlett factor scores were estimated

inequality (Factor 1) accounts for more than 50% of variances between municipalities. Moreover, Factor 1 is negatively related to population of over age 65, while it is positively related to other items. This means that advantaged municipalities have a high score for Factor 1 and disadvantaged municipalities have a low score for

Table 8.5 Results of factor analysis with varimax rotation for social capital

Item	Factor 1	Factor 2	Uniqueness
1. Average score of generalized trust	0.034	**0.399**	0.840
2. Average score of solidarity	0.175	**0.889**	0.178
3. Average score of reciprocity	0.251	**0.724**	0.414
4. Average score of political activities	**0.614**	0.110	0.611
5. Average score of civic activities	**0.825**	0.093	0.311
6. Average score of volunteer activities	**0.673**	0.120	0.532
7. Average score of residents' association	**0.517**	0.357	0.605
Eigen value	2.966	1.404	
Proportion variance	0.268	0.234	
Cumulative variance	0.268	0.501	

Note Bartlett factor scores were estimated

Factor 1. Accordingly, I calculated the regional disadvantage score (regional disadvantage = 1 − Factor 1) for each municipality. Regional disadvantage has a high value in disadvantaged municipalities and a low value in advantaged municipalities.

On the other hand, Table 8.5 shows results of factor analysis for social capital with varimax rotation. One factor that was extracted from the items related to social capital (Factor 1) accounts for 26.8% of variances between municipalities and another factor (Factor 2) accounts for 23.4%. Moreover, Factor 1 is positively related to items for activities (political, civic, volunteer, and resident association activities), while Factor 2 is positively related to items for norms (solidarity, reciprocity, and generalized trust). This indicates that Factors 1 and 2 reflect aspects of association and norm in social capital, respectively. Based on this, I treated Factor I score as an association score for social capital [Social Capital (association)] and Factor 2 score as a norm score for social capital [Social Capital (norm)].

Regional disadvantage, social capital (association), and social capital (norm) were used as independent variables at the municipality level. As mentioned above, the items of regional disadvantage and social capital were highly correlated to each other. If I included all of them into my statistical model simultaneously, multicollinearity would have appeared between them, which might lead me to misinterpret their effects on support for social policies. Therefore, I used the factor scores [regional score, social capital (association), and social capital (norm)] is an effective strategy to avoid a problem of multicollinearity. Table 8.6 shows descriptive statistics of regional disadvantage, social capital (association), and social capital (norm).

Table 8.6 Descriptive statistics of regional disadvantage and social capital

Variable	Mean	SD	Min	Max
Regional disadvantage	−0.75	0.95	−3.30	2.04
Social capital (norm)	0.00	1.13	−2.92	5.97
Social capital (association)	0.00	1.09	−5.77	4.02
N = 631				

8.4.3 Support for Redistribution

To examine effects of regional disadvantage and social capital on support for redistribution, I analyzed the SSM 2015 data by using a multi-level ordered probit model. Table 8.7 shows the results of the multi-level ordered probit models that predict support for redistribution: Models 1, 2, and 3. Model 1 tested the effect of regional disadvantage on support for redistribution. Model 2 tested the effects of social capital (association) and social capital (norm) on support for redistribution. Model 3 examined the interaction effect of regional disadvantage and social capital on support for redistribution. Lastly, Model 4 checked whether the effects of regional disadvantage and social capital at the municipality level on support for redistribution remain even after controlling for individual characteristics and socioeconomic status.

The coefficient of regional disadvantage in Model 1 is statistically significant and positive (0.121, $p < 0.001$). This indicates that people living in disadvantaged municipalities, which suffer from high population aging and weak fiscal power, are more likely to support redistribution. Moreover, the positive effect of regional disadvantage on support for redistribution (0.112, $p < 0.001$) could be still found in Model 3, which included variables of regional disadvantage and social capital simultaneously. This clarified that regional disadvantage has independent influences on support for redistribution from the influences of social capital (association and norm). Therefore, it can be said that people living in disadvantaged municipalities are more likely to support redistribution regardless of social capital.

On the other hand, the coefficients of social capital (association) and social capital (norm) in Model 2 are statistically significant and positive (for social capital (association), 0.039, $p < 0.01$; for social capital (norm), 0.051, $p < 0.001$). This seems to imply that people with high social capital at the municipality level are more likely to support redistribution. Thus, the directions of the effects of social capital (association) and social capital (norm) in Model 2 are not consistent with Hypothesis 2a, but they are consistent with Hypothesis 2b. Moreover, the coefficients of social capital (association) and social capital (norm) lost their statistical significance in Model 3. This implies that the influences of social capital on support for redistribution are explained as an indirect effect via regional disadvantage. In other words, people living in disadvantaged municipalities are more likely to support redistribution and simultaneously are keen to create social capital to compensate for their lack of social security. Rather, social capital and support for redistribution seem to not have a direct relationship with each other, but an indirect relationship through regional disadvantage.

Table 8.7 Results of Multi-level Ordered Probit Models That Predict Support for Redistribution

	Model 1		Model 2		Model 3		Model 4	
	Coeff	SE	Coeff	SE	Coeff	SE	Coeff	SE
Fixed effect								
Regional disadvantage	0.121***	(0.015)			0.112***	(0.017)	0.075***	(0.017)
Social capital (norm)			0.051***	(0.012)	0.016	(0.012)	0.012	(0.012)
Social capital (association)			0.039**	(0.014)	0.013	(0.015)	0.005	(0.015)
Age							−0.744	(0.651)
Age^2							1.305*	(0.626)
Women							0.204***	(0.028)
Married							–	–
Unmarried							0.021	(0.046)
Divorced/Bereaved							0.052	(0.046)
Primary education							0.169***	(0.042)
Middle education							–	–
Higher education							−0.175***	(0.034)
Self-employed							−0.139**	(0.046)
Regular employment							–	–
Non-regular employment							0.028	(0.044)
Upper white collar							−0.038	(0.048)
Lower white collar							–	–
Blue collar							0.179***	(0.037)
No job							−0.008	(0.049)

(continued)

Table 8.7 (continued)

	Model 1		Model 2		Model 3		Model 4	
	Coeff	SE	Coeff	SE	Coeff	SE	Coeff	SE
Job seeker							0.138	(0.085)
Household income (log)							−0.098***	(0.021)
Random effect								
(Intercept)	0.005	(0.005)	0.013*	(0.006)	0.005	(0.005)	0.000	(0.004)
1/2	−1.665***	(0.027)	−1.574***	(0.026)	−1.658***	(0.028)	−2.153***	(0.210)
2/3	−0.955***	(0.021)	−0.865***	(0.018)	−0.949***	(0.022)	−1.425***	(0.210)
3/4	0.118***	(0.018)	0.206***	(0.016)	0.124***	(0.020)	−0.319	(0.211)
4/5	0.984***	(0.020)	1.073***	(0.020)	0.990***	(0.022)	0.574**	(0.211)
AIC	−9889.08		−9915.01		−9890.08		−9706.62	
BIC	−9902.42		−9930.58		−9907.87		−9755.54	

N = 6,888. ***$p < 0.001$, ** $p < 0.01$, *$p < 0.05$ (two-tailed test)

8.4.4 Support for Free Competition

Next, I examined the effects of regional disadvantage and social capital on support for free competition. Table 8.8 reveals the results of the multi-level ordered probit models that predict support for free competition. Model 1 confirms the effect of regional disadvantage on support for free competition. On the other hand, Model 2 confirms the effects of social capital (association) and social capital (norm) on support for free competition. Furthermore, Model 3 examined the interaction effect of regional disadvantage and social capital on support for free competition. Lastly, Model 4 checked whether the effects of regional disadvantage and social capital at the municipality level on support for free competition remain even after controlling for individual characteristics and socioeconomic status.

Model 1 in Table 8.8 clarifies that the coefficient of regional disadvantage has a statistically significant and negative effect on support for free competition (-0.096, $p < 0.001$). In other words, people living in advantaged municipalities are more likely to support free competition. This finding coincides with Hypothesis 3. Moreover, Model 3 in Table 8.8 reveals that, even after controlling for social capital (association) and social capital (norm), the effect of regional disadvantage remains statistically significant. Additionally, Model 4 in Table 8.8 reveals that, even after controlling for respondents' demographic characteristics and socioeconomic status, the effect of regional disadvantage keeps its statistical significance. Based on this finding, we can conclude that the effect of regional disadvantage on support for free competition is independent from the other factors, and regional disadvantage itself directly influences respondents' policy preferences, support for redistribution, and support for free competition.

On the other hand, Model 2 in Table 8.8 shows that, while the coefficient of social capital (norm) is statistically significant and negative (-0.037, $p < 0.01$), the coefficient of social capital (association) on support for free competition has no statistical significance. Moreover, after controlling for the effect of regional disadvantage, the statistical significance of the coefficient of social capital (norm) also disappeared. This means that disadvantaged municipalities, which tend to depend on social capital, have negative influences on support for free competition. Thus, social capital does not mitigate or reinforce the negative effects of regional disadvantage on support for free competition. Therefore, neither Hypotheses 4a nor 4b were supported by the analyses based on the data from SSM 215 and the 2015 Population Census.

8.4.5 Interaction Effects of Regional Disadvantage and Social Capital on Political Attitudes

I more directly examined the interaction effects of regional disadvantage and social capital on support for social policies. Table 8.9 reveals the results of the analyses for the interaction effects of regional disadvantage and social capital using multi-level

Table 8.8 Results of multi-level ordered probit models predicting support for free competition

	Model 1		Model 2		Model 3		Model 4	
	Coeff	SE	Coeff	SE	Coeff	SE	Coeff	SE
Fixed effect								
Regional disadvantage	−0.096***	(0.014)			−0.093***	(0.015)	−0.075***	(0.015)
Social capital (norm)			−0.037**	(0.012)	−0.009	(0.013)	−0.011	(0.013)
Social capital (association)			−0.018	(0.012)	0.003	(0.012)	0.006	(0.013)
Age							−2.128**	(0.656)
Age^2							1.672**	(0.631)
Women							−0.283***	(0.029)
Married							–	–
Unmarried							−0.024	(0.044)
Divorced/Bereaved							0.070	(0.045)
Primary education							−0.047	(0.042)
Middle education							–	–
Higher education							0.142***	(0.035)
Self-employed							0.177***	(0.045)
Regular employment							–	–
Non-regular employment							−0.031	(0.041)
Upper white collar							−0.008	(0.045)
Lower white collar							–	–
Blue collar							−0.086*	(0.038)
No job							0.038	(0.050)

(continued)

Table 8.8 (continued)

	Model 1		Model 2		Model 3		Model 4	
	Coeff	SE	Coeff	SE	Coeff	SE	Coeff	SE
Job seeker							−0.029	(0.087)
Household income (log)							0.043*	(0.021)
Random effect (Intercept)	0.005	(0.005)	0.008	(0.006)	0.002	(0.006)	0.001	(0.006)
1/2	−1.299***	(0.024)	−1.369***	(0.023)	−1.300***	(0.025)	−1.794***	(0.211)
2/3	−0.866***	(0.021)	−0.936***	(0.019)	−0.867***	(0.021)	−1.359***	(0.210)
3/4	0.000	(0.017)	−0.071***	(0.015)	−0.002	(0.018)	−0.480*	(0.210)
4/5	1.072***	(0.020)	1.001***	(0.019)	1.071***	(0.021)	0.619**	(0.210)
AIC	−9957.45		−9976.77		−9959.19		−9852.86	
BIC	−9970.79		−9992.34		−9976.98		−9901.78	

N = 6,888. ***$p < 0.001$, **$p < 0.01$, *$p < 0.05$ (two-tailed test)

Table 8.9 Interaction effects of regional disadvantage and social capital

	Support for redistribution		Support for free competition	
	Coeff.	SE	Coeff.	SE
Fixed effect				
Regional disadvantage	0.057**	(0.019)	−0.074***	(0.015)
Social capital (norm)	0.004	(0.014)	−0.025	(0.014)
Social capital (association)	0.027	(0.018)	−0.011	(0.016)
Regional disadvantage × Social capital (norm)	−0.014	(0.015)	−0.023	(0.011)
Regional disadvantage × Social capital (association)	0.029	(0.017)	−0.021*	(0.013)
Age	−0.979	(0.705)	−2.110**	(0.655)
Age^2	1.473*	(0.681)	1.655**	(0.631)
Women	0.202***	(0.031)	−0.283***	(0.029)
Married	–	–	–	–
Unmarried	0.024	(0.050)	−0.023	(0.044)
Divorced/Bereaved	0.074	(0.050)	–	–
Primary education	0.181***	(0.047)	−0.047	(0.043)
Middle education	–	–	–	–
Higher education	−0.198***	(0.036)	0.143***	(0.035)
Self-employed	−0.172***	(0.050)	0.180***	(0.045)
Regular employment	–	–	–	–
Non-regular employment	0.045	(0.047)	−0.031	(0.041)
Upper white collar	−0.045	(0.051)	−0.006	(0.045)
Lower white collar	–	–	–	–
Blue collar	0.187***	(0.040)	−0.087*	(0.038)
No job	−0.003	(0.052)	0.038	(0.050)
Job seeker	0.076	(0.092)	−0.030	(0.087)
Household income (log)	−0.090***	(0.023)	0.043*	(0.021)
Random effect (Intercept)	0.000	(0.000)	0.000	(0.006)
1/2	−2.172***	(0.226)	−1.800***	(0.212)
2/3	−1.449***	(0.226)	−1.365***	(0.210)
3/4	−0.341	(0.227)	−0.486*	(0.210)
4/5	0.570*	(0.228)	0.613**	(0.210)
AIC	−80,209.57		−9852.289	
BIC	−80,262.93		−9905.657	

N = 6,888. ***$p < 0.001$, **$p < 0.01$, *$p < 0.05$ (two-tailed test)

ordered probit regression models. The model for predicting support for redistribution in Table 8.9 includes two interaction terms added onto Model 4 from Table 8.7: the interaction term of regional disadvantage score and social capital (norm) score, and the interaction term of regional disadvantage score and social capital (association) score. Similarly, the model for predicting free competition in Table 8.9 includes the same interaction terms added to Model 4 from Table 8.8.

The model predicting support for redistribution did not show a significant interaction effect for regional disadvantage and social capital (norm) or regional disadvantage and social capital (association) on support for redistribution. In other words, regional disadvantage influenced support for redistribution independently from social capital, and this finding means that neither Hypotheses 2a nor 2b were supported by the data from SSM 2015 and the 2015 Population Census. On the other hand, while the model predicting support for free competition did not show a significant interaction effect for regional disadvantage and social capital (norm) on support for redistribution, it did show a statistically significant interaction effect for regional disadvantage and social capital (association) on support for redistribution at 0.05. As the sign of the interaction effect of regional disadvantage and social capital (association) on support for free competition was negative (−), that analytical result based on the data from SSM 2015 and the 2015 Population Census supported Hypothesis 4a but not Hypothesis 4b.

As above mentioned, regional disadvantage had significant effects on support for social policies even after controlling for social capital and individual characteristics, whereas social capital had no significant effects on them after controlling for regional disadvantage. Additionally, these effects of regional disadvantage at the municipality level on support for social policies did not depend on social capital at the municipality level. Certainly, the interaction effect of regional disadvantage and social capital (association) on support for free competition was found. However, the other interaction effects of regional disadvantage and social capital except that was not observed. Therefore, it is concluded that there were no or weak interaction effects of regional disadvantage and social capital on social policies in Japan.

8.4.6 Summary

Through the analyses using SSM 2015 data, I confirmed that regional disadvantage had significant effects on support for social policies. However, people living in disadvantaged municipalities regarding population structure and fiscal power were more likely to support redistribution and less likely to support free competition. It should be noted that the significant effects of regional disadvantages on support for social policies can be observed even after controlling for social capital, respondents' demographic characteristics, and their socioeconomic status. This means that regional disadvantage at the municipality level has influence on social policy preferences by itself. In the case of determining social policy preferences, individuals tend to consider common interests at the municipality level regardless of their social position.

On the other hand, I could not confirm that social capital influenced social policy preferences by itself. Certainly, social capital had statistically significant correlations on support for social policies. People with high social capital at the municipality level were more likely to support redistribution and less likely to support free competition. Even though social capital significantly correlated with support for social policies, however, such correlations of social capital and support for social policies disappeared after controlling for regional disadvantage. In other words, social capital was indirectly related to social policy preferences via regional characteristics, but it did not have a direct effect on social policy preferences. Therefore, it cannot be concluded that social capital mitigates or reinforces negative effects of regional disadvantage.

This study, therefore, clarified that residents' common interests at the municipality level significantly influenced political attitudes. Here, it is noteworthy that common interests at the municipality level continued to influence political attitudes even after controlling for residents' demographic characteristics and socioeconomic status. This finding suggests that, for residents, common interests related to a municipality have an important meaning beyond self-interest. Additionally, the results indicated that influences of common interests at the municipality level can be observed regardless of the level of social capital within the municipality. Namely, negative influences of regional disadvantage (i.e., population aging, population declining, or lack of fiscal power) cannot be mitigated or reinforced by social capital against the predictions in this study.

8.5 Discussion and Conclusion

Through this study's analyses, I confirmed that individuals' policy preferences are determined multi-dimensionally, such as by common interests at the municipality level and self-interest at the individual level. This study's results reveal that regional disadvantage, such as population aging, tends to promote residents' support for redistribution, while it encourages residents to reduce their support for free competition. This finding indicates that, in the case of determining policy preferences, individuals would consider common interests at the municipality level as well as self-interests at the individual level. As a result, individual policy preference could have complicated characteristics, which may seem to be inconsistent or contradictory (Sudo, 2020).

Such complicated individual policy preference characteristics make the role of social capital on the formation process of policy preferences equivocal. In this project, social capital was assumed to have significant effects on support for social policies and that such effects could mitigate or reinforce effects of regional disadvantage on support for social policies. Nevertheless, the results of the analyses in this article showed that social capital by itself had no significant effects on support for social policies after controlling for regional inequality. This finding likely suggests that, as effects of social capital on individuals' social and political attitudes are multi-faceted

Table 8.10 Correlation matrix of regional disadvantage and social capital

	1	2	3
1. Social capital (norm)	1.000		
2. Social capital (association)	−0.077	1.000	
3. Regional disadvantage	0.290 ***	0.183***	1.000

N = 631. ***$p < 0.001$, **$p < 0.01$, *$p < 0.05$ (two-tailed test)

(Edlund, 2006; Laurence, 2011), they could not easily be specified. How I specify the effects of social capital on policy preferences remains unresolved.

Previous studies have emphasized the effects of individuals' demographic characteristics and socioeconomic status on their support for social policies, and social scholars should not overlook this relationship. In fact, the results of the analyses in this study also showed that individuals' characteristics and socioeconomic status have statistically significant effects on support for redistribution and/or free competition. However, overemphasizing the effects of individuals' characteristics and socioeconomic status on social policies might mislead social researchers because individuals' self-interest alone does not determine their policy preferences. These scholars must consider the role of common interests (Arndt, 2018; Gonthier, 2017), such as regional inequality, as well.

As one of reasons why regional inequality influences support for social policies, the following aspect should be considered: social problems resulting from regional inequality affect all residents in the region. If individuals can choose where to live more freely, they may not focus on problems caused by regional disadvantage. If their region has various problems, they may escape instantly. However, individuals typically do not change their location that frequently due to family and neighborhood relations, occupational conditions, and moving costs. As individuals must continue to live in the region, they have a vested interest in combatting regional inequality.

Regional disadvantage is significantly correlated with social capital. Table 8.10 shows the correlation matrix of regional disadvantage and social capital. The correlation coefficients between regional disadvantage and social capital (norm) scores and regional disadvantage and social capital (association) scores were statistically significant and positive. Regional disadvantage by itself had significant effects on support for social policies, and it is also positively associated with social capital at the municipality level. I therefore suggest that regional disadvantage can force residents to create social capital among themselves to compensate for the lack of social welfare services provided by the local government (Mitani & Hiramatsu, 2020). Presumably, residents try to use social capital to resolve the problems imposed by their regional disadvantage. However, such effects of regional disadvantage on social capital were not strong enough to mitigate the negative effects of regional disadvantage (O'Connell, 2003). As a result, social capital ostensibly has significant effects on support for social policies: the negative effect on support for redistribution and the positive effect on support for free competition.

Thus, regional inequality has independent effects on support for social policies regardless of individuals' characteristics and socioeconomic status. If advantaged people living in disadvantaged regions consider common interests at the regional level when determining their policy preferences, social inequality will have weak or no effect on their policy preferences. Similarly, if disadvantaged people living in advantaged regions consider common interests at the regional level when determining their policy preferences, social inequality will have weak or no effect on their policy preferences. In either case, however, social inequality is important in determining their policy preferences. When social researchers investigate social inequality's effects on political attitudes, they should be cautious about what type of inequality they are considering: at the individual or regional level, or they might misconstrue the effects of social inequality on the formation of policy preferences.

8.5.1 Limitations

Lastly, this study has some limitations. First, this study adopted the municipality as its analytical unit for region. However, the adequacy of the municipality as an analytical unit of region is open to discussion. Certainly, municipality plays an important role as a basic unit for provision of social welfare services in Japan. However, as the area of municipality in Japan extends beyond the neighborhood, many residents within a municipality might be unfamiliar to each other. Additionally, municipalities' population size is smaller than that of prefectures, and so municipalities might have relatively weak political power to entice politicians to implement effective social welfare policies, compared to at the prefecture level. Therefore, the neighborhood or prefecture levels may have different effects on support for social policies, and this should be considered in future studies.

Second, only population structure and fiscal power for each municipality were used as indexes of regional inequality at the municipality level. However, there is a possibility that other factors related to regional inequality at the municipality level were overlooked in these analyses. For example, geographical factors such as social networks might have effects on regional inequality. If a municipality has a strong tie with a prosperous city, this tie will likely affect residents' support for social policies. These influences may be independent of the other factors. In other cases, institutional factors such as differences in levels of welfarism between municipalities might affect regional inequality on support for social policies (Evans & Kelley, 2018; Fernández & Jaime-Castillo, 2018). Therefore, in future studies, I need to carefully examine more adequate indexes of regional inequality.

Third, effects of regional disadvantage on support for social policies were treated as a constant effect within a municipality, assuming that regional disadvantage affects all residents within the municipality evenly. However, these effects might differ in strength between residents. For example, the effect of regional disadvantage among disadvantaged people living in a disadvantaged region might be stronger than among advantaged people living in the disadvantaged region. Such interaction effects between individuals' socioeconomic status at the micro level and regional disadvantage at the macro level were not examined in this study. Future work should include consideration of variables' interaction effects at the micro and macro levels.

8.5.2 Conclusion

This study examined how regional inequality related to support for social policies, by using data from two social surveys conducted in Japan. The results showed that regional inequality had influence on support for social policies, and these influences remained even after controlling for individuals' demographic characteristics and socioeconomic status. Namely, regional disadvantage promotes support for redistribution, while it reduces support for free competition. This means that people tend to consider common interests as well as their own interests while determining their policy preferences. As individual policy preferences are determined multi-dimensionally, they could have a multi-faceted character. In fact, although support for redistribution and support for free competition are negatively associated with each other, people could support them simultaneously.

This study also examined how social capital influences support for social policies; however, the significant effects of social capital on support for social policies was not observed. According to this study's results, social capital at the municipality level did not mitigate or reinforce the negative effect of regional inequality on support for free competition or the positive effects of regional inequality on support for redistribution. However, this might not indicate that social capital did not have any relationship to individual policy preferences. Because effects of social capital on support for social policies are equivocal, there is a possibility that these effects are offset by each other.

Regional inequality promotes the generation of social capital in the region. As a result, social capital has statistically significant influences on support for social policies, which suggests that people living in disadvantaged regions seek social capital in order to overcome social problems rooted in regional inequality. As the impact of regional inequality on support for social policies is stronger than the impact of social capital on it, the effects of social capital could not be observed clearly. However, social capital and support for social policies are indirectly related to each other via regional inequality. The significance of social capital on policy preferences studies cannot be dismissed.

Acknowledgements This research is supported by JSPS KAKENHI (JP18H03647), and I thank the 2015 SSM Survey Management Committee for allowing me to use the SSM 2015 data (Ver. 070).

References

Alesina, A., Stantcheva, S., & Teso, E. (2018). Intergenerational mobility and preferences for redistribution. *American Economic Review, 108*(2), 521–554. https://doi.org/10.1257/aer.20162015

Arndt, C. (2018). White-collar unions and attitudes towards income inequality, redistribution, and state–market relations. *European Sociological Review, 34*(6), 675–693. https://doi.org/10.1093/esr/jcy033

Becker, B. (2019). Mind the income gaps? Experimental evidence of information's lasting effect on redistributive preferences. *Social Justice Research, 33*, 137–194. https://doi.org/10.1007/s11211-019-00343-7

Beyerlein, K., & Hipp, J. R. (2005). Social capital, too much of a good thing? American religious traditions and community crime. *Social Forces, 84*(2), 995–1013. https://doi.org/10.1353/sof.2006.0004

Borisova, E., Govorun, A., Ivanov, D., & Levina, I. (2018). Social capital and preferences for redistribution to target groups. *European Journal of Political Economy, 54*, 55–67. https://doi.org/10.1016/j.ejpoleco.2018.05.006

Brady, D., & Bostic, A. (2015). Paradoxes of social policy: Welfare transfers, relative poverty, and redistribution preferences. *American Sociological Review, 80*(2), 268–298. https://doi.org/10.1177/0003122415573049

Brady, D., & Finnigan, R. (2014). Does immigration undermine public support for social policy? *American Sociological Review, 79*(1), 17–42. https://doi.org/10.1177/0003122413513022

Breznau, N., & Hommerich, C. (2019). No generalizable effect of income inequality on public support for governmental redistribution among rich democracies 1987–2010. *Social Science Research,* 1–22. https://doi.org/10.1016/j.ssresearch.2019.03.013

Burgoon, B., Koster, F., & van Egmond, M. (2012). Support for redistribution and the paradox of immigration. *Journal of European Social Policy, 22*(3), 288–304. https://doi.org/10.1177/0958928712440198

Busemeyer, M. R. (2013). Education funding and individual preferences for redistribution. *European Sociological Review, 29*(6), 1122–1133. https://doi.org/10.1093/esr/jcs085

Dallinger, U. (2010). Public support for redistribution: What explains cross-national differences? *Journal of European Social Policy, 20*(4), 333–349. https://doi.org/10.1177/0958928710374373

Dimick, M., Rueda, D., & Stegmueller, D. (2016). The altruistic rich? Inequality and other-regarding preferences for redistribution. *Quarterly Journal of Political Science, 11*(4), 385–439. https://doi.org/10.1561/100.00015099

Edlund, J. (2006). Trust in the capability of the welfare state and general welfare state support: Sweden 1997–2002. *Acta Sociologica, 49*(4), 395–417. https://doi.org/10.1177/0001699306071681

Eger, M. A. (2010). Even in Sweden: The effect of immigration on support for welfare state spending. *European Sociological Review, 26*(2), 203–217. https://doi.org/10.1093/esr/jcp017

Evans, M., & Kelley, J. (2018). Strong welfare states do not intensify public support for income redistribution, but even reduce it among the prosperous: A multilevel analysis of public opinion in 30 countries. *Societies, 8*(4), 105. https://doi.org/10.3390/soc8040105

Fernández, J. J., & Jaime-Castillo, A. M. (2018). The institutional foundation of social class differences in pro-redistribution attitudes: A cross-national analysis, 1985–2010. *Social Forces, 96*(3), 1009–1038. https://doi.org/10.1093/sf/sox068

Finseraas, H. (2009). Income inequality and demand for redistribution: A multilevel analysis of European public opinion. *Scandinavian Political Studies, 32*(1), 94–119. https://doi.org/10.1111/j.1467-9477.2008.00211.x

Finseraas, H. (2012). Poverty, ethnic minorities among the poor, and preferences for redistribution in European regions. *Journal of European Social Policy, 22*(2), 164–180. https://doi.org/10.1177/0958928711433655

García-Sánchez, E., Willis, G. B., Rodríguez-Bailón, R., Palacio Sañudo, J., David Polo, J., & Rentería Pérez, E. (2018). Perceptions of economic inequality and support for redistribution: The role of existential and Utopian standards. *Social Justice Research, 31*(4), 335–354. https://doi.org/10.1007/s11211-018-0317-6

Gidron, N., & Mijs, J. J. B. (2019). Do changes in material circumstances drive support for populist radical parties? Panel data evidence from the Netherlands during the great recession, 2007–2015. *European Sociological Review, 35*(5), 637–650. https://doi.org/10.1093/esr/jcz005

Gingrich, J., & Ansell, B. (2012). Preferences in context: Micro preferences, macro contexts, and the demand for social policy. *Comparative Political Studies, 45*(12), 1624–1654. https://doi.org/10.1177/0010414012463904

Gonthier, F. (2017). Parallel publics? Support for income redistribution in times of economic crisis. *European Journal of Political Research, 56*(1), 92–114. https://doi.org/10.1111/1475-6765.12168

Hedeker, D., & Gibbons, R. D. (1996). MIXOR: A computer program for mixed-effects ordinal regression analysis. *Computer Methods and Programs in Biomedicine, 49*(2), 157–176. https://doi.org/10.1016/0169-2607(96)01720-8

Jæger, M. M. (2009). United but divided: Welfare regimes and the level and variance in public support for redistribution. *European Sociological Review, 25*(6), 723–737. https://doi.org/10.1093/esr/jcn079

Jaime-Castillo, A. M., & Marqués-Perales, I. (2019). Social mobility and demand for redistribution in Europe: A comparative analysis. *British Journal of Sociology, 70*(1), 138–165. https://doi.org/10.1111/1468-4446.12363

Kevins, A., Horn, A., Jensen, C., & van Kersbergen, K. (2018). Yardsticks of inequality: Preferences for redistribution in advanced democracies. *Journal of European Social Policy, 28*(4), 402–418. https://doi.org/10.1177/0958928717753579

Koos, S., & Sachweh, P. (2017). The moral economies of market societies: popular attitudes towards market competition, redistribution and reciprocity in comparative perspective. *Socio-Economic Review, 17*(4), 793–821. https://doi.org/10.1093/ser/mwx045

Kwon, R., & Curran, M. (2016). Immigration and support for redistributive social policy: Does multiculturalism matter? *International Journal of Comparative Sociology, 57*(6), 375–400. https://doi.org/10.1177/0020715216685767

Kwon, S. W., Heflin, C., & Ruef, M. (2013). Community social capital and entrepreneurship. *American Sociological Review, 78*(6), 980–1008. https://doi.org/10.1177/0003122413506440

Kymlicka, W. (2016). Solidarity in diverse societies: beyond neoliberal multiculturalism and welfare chauvinism. *Comparative Migration Studies, 3*, 17. https://doi.org/10.1186/s40878-015-0017-4

Laurence, J. (2011). The effect of ethnic diversity and community disadvantage on social cohesion: A multi-level analysis of social capital and interethnic relations in UK communities. *European Sociological Review, 27*(1), 70–89. https://doi.org/10.1093/esr/jcp057

Levanon, A. (2018). Labor market insiders or outsiders? A cross-national examination of redistributive preferences of the working poor. *Societies, 8*(3), 72. https://doi.org/10.3390/soc8030072

Linos, K., & West, M. (2003). Self-interest, social beliefs, and attitudes to redistribution: Re-addressing the issue of cross-national variation. *European Sociological Review, 19*(4), 393–409+i. https://doi.org/10.1093/esr/19.4.393

Lübker, M. (2007). Inequality and the demand for redistribution: Are the assumptions of the new growth theory valid? *Socio-Economic Review, 5*(1), 117–148. https://doi.org/10.1093/ser/mwl002

Lützeler, R. (2017). The urban-rural divide in Japan: A matter of social inequality? In D. Chiavacci & C. Hommerich (Eds.), *Social Inequality in Post-growth Japan: Transformation during economic and demographic stagnation* (pp. 187–200). Routledge.

MARGALIT, Y. (2013). Explaining social policy preferences: Evidence from the great recession. *American Political Science Review, 107*(01), 80–103. https://doi.org/10.1017/s0003055412000603

MIC. (2020). Lists of major fiscal indexes of municipalities. Retrieved Nov 15, 2020, from Ministry of International Affairs and Comunications website: https://www.soumu.go.jp/iken/shihyo_ichiran.html.

Mitani, H., & Hiramatsu, M. (2020). Civil society: Who participates? In C. Hommerich, N. Sudo, & T. Kikkawa (Eds.), *Social change in Japan, 1989–2019 social status, social consciousness, attitudes and values* (pp. 73–90). https://doi.org/10.4324/9780429331077

Nagayoshi, K., & Sato, Y. (2014). Who supports redistributive policies in contemporary Japan? An integrative approach to self-interest and trust models. *International Sociology, 29*(4), 302–323. https://doi.org/10.1177/0268580914537657

Naumann, E., Buss, C., & Bähr, J. (2016). How unemployment experience affects support for the welfare state: A real panel approach. *European Sociological Review, 32*(1), 81–92. https://doi.org/10.1093/esr/jcv094

O'Connell, M. (2003). Anti "Social Capital" civic values versus economic equality in the EU. *European Sociological Review, 19*(3), 241–248+i. https://doi.org/10.1093/esr/19.3.241

Owens, L. A., & Pedulla, D. S. (2014). Material welfare and changing political preferences: The case of support for redistributive social policies. *Social Forces, 92*(3), 1087–1113. https://doi.org/10.1093/sf/sot101

Putnam, R. D. (2000). *Bowling alone: The collapse and revival of American community*. Simon and Schuster.

Putnam, R. D., Leonardi, R., & Nanetti, R. Y. (1994). *Making democracy work: Civic traditions in Modern Italy*. Princeton University Press.

R Core Team. (2018). *R: A language and environment for statistical computing*. Retrieved from http://www.r-project.org/

Reeskens, T., & van Oorschot, W. (2012). Disentangling the "New Liberal Dilemma": On the relation between general welfare redistribution preferences and welfare chauvinism. *International Journal of Comparative Sociology, 53*(2), 120–139. https://doi.org/10.1177/0020715212451987

Ruef, M., & Kwon, S. W. (2016). Neighborhood associations and social capital. *Social Forces, 95*(1), 159–190. https://doi.org/10.1093/sf/sow053

Schmidt-Catran, A. W. (2016). Economic inequality and public demand for redistribution: Combining cross-sectional and longitudinal evidence. *Socio-Economic Review, 14*(1), 119–140. https://doi.org/10.1093/ser/mwu030

Shin, J. Y. (2018). Relative deprivation, satisfying rationality, and support for redistribution. *Social Indicators Research, 140*(1), 35–56. https://doi.org/10.1007/s11205-017-1769-z

Smyth, R., Mishra, V., & Qian, X. (2010). Knowing one's lot in life versus climbing the social ladder: The formation of redistributive preferences in Urban China. *Social Indicators Research, 96*(2), 275–293. https://doi.org/10.1007/s11205-009-9478-x

SSM Survey Management Committee. (2018). 2015 SSM Reports. Retrieved March 6, 2019, from http://www.l.u-tokyo.ac.jp/2015SSM-PJ/report.html.

Stan Development Team. (2018). *RStan: the R interface to Stan*. Retrieved from http://mc-stan.org.

Statistics Bureau. (2017a). Population census. Retrieved Apr 6, 2018, from Statistic Bureau, Ministry of Internal Affairs and Communications website: http://www.stat.go.jp/data/kokusei/2015/index.html.

Statistics Bureau. (2017b). Statistical observations of Shi, Ku, Machi, Mura. Retrieved Apr 6, 2018, from Ministry of Internal Affairs and Communications website: http://www.stat.go.jp/data/s-sugata/.

Steele, L. G. (2016). Ethnic diversity and support for redistributive social policies. *Social Forces, 94*(4), 1439–1481. https://doi.org/10.1093/sf/sow021

Stegmueller, D., Scheepers, P., Roßteutscher, S., & De Jong, E. (2012). Support for redistribution in Western Europe: Assessing the role of religion. *European Sociological Review, 28*(4), 482–497. https://doi.org/10.1093/esr/jcr011

Sudo, N. (2020). Two types of support for redistribution of wealth: Consistent and inconsistent policy preferences. *Societies, 10*(2), 43. https://doi.org/10.3390/soc10020043

Sumino, T. (2018). Identity priming and public opinion on income inequality: Robustness testing of the micro-level mechanism of the paradox of redistribution. *Socio-Economic Review, 16*(3), 545–565. https://doi.org/10.1093/SER/MWX038

Teney, C., & Hanquinet, L. (2012). High political participation, high social capital? A relational analysis of youth social capital and political participation. *Social Science Research, 41*(5), 1213–1226. https://doi.org/10.1016/j.ssresearch.2012.03.012

United Nations, Department of Economic and Social Affairs, P. D. (2019). World population prospects 2019. Retrieved Dec 10, 2020, from https://population.un.org/wpp/.

van Oorschot, W., & Arts, W. (2005). The social capital of European welfare states: The crowding out hypothesis revisited. *Journal of European Social Policy, 15*(1), 5–26. https://doi.org/10.1177/0958928705049159

Van Heuvelen, T. (2017). Unequal views of inequality: Cross-national support for redistribution 1985–2011. *Social Science Research, 64*, 43–66. https://doi.org/10.1016/j.ssresearch.2016.10.010

Wietzke, F. B. (2016). Kicking away the ladder? Poverty reduction and public support for redistribution in emerging economies. *Socio-Economic Review, 14*(3), 419–442. https://doi.org/10.1093/ser/mwv027

Wilkinson, R., & Pickett, K. (2010). *The spirit level: Why more equal societies almost always do better*. Allen Lane.

Naoki Sudo is Professor of Sociology in the Graduate School of Social Sciences at Hitotsubashi University. He received a Ph.D. in Sociology from the University of Tokyo. He has done work in the fields of mathematical sociology and sociological theory. His recent studies concern the effects of social changes on social inequality, social class identification, and subjective wellbeing. He has published in outlets including *Social Forces*, *Social Indicators Research*, *Journal of Mathematical Sociology*, *Social Science Japan Journal*, and *Socius: Sociological Research for a Dynamic World*. He is the former president of *Japanese Association for Mathematical Sociology* (JAMS), and the former editor-in-chief of *Sociological Theory and Methods* (the official journal of JAMS). He currently serves as the Board member of the Research Committee on Rational Choice of the *International Sociological Association*.

Chapter 9
Explanation of Socioeconomic Inequality Among the Male Elderly: An Approach Based on Estimated Income History

Shin Arita

Abstract Population aging necessitates new approaches to understanding and explaining inequality in a society. If so, what approaches should be taken to deal with social disparity issues in a society with an increasing number of elderly people? What kinds of information and research data are needed for this purpose? To address these issues, this chapter endeavors to estimate male elderly people's income history, that is, income at all age points in the past, based on their job history data. Furthermore, this chapter analyzes how the elderly people's estimated income history affects their current socioeconomic status. Through these analyses, this chapter proposes a new approach to understanding inequality among elderly people based on the perspective that employment positions, from the past to the present, determine one's socioeconomic status.

9.1 Introduction

Japan is one of the most rapidly aging countries in the world. In 2019, the proportion of the population aged 65 or older was 28.4%, which is the highest in the world. This proportion is estimated to reach 35.4% in 2040; as such, elderly people could occupy more than one-third of the entire population. (Statistics Bureau, Ministry of Internal Affairs and Communications, 2020).

How, then, does population aging impact social inequality? First, a relative increase in the elderly population in society could increase inequality in the society as a whole, because inequality is more prominent among the elderly population than it is among younger people; income inequality is a good example. Scholars have asserted that the recent deterioration in the income distribution indexes, such as the Gini coefficient in Japan, has been primarily caused by population aging—namely, an increase in the elderly population, a group that has higher internal income inequality (Otake, 2005). As this example indicates, changes in the demographic composition could affect the extent of inequality in this way.

S. Arita (✉)
Institute of Social Science, University of Tokyo, 7-3-1 Hongo, Bunkyo-ku, Tokyo 113-0033, Japan
e-mail: sarita@iss.u-tokyo.ac.jp

S. Shirahase (ed.), *Social Stratification in an Aging Society with Low Fertility*,
Economy and Social Inclusion, https://doi.org/10.1007/978-981-19-3647-0_9

Another important effect is that population aging can increase the difficulty in identifying the factors to explain the occurrence of inequality in a society. For example, let us assume that we intend to clarify the causes of income inequality in society to deal with worsening inequality, as a social problem. To investigate issues regarding income inequality among younger people, we would focus on whether they are currently employed and, if so, what kind of jobs they have. This is because the majority of income inequality among younger people stems from inequality in their employment compensation. In fact, social stratification studies have so far focused on occupation and employment statuses when determining people's positions in the social hierarchy. However, as many elderly people have already left the labor market, income inequality in an aging society cannot be explained by simply focusing on whether people are employed or what kind of jobs they have.

Thus, population aging necessitates new approaches to understanding and explaining inequality. As such, what approaches should be taken to deal with social disparity issues in a society with an increasing number of elderly people? What kinds of information and research data are needed for this purpose? This chapter considers these issues by examining the effects of job history on socioeconomic disparities among male elderly people in Japan, based on the Social Stratification and Social Mobility (SSM) survey data.

We can expect an elderly person's socioeconomic status to be influenced largely by their past jobs (Kimura, 2002; Mugiyama, 2018; Shirahase, 2021). However, because the data structure of the respondents' job histories is extremely complicated, no specific method has been established for using this wealth of information to understand the current socioeconomic status of elderly people. This is particularly true for Japan, where people's status in the labor market is largely affected by not only their occupation and employment statuses but also their firms' sizes and employment type, namely, a distinction between regular and non-regular employment, as discussed later.

To address this issue, this chapter endeavors to estimate people's income history, that is, income at all age points in the past, based on their job history data. One of the major advantages of the SSM survey is that it collects detailed information on the respondents' job history throughout their careers. By utilizing this valuable information, we can expect to estimate the respondents' income, at all age points in the past, with a high degree of accuracy, enabling us to capture their entire income history.

Furthermore, the chapter analyzes how the elderly people's estimated income history affects their current socioeconomic status and provides a more detailed examination of how disparities in the elderly people's socioeconomic status unfold in Japan. Through these analyses, this chapter proposes a new approach to understanding inequality among elderly people, while also highlighting the characteristics of the Japanese labor market based on the perspective that employment positions, from the past to the present, determine one's socioeconomic status.

9.2 Socioeconomic Stratification in the Japanese Labor Market

This section examines the socioeconomic stratification in the Japanese labor market to explore the information necessary for the proper estimation of elderly people's income history using job history data. Most previous studies that attempt to explain people's socioeconomic statuses based on their employment positions have focused on employment status and occupation. This is because it has been assumed that employment status, which represents the position in the industrial relations, and occupation, which represents the position in the labor market and individuals' resources, such as their skills, have a great influence on people's socioeconomic status. In fact, conventional social class models have operationally classified people's classes based on their employment statuses and occupations.

On the other hand, scholars have focused on other conditions of employment opportunities in the Japanese labor market. One of these is firm size. Late industrialization resulted in Japan's two-tier economic structure between modern large firms and traditional small-to-medium-sized firms, resulting in large wage gaps between sectors with different firm sizes (Kalleberg & Lincoln, 1988; Sakamoto & Powers, 1995). The large wage gaps, based on firm size, have been maintained due to the Japanese employment practices, characterized by long-term secure employment, which prevent frequent job changes across firms, and the social norm that corporate profits, which vary based on firm size, should be distributed to employees of the firm. Thus, firm size is considered as one of the major determinants of the socioeconomic statuses of workers in the Japanese labor market. For instance, the SSM Comprehensive Job Classification, which is the job classification scheme frequently used in Japan, classifies workers' statuses based on not only their occupation and employment statuses but also firm size (Hara & Seiyama, 2005).

Furthermore, employment type has become an important factor for socioeconomic status in the Japanese labor market. In Japan, a large disparity in rewards exists between regular employees, who are treated as core members of the firm, and non-regular employees, who are not. Under the male breadwinner model and the social norms that firms should provide employees' households with livelihood security, regular employees, who are mainly males assumed to be their households' breadwinners, are rewarded generously to sustain their families, while non-regular employees, who are exemplified by fixed-term and part-time workers and assumed to be supplementary earners in their households, are given only small rewards (Imai, 2011; Osawa, 2011). Considering the large reward difference between regular and non-regular employees in Japan, some scholars assert that employment type should be considered when classifying employees' status, in addition to occupation, employment status, and firm size (Hashimoto, 2009; Tarohmaru, 2009).

In summary, both employment status and occupation, as well as firm size and employment type, namely, the distinction between regular and non-regular employment, have significant impacts on stratification in the Japanese labor market. The effects of employment position on socioeconomic status are multidimensional in

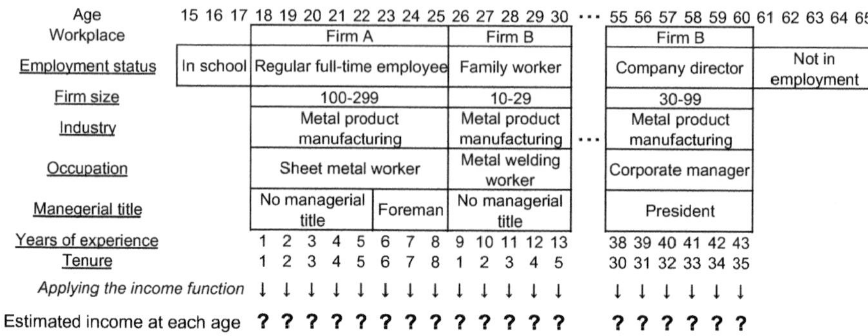

Fig. 9.1 Example of estimation of income history based on individual job history. *Note* Educational attainment and unemployment experience are also used for the estimation

nature; meaning, the various conditions of individuals' employment positions independently affect their status in Japan (Arita, 2016, 2017; Kanomata, 2001). Therefore, when examining the effect of job history on the socioeconomic status of elderly people, throughout their working years, it is necessary to not only focus on employment status and occupation, but also on the effect of firm size and type of employment.[1] We believe that reducing the multidimensional conditions of a job to a single variable—estimated income—is a suitable method to understand the effects of job history on the socioeconomic status of the elderly in the Japanese labor market.

9.3 Data and Methods

9.3.1 Methods for Estimating Income History

The SSM survey collects details regarding employment status, occupation, industry, firm size, employment type, and managerial title for each job a survey respondent has held and for each workplace, as well as the respondent's age when starting and leaving each job. No long-term panel surveys track individuals throughout their entire careers in Japan; therefore, retrospective survey data regarding past jobs is the only available source for analyzing the respondents' entire job histories and the effects on the current socioeconomic status of elderly people.

As shown in Fig. 9.1, the respondents' job history data contains extensive information for the analysis, because of the accumulation of the various conditions for each job a person has held at all ages. Furthermore, there are many categorical variables among the job conditions, such as occupation and employment status, which

[1] The amount of retirement allowance and pension also largely vary according to their type of employment and firm size. This is another reason that we should pay special attention to the effects of these employment conditions in the job history on the socioeconomic status of elderly people.

makes it difficult to represent these conditions on a one-dimensional scale; it also makes it difficult to analyze all of them in a comprehensive manner. Therefore, most previous studies regarding the effect of job history on elderly people's socioeconomic statuses have concentrated on past employment at a particular age or on a person's "primary job" in the past; even when using the entire job history information, these studies focused on just one of the many possible job conditions, such as occupation or employment status.

However, limiting the analysis to employment at a particular age or job condition may not adequately capture the effect of entire job histories on the socioeconomic statuses of elderly people. In other countries, one's occupation has a greater effect on socioeconomic status than other job conditions do; any conditions other than occupation may not need to be considered. However, in Japan, other job conditions, such as firm size and employment type, have a major effect on socioeconomic status, as discussed in the previous section. Considering these distinctive features of the Japanese labor market, this chapter analyzes the influence of job history, not by simply focusing on a job at a specific age or a specific employment condition, but rather by using all job conditions available in the SSM survey data to investigate the effects of those factors comprehensively.

To achieve this goal, this chapter uses a method in which the various job conditions in the individuals' job histories are reduced to a single continuous variable: estimated income at each age. More specifically, information in the SSM survey on current employment and income was first used to estimate an income function. Next, personal income at each age in the past is estimated by applying the income function to an elderly person's job information, at a specific age. Linking this estimated income at specific ages in the past produces an individual's income history.[2] This chapter uses this method to capture the overall picture of an elderly person's job history and investigate its effects on their current socioeconomic status. From a different perspective, this analysis is equivalent to evaluating people's jobs and their histories from the perspective of the "income-generating power" of those jobs.

9.3.2 Procedure and Data

The analyses performed in this chapter are summarized again in the three processes described below. First, the income function is estimated using the information on

[2] Some countries allow government information on income and taxation to be used for academic purposes. For example, Guvenen et al. (2017) used sample data extracted from an income list belonging to the US Social Security Administration to directly calculate people's actual lifetime incomes. However, as Japan does not yet permit such data usage, the method described in this chapter is the only way to analyze an individual's income history. In this chapter, the attempt to estimate income history based on a person's past employment at various ages is similar to that by Sato & Yoshida (2007) and Lefranc, Ojima, & Yoshida (2014), with which they estimated fathers' incomes, based on their employment information, to analyze intergenerational income mobility in Japan.

current personal income, for those in the working generation (aged 65 and under). Second, income at specific ages in the past is estimated by applying the income function to elderly people's job history data (person-year data from age 15 to 65).[3] Third, the income history obtained was used to explain the socioeconomic status of the elderly. The elderly people analyzed in this chapter are those aged 65 or older, a life stage in which most people's vocational careers have ended.

Data on the job history of elderly people were obtained from the 2015 SSM survey. Available elderly samples in past SSM surveys were small, because the maximum age of respondents was 70; therefore, the maximum age was raised to 80 for the 2015 SSM survey, making it possible to obtain an adequate sample size for conducting such an analysis. Additionally, in the 2015 SSM survey, it was not common for women aged 65-or-older to continue working after marriage or after having children; thus, the scope of this analysis is limited to men.

In this analysis, it is assumed that the shape of the income function is the same for different time points, and the same income function is applied to job history at specific ages in the past.[4] Data from the 2015 and the 2005 SSM surveys, which used nearly the same questions and categories, were used to estimate the income function.

9.4 Estimating and Applying the Income Function

9.4.1 Estimating the Income Function

First, this section estimates the income function using responses on current income and employment, in the SSM survey data. The income function is estimated by applying OLS to individual annual incomes at the time surveyed, and to various conditions of the male respondents' current employment, for those aged 65 and under, using the pooled data from the 2005 and 2015 SSM surveys. The natural logarithm value of individual income is used as the dependent variable. The independent variables are educational attainment, employment status with the distinction of employment type for employees, occupation, industry, firm size, managerial title, years of experience, tenure, and unemployment experience.[5] Among these, years

[3] To compile person-year data, the SPSS syntax for person-year-data conversion (ver. 2.0 for SSM 2015 v070 data) by Professor Tokio Yasuda was modified and used. I would like to express my gratitude to Professor Yasuda.

[4] However, it has been demonstrated that the effects of various job conditions, as well as age and education, on income are somewhat different at different points in time (Kanomata, 2001, 2008; Yoshida, 2005). The differences in the shape of the income function at different times should be considered in the future research.

[5] Years of experience were calculated as the number of employment years, starting from a person's first job, minus the number of unemployment years, while tenure was calculated as the number of employment years at the current workplace. Experience of unemployment was ascertained based on job history data. The timing of the survey was controlled for by incorporating a 2005 dummy variable.

of experience and tenure were incorporated into the model as continuous variables, while the other conditions were incorporated as dummy variables corresponding to the categories (see Table 9.1). Furthermore, for these variables, the main effect terms

Table 9.1 Categorical variables used in income estimation

Educational attainment	Junior high school, High school, Junior or technical college, College/University, Graduate school
Employment status (with distinction of regular and non-regular employment)	Company director/Company executive, Regular full-time employee, Temporary employee/Part-time employee, Employee dispatched by a temporary employment agency, Contract employee/Employee on a short-term contract, Self-employment/Freelance worker, Family worker
Occupation	Professionals and technicians, Managerials, Clerks, Sales workers, Service workers, Security workers, Agricultural and fishery workers, Transport and communication workers, Metal/Chemical/Mechanical manufacturing workers, Other manufacturing workers, Machinery operators and electricity workers, Mine workers and construction workers, Laborers
Industry	Agriculture/Forestry/Fishing, Construction/Mining/Quarrying, Electricity/Gas/Water supply, Manufacturing, Information and Communications, Transport, Finance/Insurance/Real estate/Renting and business activities, Scientific research professional and technical services, Wholesale and retail trade, Hotels and restaurants/Living-related services, Education learning support, Medical health care and welfare, Other community/social/personal services/DK
Firm size	1, 2–4, 5–9, 10–29, 30–99, 100–299, 300–499, 500–999, 1000 or more, Government or other public office, DK
Managerial title	No managerial title/DK, Supervisor/Foreman/Group leader, Subsection chief, Section chief, Department head, President/Director/Exective officer/Board of directors

as well as the interaction terms and squared terms were incorporated into the model.[6]

To fit the age range for income history estimation, the income function was estimated from male samples in employment aged 65 or under at the time of the survey (N = 3836). The number of parameters in the model was 103, and the coefficient of determination was 0.479. This means that the independent variables explain about half of the dispersion of their logarithmic personal income.[7]

Next, we provide an overview of the relative strength of the independent variables' effect on the estimated income function. The effects of educational attainment and employment conditions were estimated using dummy variables corresponding to each of the categories in Table 9.1. Because educational attainment and employment conditions comprise several to a dozen categories, each of which corresponds to a dummy variable, it is impossible to discern the strength of the effect of each employment condition or educational attainment as a whole on individual income simply by examining the estimated coefficient of individual dummy variables; for example, discerning which condition, between occupation and firm size, has a larger effect on income is impossible. To address this issue, this section compares the relative magnitudes of the effects of employment conditions and educational attainment by focusing on the extent to which the determination coefficient increases when a group of dummy variables, corresponding to each condition, is added. Specifically, this analysis focuses on the increase of the determination coefficient at the initial and final addition to the model. The increase when dummy variables are added first represents the total effect, including the correlations arising from the effects of underlying confounding variables and the mediating effects through the other variables, while the increase when they are added last represents the original independent effect, not including the confounding and mediating effects.[8]

Table 9.2 shows the increase in the determination coefficients, when dummy variables corresponding to categories of each condition are added. Comparing the amount of increase at the final addition, based on the table, shows that employment status—including differences in the type of employment for employees—and firm size have a large original effect on income. Regarding the amount of increase at the initial

[6] The following interaction terms and squared terms are incorporated: educational attainment × years of experience, educational attainment × the square of years of experience, status in employment × tenure, occupation × tenure, industry × tenure, firm size × tenure, the square of years of experience, the square of tenure.

[7] This coefficient of determination is almost as high as those in previous studies in Japan are, such as Sato and Yoshida (2007). Furthermore, when solely using the data for a single survey year, the model's coefficient of determination rises further; for 2015, it exceeds 0.5 (Arita, 2018).

[8] Given the hierarchy of variables in the model, in the initial addition, the interaction terms for years of experience/tenure are not included and only the main effect terms are added to the base model, which only includes the 2005 dummy variable. In the final addition, interaction terms for years of experience/tenure are added simultaneously with the main effect terms.

Table 9.2 Increase in the coefficient of determination when dummy variables are added (⊿R2)

	Educational attainment	Employment status	Occupation	Industry	Firm size	Managerial title
Increase at the initial addition	0.071	0.185	0.176	0.074	0.091	0.193
Increase at the final addition	0.012	0.045	0.015	0.009	0.033	0.015

addition, employment status, occupation, and managerial title have a strong effect.[9] These results indicate the multidimensional nature of stratification in the Japanese labor markets discussed earlier. However, the effects of educational attainment and industry are relatively weak.

9.4.2 *Estimating Income History*

Next, the income function estimated above is applied to the respondents' job histories to estimate individual income history. Specifically, logarithmic personal income at ages 15–65 is estimated by applying the income function obtained in the section above to the jobs at specific ages in the past and the educational attainment of respondents. The logarithmic income values are then exponentially transformed back to non-logarithmic income amounts.[10] Income is estimated by applying the function only when a subject is in employment, and the estimated income at times of unemployment is set to 0.

Figure 9.2 shows the average estimated annual income by age for men aged 65 years or older, when they were between the ages of 15 and 65. The target estimation sample consists of 1091 cases, without omissions in the job history information during that period. The solid line in the figure represents the respondents' average income, including those who were not in employment at each age (the estimated income of unemployed people is zero), while the dashed line represents the average income using only the sample of people who were in employment. Both lines indicate that the average estimated income steadily increased, peaking in their early 50s, after which it gradually decreased and dropped off dramatically in their 60s. The average of total estimated income, calculated by adding the estimated incomes at specific ages

[9] The large effect of managerial title on income in Japan was also indicated by Kanomata (2001). Few surveys, other than the SSM surveys, have asked for a detailed history of the managerial titles held by an individual; therefore, SSM survey data is extremely useful for estimating people's income histories in Japan.

[10] Because income is estimated based on information concerning jobs held at specific ages in the past, this chapter essentially estimates earned income. The analyses estimate the income earned in jobs as the value in 2015.

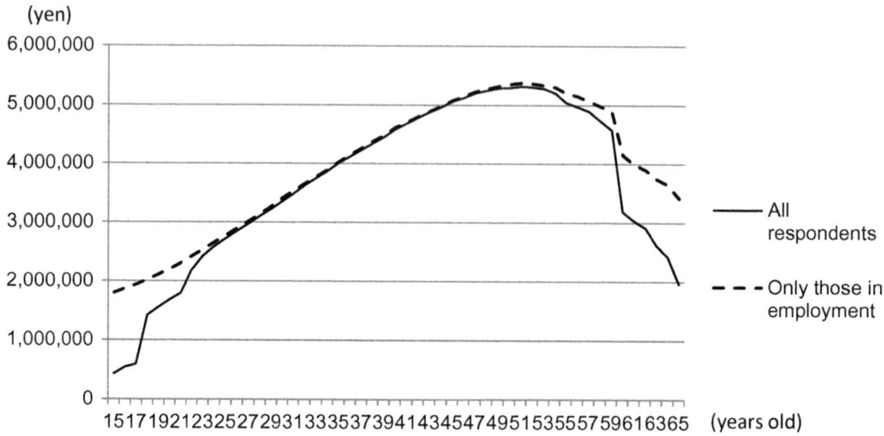

Fig. 9.2 Average estimated income by age for men 65 or over

for each individual, was 190.78 million yen (minimum: 58.53 million yen, maximum: 392.58 million yen), with a standard deviation of 57.27 million yen. Adding to the retirement allowance, whose analysis is not conducted in this chapter, and the earned income after age 65 results in a value consistent with the lifetime earned income of individuals.

The solid line in Fig. 9.2 shows that the average estimated income increased considerably at ages 18 and 22, and decreased considerably at age 60. The increase at ages 18 and 22 are due to the large number of people who start working when they graduate from high school and college, respectively. The decrease occurs at age 60 because many companies and organizations in Japan had chosen 60 as the age of mandatory retirement. The zigzagging at ages 18 and 22 disappears almost entirely, as shown by the dashed line, which represents the average estimated income only for those in employment at that period. Meanwhile, at age 60, the income shown by the dashed line still decreases by approximately one million yen. This major drop in the average estimated income implies that even when people continue working after age 60, their employment situation changes considerably upon reaching the retirement age, with many people likely transitioning from being regular employees to non-regular employees, such as fixed-term employees, leading to a major decrease in income.

9.5 Explaining the Socioeconomic Status of the Male Elderly Using Income History

9.5.1 Socioeconomic Disparities Among the Male Elderly

This section investigates how well the current socioeconomic status of the male elderly can be explained using the estimated income history. Here, the socioeconomic status of the elderly people is assessed in three ways: (a) subjective identification of social status, (b) total assets, and (c) monthly living expenses. Subjective identification of social status is an indicator of the social status of elderly people, while total assets and monthly living expenses are indicators of economic status in terms of stock and flow, respectively. For the subjective identification of social status, respondents were asked to rate their social position on a ten-point scale. Reversing the original values, a higher number indicates a higher social position. Total assets are the total monetary value of a household's assets, including all financial assets and real estate, while monthly living expenses are the monetary value of living expenses per household per month, excluding occasional expenses.

Table 9.3 shows the averages and standard deviations of dependent variables for male respondents in both the elderly group and other age groups. As shown in the table, although the averages and standard deviations for the subjective identification of social status do not differ considerably, there is a great deal of dispersion for total assets and monthly living expenses overall, between the age groups that are 49 years and below and those with 50 years and above. A comparison between those aged 50–64 and those aged 65–79 shows that the standard deviations of total assets and monthly living expenses in the latter group are larger than in the former, indicating a great deal of dispersion for those aged 65 and above. Comparing the average and standard deviation of personal income, which is not included in the table, despite the average personal income for men being lower in the 65–79 age group than the 50–64

Table 9.3 Summary statistics of dependent variables (by age group)

		20–34	35–49	50–64	65–79	Total
(a) Subjective identification of social status	Average	5.25	5.37	5.54	5.40	5.41
	Standard deviation	1.78	1.63	1.70	1.61	1.67
	N	562	888	972	1075	3497
(b) Total assets (10 million yen)	Average	1.16	1.68	2.55	2.97	2.27
	Standard deviation	2.02	1.91	2.92	3.07	2.71
	N	308	604	697	711	2320
(c) Monthly living expenses (10 thousand yen)	Average	15.67	19.68	21.69	21.56	20.22
	Standard deviation	9.60	9.72	11.70	13.22	11.63
	N	472	798	888	964	3122

age group, the standard deviation was larger for those aged 65 and up.[11] The above results also indicate that socioeconomic disparities in the elderly population tend to be greater than the disparities among younger people.

9.5.2 Analysis Using the Total of Estimated Income

This section investigates the extent of the dependent variables' dispersion that can be explained by individual income history. For this purpose, a regression analysis is performed using the above three socioeconomic status variables, as dependent variables for male samples aged 65 and over, with no missing job history data from the age of 15–65 years.

To conduct the analysis, we need to establish a form in which individual income history should be integrated into the regression model. Here, a straightforward form is chosen; we use the simple total estimated income at ages 15–65 as the independent variable. The estimation is also performed with models using educational attainment and age, factors that are often used to explain the socioeconomic status of elderly people who are not in employment, as the independent variables. Subsequently, the fitness of the models was compared.

Table 9.4 shows the regression analysis results of the socioeconomic status of elderly men. First, the coefficient of determination for (a) subjective identification of social status was much larger in Model 2, which included the total estimated income, than in Model 1, which included age and educational attainment. The subjective identification of social status among the elderly is largely determined by the amount of income each subject has earned thus far. Additionally, although the coefficient of determination for Model 3, which incorporates all of these factors, was slightly larger than that for Model 2, the effects of the dummy variables for educational attainment were not statistically significant in Model 3. A considerable portion of these effects in Model 1 can be attributed to the correlation between educational attainment and income history.[12]

The analysis results of (b) total assets are nearly the same. Model 2 had a larger coefficient of determination than Model 1, and total estimated income explained 14% of the dispersion in the total assets of the male elderly. Concerning (c) monthly living expenses, although Model 1 had a larger coefficient of determination than Model 2, the difference was small. Based on the above results, we can conclude that the total estimated income is a good indicator of the socioeconomic status of elderly people.

---

[11] Average personal income was 4.86 million yen and 3.31 million yen for the 50–64 age group and 65–79 age group, respectively, and the respective standard deviations for the groups were 3.58 million yen and 4.12 million yen.

[12] Compared to Model 3, Model 2 has a smaller AIC and BIC, indicating better model fitness.

Table 9.4 Regression analysis of socioeconomic status using total estimated income

	(a) Subjective identification of social status			(b) Total assets (10 million yen)			(c) Monthly living expenses (10 thousand yen)		
	Model 1	Model 2	Model 3	Model 1	Model 2	Model 3	Model 1	Model 2	Model 3
Constant	4.632***	3.648***	3.628***	−2.080	−1.307**	−4.116*	22.092**	9.990***	17.022*
Age	0.006		0.001	0.054*		0.042	-0.061		−0.080
Education (ref. Junior high school)									
High school	0.355**		0.102	1.164***		0.574*	3.730***		2.459*
Junior college	0.905*		0.347	3.102***		1.860*	4.758		2.057
College	0.871***		0.240	2.365***		0.883*	8.220***		5.108***
Total estimated income (10 million yen)		0.094***	0.085***		0.226***	0.189***		0.612***	0.414***
N	1069	1069	1069	713	713	713	966	966	966
R^2	0.039	0.086	0.088	0.086	0.139	0.152	0.053	0.055	0.070
Adj. R^2	0.036	0.085	0.084	0.081	0.138	0.146	0.049	0.054	0.065
AIC	4001.8	3942.7	3948.0	3569.2	3520.7	3517.5	7668.8	7660.8	7652.8
BIC	4026.7	3952.6	3977.9	3592.1	3529.8	3545.0	7693.2	7670.6	7682.0

Note The subjects of this analysis were male respondents aged 65 and over with no omissions in their job histories from age 15–65

9.5.3 A Comparison with Models Based on Information at Specific Ages

This section compares the results from the previous model using total estimated income, with models based only on occupation or estimated income at a particular age. Specifically, subjective identification of social status, total assets, and monthly living expenses are estimated using the SSM Comprehensive Job Classifications and the occupational prestige score at ages 40 and 50, which are commonly used in previous studies as ages in which individuals hold their main jobs, in addition to the estimated income at those ages. Afterward, the results are compared with those from a model based on the total estimated income. This confirms whether income history that incorporates an entire job history is an indicator that is truly better than occupation or estimated income at only a specific age in explaining the current socioeconomic status of the male elderly.

In Table 9.5, the results of these models are summarized. Model 1 shows the estimation results for Model 2, from Table 9.4, that is, the model that incorporates only the total estimated income. Models 2 and 3 are the models that only incorporate estimated income (0 when unemployed) at ages 40 and 50, respectively. Models 4 and 5 are the models that incorporate dummy variables for the eight-category version of the SSM Comprehensive Job Classifications, which is commonly used in Japan, and an unemployment dummy variable at these ages.[13] Models 6 and 7 show the estimation results for the models that incorporate occupational prestige scores[14] and an unemployment dummy variable at ages 40 and 50, respectively.

This table shows that the models based on occupational prestige scores at ages 40 and 50 (Models 6 and 7) have a substantially smaller coefficient of determination, compared to the other models. Given that the occupational prestige score is an indicator focused solely on occupation, it is reasonable to posit that the socioeconomic status of elderly people is determined not only by their past occupations but also by conditions such as employment status, employment type, and firm size. Such results reflect the multidimensional nature of the hierarchy of employment opportunities in Japanese society.

The coefficient of determination for Models 4 and 5, based on the SSM Comprehensive Job Classifications, is larger than that of the models based on occupational prestige scores; however, it is less than that of the models based on estimated income (Models 2 and 3). This is likely because although SSM Comprehensive Job Classifications account for employment conditions, other than occupation, such as employment status or firm size, the classifications are fairly rough and the distinction between

[13] The eight categories of SSM Comprehensive Job Classifications are as follows: professionals, white-collars in large firms, white-collars in middle to small firms, self-employed white-collars, blue-collars in large firms, blue-collars in middle to small firms, self-employed blue-collars, and farmers. The unemployment dummy variable in the models also applies to cases in which occupation is unknown.

[14] Unemployment was assigned a value of 0. However, the effect of being unemployed is estimated by the unemployment dummy variable that is also incorporated into the model.

Table 9.5 Regression analysis using estimated income and job information at specific ages (Summary of results)

	Independent variable	Model 1	Model 2	Model 3	Model 4	Model 5	Model 6	Model 7
		Total estimated income	Estimated income at 40	Estimated income at 50	SSM job class at 40	SSM job class at 50	Occupational prestige at 40	Occupational prestige at 50
(a) Subjective identification of social status (N = 1069)	R^2	0.086	0.063	0.079	0.045	0.063	0.021	0.033
	adj. R^2	0.085	0.063	0.078	0.038	0.056	0.019	0.032
	AIC	3942.7	3968.8	3951.5	4003.3	3983.8	4018.6	4004.5
	BIC	3952.6	3978.8	3961.4	4048.1	4028.6	4033.5	4019.4
	Number of parameters	2	2	2	9	9	3	3
(b) Total assets (N = 713)	R^2	0.139	0.116	0.114	0.070	0.091	0.020	0.043
	adj. R^2	0.138	0.114	0.112	0.059	0.081	0.017	0.040
	AIC	3520.7	3539.8	3541.3	3589.8	3573.0	3614.7	3598.0
	BIC	3529.8	3548.9	3550.4	3630.9	3614.1	3628.4	3611.7
	Number of parameters	2	2	2	9	9	3	3
(c) Monthly living expenses (N = 966)	R^2	0.055	0.050	0.061	0.031	0.045	0.015	0.024
	adj. R^2	0.054	0.049	0.060	0.023	0.037	0.013	0.022
	AIC	7660.8	7666.1	7654.7	7698.7	7684.8	7702.7	7693.7
	BIC	7670.6	7675.8	7664.5	7742.6	7728.7	7717.3	7708.3
	Number of parameters	2	2	2	9	9	3	3

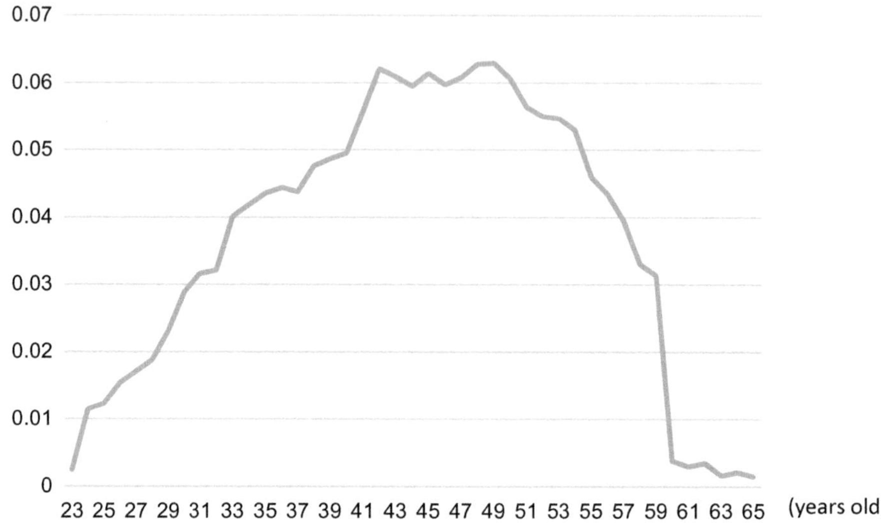

Fig. 9.3 Coefficient of determination of models for monthly expenses using estimated income at specific ages

regular and non-regular employment is not considered.[15] Thus, the estimated income history, which reduces a respondent's multidimensional job history to a single quantitative variable, based on its income-generating power, is a convenient and useful indicator.

Lastly, we compare the fitness of Models 2 and 3, based on the estimated income at a specific age, with the fitness of Model 1 containing the sum of estimated incomes at all ages. Model 1 has a larger coefficient of determination for the subjective identification of social status and total assets, and the difference is particularly noticeable for total assets. It is understandable that the stock aspect of economic status is more strongly affected by cumulative income than by the estimated income for a single point in time. Meanwhile, the results for monthly living expenses are slightly different in that the coefficient of determination is slightly larger for Model 3 that only includes estimated income at age 50 than the model based on total estimated income (Model 1).

To investigate the fitness of models on monthly living expenses further, models using estimated income at each of ages 15–65 were estimated. Figure 9.3 shows the coefficients of determination for the model based on the estimated income at an age from 15 to 65 years.[16] As this figure shows, starting from the model based on estimated income during youth, the coefficient of determination increases as age increases, peaking in the late 40s (0.063 at ages 48 and 49). Afterward, the

[15] Additionally, because the SSM Comprehensive Job Classifications are categorical variables, applying them to respondents' entire job histories is not practically useful.

[16] The coefficients of determinant are shown only for the period from age 23 to age 65, when the estimated income at the age has a positive coefficient in the model.

coefficient of determination steadily decreases to almost zero in the 60s. In other words, monthly living expenses in old age are affected most strongly by the level of estimated income in the 40s and the early 50s, while estimated income in other periods, particularly in the 60s and beyond, does not make much of a difference. As demonstrated in Fig. 9.2, the period from the 40s to the early 50s is close to the period in which the estimated income by age peaks. This is interpreted to mean that people's income and consumption in a person's most productive years determines their level of consumption even after they enter old age with a lower income.

9.6 Discussion and Conclusion

This chapter has attempted to explain socioeconomic disparities among the male elderly by respondents' income history, estimated based on detailed job history data from SSM surveys. Based on the analysis results in this chapter, this approach—which captures the overall picture of individual job history, from the perspective of income-generating power, and uses that to explain the socioeconomic status of elderly people—is highly effective for understanding inequality among elderly people. As an indicator that represents a respondent's multidimensional job history, the estimated income is useful in explaining the socioeconomic status of the male elderly. The total estimated income calculated by adding all of the estimated incomes at each age can better explain the socioeconomic status of the elderly, particularly economic conditions in terms of stock (e.g., total assets). This is the case even when compared to models based on educational attainment, occupational prestige scores, and comprehensive job classifications at specific ages. Additionally, estimated income during a person's most productive years is effective in explaining the monthly living expenses of the elderly.

As argued in this chapter, one reason why individual income history has a stronger effect on the socioeconomic status of elderly people, compared with factors such as educational attainment or past occupational prestige scores, is the multidimensional nature of the hierarchy of employment opportunities in the Japanese labor market. In Japan, socioeconomic status is strongly affected not only by the conditions focused on by social stratification studies, employment status, and occupation (or education levels, which are closely related to them) but also by firm size and employment type. The estimated income used in this chapter makes it possible to ascertain the comprehensive picture of a person's position, within this kind of multidimensional social stratification structure, qualifying it in a highly descriptive manner.

Japan has the most rapidly aging population in the world, and this chapter endeavors to provide a Japanese-based answer to one of the big questions in social stratification studies: how to determine an elderly person's status in the social hierarchy. Evidently, most elderly people are not in employment, and it is often impossible to apply the conventional approach of social stratification studies to the elderly population: using an individual's job as the key to understanding inequality. However, this holds true only when focusing on current employment among the elderly. Few people have been unemployed throughout their entire job histories, and explanations that use past employment information have plenty of potentials. Of course, the approach adopted in this chapter—reducing multidimensional job history at various ages to a single quantitative variable of estimated income, from the perspective of its income-generating power—is only one of the many methods that could be used to achieve this. There will likely be a great accumulation of research on how and why people's job histories affect them later in life. This will enable us to better understand issues of inequality in a rapidly aging society and develop better solutions for these issues.

References

Arita, S. (2016). *Shūgyō kikai to hōshū kakusa no shakaigaku: Hiseiki koyō, shakai kaisō no nikkan hikaku (Sociology of reward inequality among employment positions: A comparison of non-regular employment and social stratification in Japan and Korea).* University of Tokyo Press. (in Japanese).

Arita, S. (2017). *A comparative analysis of social stratification in Japan, Korea and Taiwan: Where is the locus of social inequality?* ISS Discussion Paper Series, F-182.

Arita, S. (2018). Shokureki dēta ni motozuku katokureki no suitei (Estimation of income history based on job history data). In T. Moriyama (Ed.) *2015 nen SSM chōsa repōto 7: Rōdō shijō II (2015 SSM survey report 7: Labor market II)* (pp.1–21). 2015 SSM Chōsa Kenkyūkai. (in Japanese)

Guvenen, F., Kaplan, G., Song, J. & Weidner, J. (2017). *Lifetime incomes in the United States over six decades.* NBER Working Paper No.23371. National Bureau of Economic Research.

Hara, J., & Seiyama, K. (2005). *Inequality amid affluence: Social stratification in Japan.* Trans Pacific Press.

Hashimoto, K. (2009). *'Kakusa' no sengoshi: Kaikyū shakai Nihon no rireki sho (Post-war history of social inequality: The resume of Japanese society).* Kawade Shobo Shinsha. (in Japanese)

Imai, J. (2011). The limit of equality by 'Company Citizenship': Politics of labor market segmentation in the case of regular and non-regular employment in Japan. In Y. Sato & J. Imai (Eds.), *Japan's new inequality: Intersection of employment reforms and welfare arrangements* (pp. 32–53). Trans Pacific Press.

Kalleberg, A. L. & Lincoln, J. R. (1988). The structure of earnings inequality in the United States and Japan. *American Journal of Sociology, 94*(S), 121–153.

Kanomata, N. (2001). *Kikai to kekka no hubyōdō: Sedai kan idō to shotoku, shisan kakusa (Inequality of opportunities and results: Inter-generational mobility and disperities of income and asset).* Minerva Shobō. (in Japanese)

Kanomata, N. (2008). Baburu hōkai go no shotoku kakusa to shakai kaisō (Income differentials and social stratification after the collapse of the bubble economy). In Y. Sato (Ed.), *2005 nen SSM chōsa sirīzu 15: Ryūdōsei to kakusa no kaisō ron (2005 SSM research series 15: Disparities, social fluidity, and social stratification)* (pp.45–65). 2005 SSM Chōsa Kenkyūkai. (in Japanese)

Kimura, Y. (2002). 'Kako no shokugyō' ni yoru rōgo no shotoku kakusa (Does the longest-held occupation have any effects upon the income of elderly people?). *Riron to hōhō (Sociological theory and methods), 17*(2), 151–165. (in Japanese)

Lefranc, A., Ojima, F., & Yoshida, T. (2014). Intergenerational earnings mobility in Japan among sons and daughters: Levels and trends. *Journal of Population Economics, 27*(1), 91–134.

Mugiyama, R. (2018). Shokugyō keireki no eikyō ni miru kōreisha no keizai kakusa (The differential effect of job history upon income and wealth among elderly people across gender in Japan). In Sakaguchi, Y. ed. *2015 nen SSM chōsa repōto 6: Rōdō shijō I (2015 SSM survey report 6: Labor market I)* (pp.1–21). 2015 SSM Chōsa Kenkyūkai. (in Japanese)

Osawa, M. (2011). *Social security in contemporary Japan*. Routledge.
Otake, F. (2005). *Nihon no fubyōdō: Kakusa shakai no gensō to mirai (Inequalities in Japan: Illusion* and future of stratified society). Nihon Keizai Shimbunsha. (in Japanese)
Sakamoto, A., & Powers, D. A. (1995). Education and the dual labor market for Japanese men. *American Sociological Review, 60*, 222–246.
Sato, Y. & Yoshida, T. (2007). Hinkon no sedai kan rensa no jisshō kenkyū: Shotoku idō no shiten kara (An empirical study of intergenerational persistence of poverty: From the viewpoint of income mobility). *Nihon rōdō kenkyū zasshi (The Japanese journal of labour studies), 49*(6), 75–83. (in Japanese)
Shirahase, S. (2021). Social stratification theory and population aging reconsidered. *Social Science Japan Journal, 24*(2), 277–288.
Statistics Bureau, Ministry of Internal Affairs and Communications. (2020). *Statistical handbook of Japan 2020*. Statistics Bureau Ministry of Internal Affairs and Communications.
Tarohmaru, H. (2009). *Jakunen hiseiki koyō no shakaigaku (A sociology of non-standard youth employment)*. Osaka University Press. (in Japanese).
Yoshida, T. (2005). Sengo nihon no shotoku bunpai no sūsei to kakusa yōin no kentō (Study of trend of income distribution and factors of inequality in post-war Japan). In F. Ojima (Ed.), *Gendai nihon ni okeru jendā to shakai kaisō ni kansuru sōgōteki kenkyū (Comprehensive study of gender and social stratification in contemporary Japan)* (pp. 41–52). Doshisha University. (in Japanese).

Shin Arita is a professor at Institute of Social Science, University of Tokyo. He majored sociology and area studies (Korean studies) and specializes in comparative sociology. His research interests include labor market, educational system, and social stratification in East Asian countries. He and his colleagues are currently conducting a comparative research on the legitimation of income inequalities focusing on the effects of institutional settings. His recent books are *Education and Social Stratification in South Korea* (University of Tokyo Press, 2020) and *Sociology of Reward Inequality Based on Employment Positions: A Comparison of Non-standard Employment and Social Stratification in Japan and Korea* (University of Tokyo Press, 2016, in Japanese).

Chapter 10
Another Aspect of Social Inequality, Wealth, in a Super-Aged Society, Japan: Re-examining the Conventional Framework of Social Stratification

Sawako Shirahase

10.1 Introduction

Japan is now the world's most aged society. The percentage of those aged 65 and over was 28.7% in 2020, and that of those aged 75 and over was 14.9%, the increase in the latter having been particularly accelerated.[1] In contrast, the total fertility rate in 2020 was 1.34, which has remained below the replacement rate of the population (2.07) since the mid-1970s. The most recent figure of the number of newborn babies was 840,832 in 2020, which was the lowest ever recorded.[2] A demographic transformation has taken place since the 1950s wherein the total fertility rate dropped by 1.65 points from 3.65 to 2.00. At the same time that Japan has suffered a declining birth rate, longevity has expanded. As a consequence, the growth of the proportion of the aging population has accelerated, particularly since the mid-1980s. Associated with such a rapid change in the demographic structure are two main issues that require special attention when examining social stratification: the growth in the number of elderly people who are out of the labor market and the increase in the number of young people who postpone forming their family due to delays in marriage or who even shy away from it. These demographic changes would lead to some revision of the basic framework of social stratification, which has been discussed based on the association with the labor market of the household head.

The increase in the number of retired people associated with the increase in the number of people aged 65 and over raises questions about the orthodox approach to social stratification closely associated with the labor market positions of the household heads. A major question is how to determine the social status of those who are not employed and whether we should consider the change of how to determine the structure of social stratification due to such transformation of demographic structure. For instance, when the first national survey of social stratification and social

S. Shirahase (✉)
The University of Tokyo, Tokyo, Japan
e-mail: sshiraha@l.u-tokyo.ac.jp

S. Shirahase (ed.), *Social Stratification in an Aging Society with Low Fertility*, Economy and Social Inclusion, https://doi.org/10.1007/978-981-19-3647-0_10

mobility (SSM) was conducted in Japan, the majority were of working age, that is, 15–64 years old, and the overwhelming majority of the male heads of household worked and supported their families. Thus, it was reasonable to assume the structure of social stratification and inequalities to be closely associated with the labor market position. However, more than one-fourth of the population is now aged 65 and older, and the number of them at work declines as they age. As the population ages and an increasing number of people have retired from the labor market, the number of households living mainly on social security benefits, exemplified by public pensions, has also increased (Cabinet Office, 2020), and measuring the economic well-being of households based solely on the status in the labor market of the head of the household has reached its limit.

In sociology, occupation has been viewed as an important determinant of social stratification, indeed as a backbone of social stratification (Parkin, 1971), and in fact, Weber also claimed that "the class situation is ultimately the market situation" (1946, p. 182). However, they did not take into account the aging of the population, in which the number of those leaving the labor market has increased, and it has not been seriously discussed how their positions in the labor market when they are of working age form their substantial socio-economic status in their later life.

Furthermore, old people used to live with their offspring, mainly their eldest son and their families, but now the proportions of one-person and couple-only families among older people have increased since the 1980s, when the percentage of those aged 65 and over has accelerated in Japan. Along with such a change in the household structure, the household income package pattern has also changed; public transfers, such as public pensions, have played an important role in explaining the economic well-being of the elderly. Thus, as the demographic structure changed, the household structure and the pattern of individual life courses also changed. It would be no surprise then that there is need to question the conventional framework of how social stratification generates social inequality in a society in which the demographic structure has largely changed. In this chapter, I discuss whether the mechanism generating social stratification changes when we consider the aging population as well as the change in the household structure.

Japan is currently the world's most aged society, and it is advantageous to examine this super-aged country in connection with our research question: How is social inequality generated from the perspective of social stratification in an aging society where the numbers of old people and of those who are out of the labor force are increasing? In Japan, there are major empirical studies of social stratification that have been conducted on the basis of the National Survey of Social Stratification and Social Mobility (SSM survey), which has been conducted every 10 years since 1955. However, it originally targeted the working-age population aged 20–69, who are mostly at work, and considered socio-economic inequalities with a focus on the labor market. For example, when the first SSM survey was conducted in 1955, much attention was paid to Japan's rapid growth in attempts to verify the industrialization hypothesis in Asia (Cole & Tominaga, 1976), the percentage of the working-age population (15–64 years) was 61.2%, and the percentage of the older population (65 years or older) was only 5.3%. Today, the percentage of those aged 65 or older is 28.1%, which is more than one-fourth of the entire population of Japan, and the percentage of the younger population (14 years or younger) is 12.2%, a significant decrease from the figure of 33.4% recorded 75 years ago.[3]

Since the 1990s, population aging has been actively discussed among economists in close association with the widening of income inequality (Tachibanaki, 1998; Ohtake, 2005). According to Ohtake (1994), a leading economist, a major reason for expanding the scope of income inequality since the 1980s is the increase in the number of elderly people, causing relatively large income inequality. Thus, once the aging population is considered, Ohtake claimed that there was no substantial increase in the extent of income inequality. It has since indeed been confirmed that it is necessary to consider the differences in the demographic structure when comparing the extent of income inequality over time, and we should be cautious in concluding whether the overall extent of income inequality is larger in one country than another or whether income inequality has continuously expanded. Shirahase (2002, 2015) pointed out that there were no detailed arguments about the relationship between the aging population and the growth of economic inequality in previous arguments by economists. As a critical aspect of explaining the expanded income inequality in Japan, she emphasized that the change in the household structure in which the elderly live explains why the elderly show a relatively high extent of economic inequality. Economic well-being is largely explained by different living arrangements for older people, and in fact, those living alone and those in three-generation households are largely different in this respect (Shirahase, 2002). The elderly living alone suffered the most from economic hardship; their poverty rate was almost 70% in the 1980s, and although recently the corresponding figure has improved due to the recent improvement in the social security system, the poverty rate for one-person households of old women still remains high. Such a large change in household structure is also related to changes in the household income package. The percentage of social transfers is increasing, while earned income is decreasing among older people. In old age, the number of those who are out of the labor market is increasing, which leads us to consider whether social status can be accurately understood only by market income and occupation as in working age.

Income is not the only component that determines the economic well-being of people; wealth would be as important as income, particularly among those who leave the labor market. The level of economic well-being should be measured not only by income level but also by the level of wealth accumulated throughout their life course. Even if many old people leave the labor market, their economic well-being differs in terms of non-earned income, such as social transfer and wealth.

In this chapter, I discuss wealth inequality from the perspective of cumulative inequality, in addition to a discussion of income inequality. It has been pointed out that the extent of wealth inequality is much higher than that of income inequality, and the generational gap in wealth is also much larger than in income per se (Kitao & Yamada, 2019; Shirahase, 2017b). As mentioned earlier, a substantial number of older people live only with a public pension or social security benefits, and such a phenomenon would lead to reducing income inequality among the elderly, mainly because market income is one of the driving forces to increase income inequality.

Contrariwise, wealth is cumulative across the life course, and it would show greater inequality between those who have and those who do not. In this chapter, I focus on what determines wealth in relation to an aging population.

Income and wealth are closely associated, and as the amount of total assets or property increases, the chance to inherit parental bequests also becomes high. Wealth is a good criterion not only for what kinds of jobs/occupations one engages in but also what kind of family background one has. Thus, wealth comprises cumulative assets and, at the same time, the inheritance of parental advantages/disadvantages over generations. I would like to discuss social stratification with a focus on wealth as a stock in relation to the aging population, in which a substantial number leave the labor market and become dependent on non-earned income for their lives. Wealth includes not only financial assets but also non-financial assets, including real estate. In this chapter, I focus on financial assets (savings) as a proxy of wealth, and the main research question in this chapter is to examine what we can see as a new perspective in social stratification by taking into consideration wealth in addition to income in the super-aged society of Japan.

In discussing social inequality, it has been noted that not only flow aspects such as income but also stock aspects such as savings should be taken into account (Sorensen 2000), while previous major attention in social stratification studies focused on occupation as the backbone. As I mentioned earlier, it is necessary to pay greater attention to what people have amassed previously, rather than what they have. Spilerman (2000) pointed out that assets occupy an important place in examining social stratification, and Pfeffer (2018) showed that assets have a significant impact on educational attainment and pointed to the existence of wealth gaps associated with intergenerational transfers (Pfeffer & Killewald, 2018). While dependence on financial assets, including savings that have been accumulated until old age, is expected to increase for the retired elderly, Horioka and Niimi (2018) found that even though the retired elderly are more likely to consume their savings, the consumption rate does not increase as much as the simple life cycle hypothesis predicts.[4] Furthermore, there is another important channel for wealth, namely private transfers. With respect to income, social transfers are significant from the perspective of redistribution and income security. In fact, most elderly people live on public pensions. This is more of a social transfer than the compensation for labor, even though there is an aspect of income security in transfers, which have been built up through their past occupational career. There is yet another form of private transfer, the typical example of which is inheritance. Kitamura (2019) estimates the amounts of inheritance and in vivo gifts to be 50 trillion yen and 30 trillion yen, respectively, accounting for 37.5% of total intergenerational transfers of assets, much of which is inherited upon the death of parents (relatives). Hence, in this chapter, wealth, which has not been fully explored in the study of social stratification, will also be discussed in association with asset transfers from parents.

This chapter discusses three topics: (1) economic inequality in terms of income and savings, (2) the relationship between intergenerational occupational mobility and wealth inheritance, and (3) determinants of the economic well-being of the elderly, represented by the total value of household income and real savings. With regard to the second and third points, we also pay attention to the gender gap. It has been pointed out that there have been substantial gender-based differences in work histories, including working style and division of labor within the family. Before starting analyses of the main questions as mentioned above, let us take a brief look at changes in the post-war household structure, which are essential when looking at population aging.

10.2 Changes in Population and Household/Family[5] Structure

The population structure is divided largely into three age groups: young-age group (0–14 years), working-age group (15–64 years), and old-age group (65+ years). Recently, the old age group has often been divided into a younger segment (65–74 years) and an older segment (75+) to reflect the accelerated increase in the number of elderly people, particularly since the 1980s. The young-age and old-age populations are defined as the dependent population, and the dependent population index was calculated as the ratio of the dependent population to the working-age group. In 1950, when Japan's high economic growth took off, the ratio of the young-age group to the working-age was 59.4, and that of the old-age group was 8.3. Approximately 90% of the dependent population was the young-age group. In 2015, the dependent population index was 64.5, which is not much different from 65 years ago, but the age composition of the dependent population has changed dramatically; the old-age group accounts for nearly two-thirds of the dependent population. The reversal between the young-age group and the old-age group in the dependent population was observed in 2000. Even if both the young and the old populations are considered dependent, these two are quite different in meaning: the young people are going to join the working-age population and to support society, while the old stay longer once they enter the late stage of their life course and eventually become frail and need help from others. The other problem that has newly emerged for young people is that it is no longer guaranteed that young people will enter the labor market on a full-time basis due to worsening of the labor market, many instead remaining dependent on their parents regardless of age.

The total fertility rate was 3.65 in 1950, but the rapid decline in fertility during the 1950s reduced it to 2.00 in 1960, and in 1975, the total fertility rate fell below the replacement level fertility and the birthrate began to decline in earnest. Ten years later, in 1985, the population aged 65 years or older surpassed 10% and reached 15% in 1995. In 1985, Japan's average life expectancy was highest among OECD countries, and the recent increase in average life expectancy was due in large part to the decline in the mortality rate of those aged 65 years or older.[6]

These demographic shifts were linked to changes in the actual living arrangements, that is, households. In 1950, the total number of households in Japan, excluding Okinawa, was 16,580,000, which more than tripled in 2015 to 53,449,000.[7] On the other hand, the average number of household members was reduced by more than half from 5.02 in 1950 to 2.38 in 2015.[8] Closer observation of the content of household structure shows that the number of married-couple households with children decreased, while the number of married-couple-only households and the number of one-person households largely increased. In 2015, of total households, the share of married-couple-only households was 20.1% and the share of one-person households was 34.5%, together accounting for the majority of all households. With regard to the elderly in particular, the structure of living arrangements has changed from households where they mostly live with their children to one-person households (27.3%) or married-couple-only households (29.6%). Furthermore, of households with children under the age of 17, which are decreasing in number, as of 2015, the share of households with only parents and children is 83.7%, of which the share of single-mother households is 9.6%, which is roughly 10% of all such households.

After World War II, the number of married-couple households with children, symbolic of the modern family, decreased with decreases in the size of households (Shiharase, 2017a). For example, among households where members share their residences and livelihoods, the share of married-couple households with children was 43.1% in 1955, which was reduced to 27.3% in 2015. Meanwhile, the proportion of married-couple-only households increased from 6.8% in 1955 to 20.5% in 2015.[9] The increase in the number of married-couple-only households is related to population aging and the division of the households with the elderly into one-person and couple-only households among elderly households; the decrease in the number of married-couple households with children is related to the tendency of young people to marry later or shy away from it in life. These transformations in the household structure are assumed to impact their positioning in social stratification in accordance with changes in the age and gender composition of household members. Paying attention to dynamic transformations within households leads to an important question in reconsidering the social stratification theory. More concretely, the increase in the number of household heads who are single parent or retired is not seriously considered when constructing the social stratification theory. Thus, it is important to examine the pattern of social stratification by considering such a large demographic transformation, that is, the aging population and lowering fertility rates.

10.2.1 Data and the Inequality Measurement

The data used in this section are derived from the 2001 and 2016 surveys of the Comprehensive Survey of People's Living Conditions (CSPLC) conducted by the MHLW.[10] The CSPLC has been conducted every year since 1986, and a large-scale survey including detailed information on the income sources of every member has been conducted every three years. Questions on actual savings started being asked from 2001 only in the large-scale survey years, so we compared 2001 with 2016 in this study. The CSPLC asks about the detailed income of all members of the household for the previous year of the survey, and an advantage of these data is that they allow us to decompose the personal incomes of all household members and identify a detailed income source for each. I also emphasize that the CSPLC has a relatively large sample size, allowing us to examine income inequality by considering the differences in household types. The sample sizes analyzed in this study were 30,389 in 2001 and 24,600 in 2016.[11]

The actual savings calculated by subtracting rental loan from total savings were used in our analyses. Regarding income, disposable income is calculated by subtracting the direct taxes, such as income tax and social insurance contributions, from the total income and divided by the square root of the number of household members living together. It is necessary to take into account the change in demographic structure when examining the degree of income and wealth inequalities. Therefore, we resort to the decomposition method derived from Shorrocks (1984) as shown below. The change in the degree of income/wealth inequalities can be decomposed into three components: (1) the change in inequalities within the age group, (2) the change in the age structure of the household head, and (3) the change in inequalities between the age groups.

$$\Delta MLD = MLD^{2015} - MLD^{2000}$$

$$= \sum_i \overline{\alpha_i} \Delta MLD_i + \left[\sum_i \overline{MLD_i} \Delta \alpha_i + \sum_i \overline{\ln \frac{\mu}{\mu_i}} \Delta \alpha_i \right] + \sum_i \overline{\alpha_i} \Delta \ln \left(\frac{\mu}{\mu_i} \right).$$

$\overline{\alpha_i}$ and $\overline{MLD_i}$ are the mean values of α_i and MLD_i of the ith age group in 2000 and 2015. Δ denotes the difference in the ith age group between 2000 and 2015.

10.3 Population Aging and Changes in Income and Asset Distribution

The degree of economic inequality measured by disposable income as a flow aspect of economic well-being and savings as a stock aspect differs greatly. The Gini coefficients of equivalent disposable income and equivalent savings were 0.245 and 0.742, respectively, in 2000, while the corresponding values showed a downward trend to 0.224 and 0.614, respectively, in 2015. What explains this decrease in the extent of the two kinds of economic inequalities? To see the effect of the age distribution of the head of the household, mean log deviation was used to perform factor decomposition in the following manner (Shorrocks, 1984), as discussed in the previous section. We examine three factors to determine whether the difference in the degree of disparity (2000 and 2015) is due to changes in the disparity within age groups, the disparity between age groups, or structural changes in the age distribution of the household heads.

First, let us consider the results of economic inequality based on disposable income (left side of Table 10.1). The degree of income inequality decreased on the whole, but

Table 10.1 Decomposition analysis into three factors on the change in the extent of inequality between 2000 and 2015

	Change in disposable income			Change in savings		
	Within-age effect	Change in age structure	Between-age effect	Within-age effect	Change in age structure	Between-age effect
20s	0.0005	−0.0166	−0.0037	−0.0025	−0.0745	0.0097
30s	−0.0014	−0.0080	−0.0080	0.0004	−0.0583	0.0134
40s	−0.0010	−0.0018	−0.0059	−0.0130	−0.0207	0.0133
50s	−0.0016	0.0013	−0.0064	−0.0332	−0.0357	0.0214
60s	−0.0106	0.0067	−0.0070	−0.0297	0.0084	0.0209
70s+	−0.0129	0.0569	−0.0010	−0.0248	0.0429	0.0310
計	−0.0271	0.0386	−0.0322	−0.1028	−0.1379	0.1098

Source Comprehensive Survey of People's Living Conditions

the decrease was brought about mainly by reduction in the gaps within and between age groups, and the structural factor due to changes in age group distribution changed in the direction of widening the income gap. The widening of the gap due to structural changes in age was canceled out by the narrowing of the gap within and between age groups, and the overall income gap was decreased compared to 2000. Thus, the overall decrease in income inequality is explained by the reduction in the gaps within age groups and between them, although the aging of household heads leads to an increase in the degree of income inequality.

The same analysis was conducted for savings, and the right side of Table 10.1 shows the results. The wealth inequality was narrowed, similar to income inequality, while the degree of its reduction was significantly larger than that of income inequality. Such reductions in wealth inequalities can be explained mainly by the narrowing gap in wealth within age groups and the change in the age structure of household heads. Aging in household heads narrowed wealth inequality, unlike income inequality, while the wealth gap between age groups has widened. It has been confirmed that the income gap among the elderly headed households has narrowed, as the low-income group among the elderly has been raised (Shirahase, 2015).

As shown in Fig. 10.1, the degree of wealth inequality by age group has been reduced across all generations, and the degree of wealth inequality within age groups has become more similar across generations. In fact, the data in Table 10.1 confirm a reduction in wealth inequality within age groups. The differences in wealth inequality across age groups have narrowed and the extent of the wealth inequality across age groups of household heads has relatively leveled off over the last 15 years.

Next, in order to examine the change in the age structure of household heads, the mean savings and the percentage of the households whose savings are none by age group are presented in Fig. 10.2. Let us first examine the change in mean savings by age groups. When we compare the average savings by age group, the pattern in which the savings of elderly households tend to be higher on average than those of non-elderly households remains the same between 2000 and 2015. However,

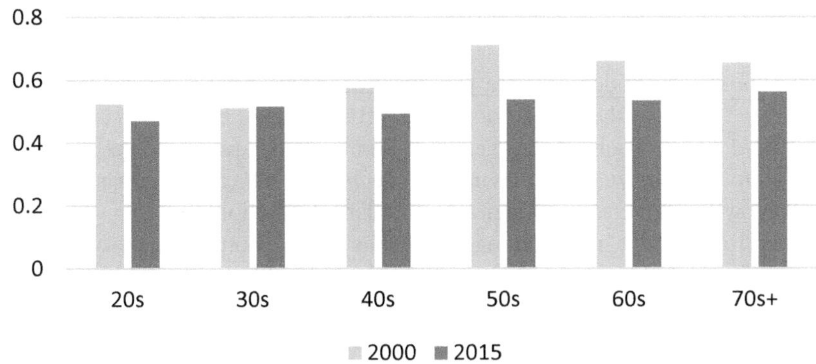

Fig. 10.1 Wealth inequality (Gini coefficients) by age group in 2000 and 2015. *Source* Comprehensive Survey of People's Living Conditions

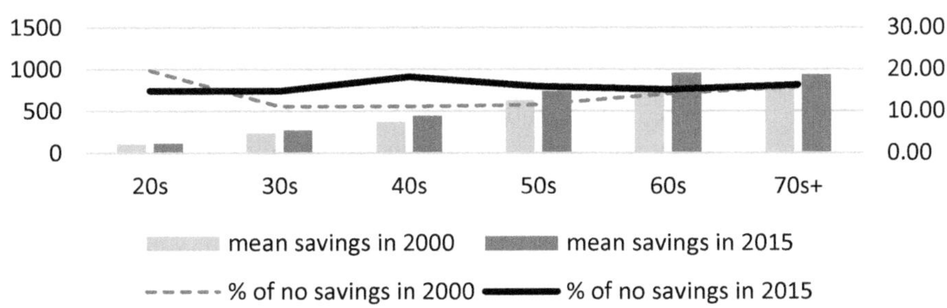

Fig. 10.2 Mean savings (10,000 JY) and the percentage of those with no savings by age group (%). *Source* Comprehensive Survey of People's Living Conditions

the advantage in savings of elderly households relative to the overall average has generally diminished, suggesting that the number of elderly households with high savings has decreased,[12] which in turn has contributed to the narrowing of the savings gap among elderly households.[13] On the other hand, the most interesting findings in Fig. 10.2 can be seen in the percentage of zero-saving households.

In 2000, the young households showed the highest percentage of zero-savings, while in 2015, those in their 40s showed the highest corresponding figure. Thus, the percentage of households with no savings is rising in working-age adults in their 30s to 50s, and the percentage of households with no savings by age group of household heads has leveled off in 2015. Such a high increase in the percentage of zero-saving families of working-age heads would imply that they have seen economically tough times since 2000.

On the other hand, the percentage of old households with zero savings did not change significantly, but it was not the case that the elderly enjoy economic security. In fact, when calculating the relative ratio of mean savings for the elderly to the overall mean, we found that the relative advantage in wealth among older people declined.

Thus, these results demonstrate that the savings of elderly households tend to be higher on average than those of non-elderly households. However, the lead in savings of elderly households has generally diminished, suggesting that the number of elderly households with high savings has decreased, which in turn has contributed to the narrowing of the savings gap among elderly households.

As mentioned above, the examination of changes in income inequality and wealth inequality found that both were affected by changes in the age structure distribution, but in different directions. Although both kinds of economic inequalities tended to decline, aging in the age structure had a positive effect on the income gap but a negative effect on the savings gap. One aspect of this different direction of change is that, in terms of income as a flow, the aging population leads to an increase in the number of households of retired old people whose main income is derived from social security benefits, represented by public pensions, and such an increased weight in the social transfer would lead to a narrow degree of income inequality. The other aspect is that the aging of the population brings about a decline in the number of old households with very high savings, and as a result, the wealth inequality would decrease due to the decline in the number of old households with very high savings.

Another concern is that the number of households in their 40s and 50s with no savings has been increasing since the 2000s. The increase in the number of working-age households with no savings means that unless their parents transfer their savings to them, the chance of having any savings in their old age is quite slim. It would be no guarantee that older households enjoy relatively higher savings when working-age households become older in the future.

10.4 Wealth Through Intergenerational Inheritance

There are cases in which stock assets are inherited from the parents. For instance, land has been inherited across generations, and it can be regarded as a family capital. Remittance is also a type of private intergenerational transfer from parents or children, but its amount is rather limited (Shirahase, 2020). In this section, we examine the intergenerational inheritance of wealth and how private assets are transferred from parents to children. Phiffer and Killewald (2018) examined five channels of asset transfers, that is, bequest inheritance, education, marriage, homeownership, and ownership of the family business, and found that wealth-related transfers begin relatively early in the life course through investment in education.

In this section, the data that are mainly analyzed are from the National Survey of Social Stratification and Social Mobility (SSM survey) conducted in 2015. Although it does not include detailed information on how various assets are transferred, the SSM survey includes questions about the total amount of assets and whether they have been inherited from parents (their own or their spouse's), and the amount if they have.[14]

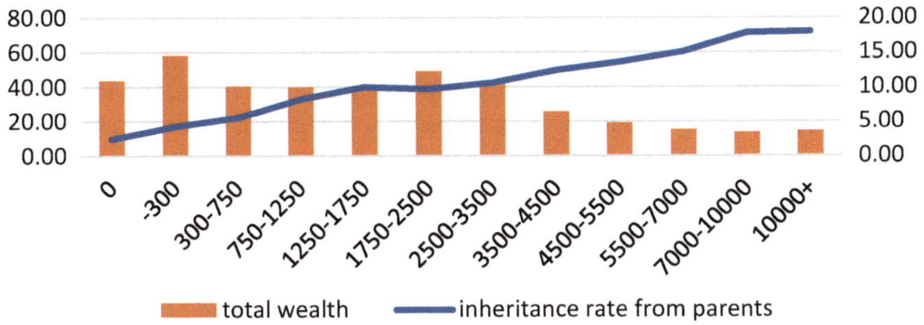

Fig. 10.3 Distribution of total wealth (10,000 JY) and the percentage of those who inherited wealth from parents (%). *Source* SSM2015 survey

Figure 10.3 presents the distribution of total wealth and the inheritance rate from parents by the total amount of assets that the respondents possess. About ten percent of the respondents have no assets, and about one-fourth of the respondents have assets of less than 10,000,000 yen, On the other hand, about 20% own assets more than 30,000,000 yen, and about 4% are very rich, owning wealth valued at more than 100,000,000 yen.

In research on social mobility, the patterns of mobility/inheritance have been observed by comparing the social status, exemplified by occupation, between fathers and children. The similarities and differences in social status between fathers and children have been used to measure the openness of society and to examine the degree of equality (Glass, 1954; Goldthorpe, 1987; Erikson and Goldthorpe, 1992; Ishida, 1993; Breen, 2004). While economics has examined the degree of inequality by focusing on the distribution of economic resources such as wages and income, sociology has examined the degree of social equality by focusing on the relationship in occupational similarities/dissimilarities between parents and children. How easily the father's education is inherited by their son/daughter has been regarded as a measure of social openness. In other words, how difficult or different it is for those with a wide variety of family backgrounds to have access to a certain favorable occupation with high prestige and reward has been regarded as a measurement of mobility barriers. If people can have access only to the occupation in which their fathers were also engaged, then there is a perfect correlation in occupation between fathers and sons, and there is no chance of having a job different from their father no matter how smart they are. In such a situation, there is no free choice of occupation. The main hypothesis that most sociologists tried to examine under industrialization was whether the degree of freedom to choose one's occupation was independent of one's father's. If we confirm that the relationship between fathers and sons in their social status represented by occupation has become significantly weaker, we could thereby confirm that industrialization brought freer choices and encouraged the openness of society. Unfortunately, however, the relationship between parents and children in their occupations and their social status remains close (Ishida, 2021). In this section,

I discuss the pattern of wealth inheritance, taking into account the occupational relationship between parents and children. The main research question is whether the chance of inheriting wealth from parents would be higher for those who inherit their fathers' occupations. I would thus like to see if occupational inheritance is closely related to wealth inheritance across generations.

In this section, we focus on the relationship between the father's occupation when the respondent was 15 and the respondent's own occupation at the age of 50, so as to make the stage of life course similar between parents and children. For this reason, from this section onward, the analysis will be limited to respondents aged 50 and above. Since about 30% of women had a job at age 50, the dummy for unemployment at age 50 was used only for women. As for men, only 0.7% were unemployed at the age of 50, so only employed men were included in the analysis.

We resort to logit analysis of whether assets have been inherited, as shown in Table 10.2. The independent variables used in this analysis were as follows. Age of the respondent was at the time of the survey. *Educational attainment* is categorized into three categories: compulsory education only, a high school diploma, and college and beyond. The first category of compulsory education was set as the reference. *Marital status* was divided into four categories: never married, married with a spouse, divorced, and widowed. The reference category for marital status was married. *Class origin* was measured by the class position of fathers when the respondents were aged 15, and it was divided into five categories: (1) professional/managerial, (2) clerical/sales, (3) skilled blue-collar, (4) semi-skilled/unskilled blue-collar, and (5) agriculture, forestry, and fishery, with semi-skilled/unskilled blue-collar as reference. *Class positions* of respondents at the age of 50 were also divided into the same five categories as class origin. For *employment status* at age 50, we also included firm size as an independent variable regardless of whether the business was small (less than 30 employees) or whether it was a public institution. Regarding *asset inheritance*, whether or not a man is the eldest son is of particular importance in the case of men. Thus, the issues of whether or not he is the eldest son if the respondent is a man, and whether or not she has male siblings if the respondent is a woman, were taken into account, in addition to the number of siblings.

First, let us look at the results for males aged 50 and over in Table 10.2. The variables that present statistically significant effects on wealth inheritance from parents are marital status (never married and divorced), eldest son or not, occupation at age 50 (professional/managerial or agricultural), and the father's being alive. There were no significant effects of class origin in the final analysis, and whether the job of the respondent at the age of 50 is the same as their fathers does not have a significant effect on inherited wealth. However, the jobs at age 50 showed a significant effect; compared with those who work semi- and non-skilled blue-collar jobs, those who were at professional or managerial work or at farm-related work are more likely to inherit wealth from parents. In inheriting family capital, whether a man is the eldest child remains very important; the eldest son is more likely to inherit parental assets. However, the timing of inheritance of family assets seems to be relatively late, particularly after the father deceases. Regarding marital status, those who have never been

Table 10.2 Logit analysis on inheritance from parents

	Male coefficients	Female coefficients
Age	−0.007	0.031**
Class origin: ref. = farmer		
White-collar job	0.033	−0.117
Blue-collar job	−0.003	−0.068
No father	0.029	0.346
Educational attainment: ref. = compulsory education		
High-school diploma	0.200	1.191**
College and beyond	0.484*	2.166**
Marital status: ref.=married		
Never-married	−1.253**	−0.604
Divorced	−0.871**	−1.223**
Widowed	−0.204	−0.430*
Eldest son/Having male siblings	0.456**	−0.362**
Number of siblings	−0.047	−0.129**
Work at the age of 50		0.308
Inheriting father's job	0.183	0.174
Job at the age of 50: ref. = semi-and non-skilled job		0.279
Professional/Managerial	0.431*	0.279
Clarical/Sales	0.329	0.384
Skilled blue-collar	−0.039	0.005
Farmers	1.096*	0.181
Farm size at the age of 50: ref.=small-size		
Medium- and large-size	0.020	−0.282
Government	−0.026	−0.655*
Father alive	−1.469**	−0.596**
Constant	−0.075	−2.726**
Cox-Snell R^2	0.101	0.129
N	1,185	1,079

Source SSM2015 survey
Note * $p < 0.05$ ** $p < 0.01$

married or divorced have a significant disadvantage in inheriting parental wealth, compared with those who are married.

As for women, variables that show statistically significant effects on receiving wealth from parents are age, education, divorced status, the presence of male siblings, and father alive. Class origin does not have a significant impact on wealth inheritance from parents, similar to males. The educational effects, particularly those of higher education, were higher than those for men. It may be the case that the role of educational attainment in searching for a spouse is important for women, and as a result, the impact of completing higher education on wealth inheritance increases.[15] Unlike men, job at the age of 50 does not show significant impacts on wealth inheritance, but whether they worked for the government when they were aged 50 showed a negative impact. In both men and women, we could not confirm a direct effect of occupational inheritance from their parents. Thus, for women, the labor market-related variables had a limited impact, although demographic factors such as marital status and the existence of male siblings matter a great deal in explaining whether they inherited family wealth. In particular, the negative impact of being divorced for women should not be overlooked.

In summary, there are gender similarities and differences in the mechanisms of inheriting wealth from parents. For both men and women, there is no direct effect of class origin and occupational inheritance, and educational attainment has a significant impact on inheriting wealth, while the impact of higher education is higher for women than for men. The impact of previous work history represented by the job at the age of 50 is significant mainly for men, while women's work histories show a limited impact, including whether they are at work at the age of 50. Finally, I would like to emphasize that demographic factors such as marital status and sibling order are statistically significant in determining the inheritance of wealth from parents. It is important that such demographic factors have been closely defined as strong social norms: The male-centered family lineage seems to be valid for wealth transfer between generations.

10.5 Economic Well-Being of Old People Including Wealth

Lastly, we examine the determinants of the overall level of economic well-being for the elderly, which is defined as the sum of household income and real savings for those aged 65 and over. In this section, we use the total household income, including stocks exemplified by savings, divided by the square root of the number of household members living together, to represent economic status, and examine the determining factors of the level of economic status. The independent variables were the same as those analyzed for wealth inheritance in the previous section. It should be noted, however, that while the 2015 SSM survey data used in this analysis have the advantage of including information about the detailed work history of respondents, they have the disadvantage of relatively high missing values for household income and savings.[16] Thus, the results of our analyses should be interpreted with caution.

Mugiyama (2018) asked a similar research question and analyzed the same 2015 SSM survey to examine the personal income, equivalent household income, and net assets (total assets minus borrowings) of respondents aged 60 and over, based on their occupation at age 40 and the longest period of employment at the workplace. He claims that the factors that determine economic well-being in old age are different for men and women. Similarly, Shirahase and Mugiyama (2019) compared the origin effects on class destinations at the different points of life courses and found that the mechanism determining social mobility patterns by birth cohort differs between men and women; the impact of class origin has remained stable for men, while it diminished after the age of 40 for women. Hence, in this section, we analyze the economic status of the elderly at the age of 65 by gender and examine the determinants of economic well-being. Let us begin with the results for old men (Table 10.3).

The variables that present statistically significant effects are the absence of the father when the respondent was aged 15, education, marital status, and job at age 50.

Table 10.3 OLS regression analysis on economic level between men and women

	Male coefficients	Female coefficients
Age	0.015**	0.020**
Class origin: ref. = farmer		
White-collar job	0.078	−0.155
Blue-collar job	−0.003	−0.084
No father	−0.535**	0.239
Educational attainment: ref. = compulsory education		
High-school diploma	0.812**	0.888**
College and beyond	1.086**	1.208**
Marital status: ref. = married		
Never-married	−0.365	−0.318
Divorced	−0.396	−0.762**
Widowed	−0.548**	−0.431**
Eldest son/Having male siblings	−0.128	0.181
Number of siblings	0.013	−0.022
Work at the age of 50		−0.029
Inheritance of father's job	−0.014	0.048
Job at the age of 50: ref. = semi-and non-skilled job		
Professional/Managerial	0.406*	0.149
Clarical/Sales	0.069	−0.016
Skilled blue-collar	0.095	−0.324
Farmers	−0.061	−0.870
Farm size at the age of 50: ref. = small-size		
Medium- and large-size	0.335**	0.157
Government	0.192	0.346
Constant	13.825	13.966
Adjusted R^2	0.186	0.141
N	545	420

Source SSM2015 survey
Note * $p < 0.05$, ** $p < 0.01$

For those aged 65 and older, a negative effect on the level of economic well-being was associated with the father being absent when the respondent was at the age of 15, and the impact of family background remains valid in determining economic well-being even in later life, with a direct positive impact remaining significant. When the respondents held professional or managerial jobs or worked at medium- or large-scale firms at the age of 50, the economic well-being of old people is likely to be better. The economic well-being tends to be lower among those who are divorced than among those who are married.

For women, on the other hand, only educational attainment and marital status of divorce or widowhood had a significant effect; those who completed high school or higher education were more likely to be better off in their late life than those whose final education ended with compulsory education, while if they are divorced or widowed, their economic well-being is less favorable than among those who are married and living with their spouse. Compared with men, women's working condition at the age of 50 does not affect the subsequent level of economic well-being. For older women, the same analysis was conducted using their husbands' education instead of their own, and the same results were obtained for their economic well-being. The economic status of elderly women is influenced by their husbands', and the absence of a husband itself has a negative effect on their economic status. Thus, the economic well-being of older women is determined largely by relational factors, such as whether or not they are married. For men, on the other hand, not only relational factors but also their own past employment status determine the level of economic well-being in later life.

10.6 Conclusion

In this chapter, we examine social stratification by focusing on wealth and savings. In the first section, to examine changes in the extent of economic inequality since 2000, we focused on disposable income as a flow and savings as a stock to measure economic well-being. As a result, both the income gap and the savings gap have been narrowing in recent years, and the fact that population aging directly contributes to expanding overall economic inequality, which was actively discussed in the 1990s, was not confirmed since at least 2000. From 2000 to 2015, population aging was found to contribute to the widening of income inequality, while the income gap among the elderly in particular narrowed, resulting in a reduction in the overall income gap within corresponding old age groups. For old households, the ratio of public pensions as a social transfer in their income package increases, while market income as a flow decreases. The increase in the social transfer ratio in their household economy leads to a narrowing of income inequality among the elderly population. Such a change in the household economy's income structure was closely related to the change in household structure; the number of elderly people living alone and in couple-only households has increased. Furthermore, the working pattern of the elderly has changed; while the overall employment rates have increased among those aged 65 and over, the percentage of non-regular workers increased, and the differences between those who earned their income from non-regular jobs and those who do not work and live only with social security benefits have become smaller due to the relatively low wage of non-regular jobs. On the other hand, although the overall income inequality has declined among old households, the income source explaining the overall income inequality among the elderly is still the income of working-age household members living with them. In other words, co-residence with working-age families still largely determines the economic well-being of the elderly (Shirahase, 2015).

Regarding the change in wealth inequality represented by savings, its degree narrowed more than that of income inequality. A clear difference in the impact of an aging household head between income and wealth inequality is the direction of the change; while the aging of households leads to expanding income inequality, it serves to narrow wealth inequality, mainly due to the decline in the relative advantage in wealth of old households compared with working-age households. While the pattern in which the mean savings among old households is higher than that among the young, the relative advantage in wealth among the old was diminished mainly because the number of super-wealthy elderly who own various assets has recently declined. Thus, we find that the impacts of the aging of the population on different aspects of economic inequality are not the same.

In examining the pattern of wealth inheritance, we find gender differences and similarities. For both men and women, the conventional family norm whereby the eldest son inherits the family assets remains valid. For women, it is important whether or not they have male siblings, and only when they do not have them are they candidates to inherit family wealth. Education is more important for women than for men in determining wealth inheritance; it appears that education can play a critical role in matchmaking with their current spouse, and educational attainment of women could be important in determining the inheritance of wealth, which is very close to the sibling order of their spouse. Previous work history affects the chance of inheriting family assets only for men.

In terms of overall economic level measured by both income and wealth, no effect of class origin was found for either men or women, but educational effects remain significant even at late life for both. In old age, the previous history of the labor market has a limited impact on women, while a significant impact of jobs at the age of 50 remains for men. The relational situation is becoming important, particularly in late-life stages. It should be noted that demographic factors such as gender, marital status, and sibling order play important roles in determining the level of economic well-being for both men and women.

What do we find when examining stratification by focusing on wealth? One is that family norms, such as being the eldest son or having male siblings, still have important implications. In particular, women's financial status is greatly affected by their marital status. The absence of the father at age 15 and employment status during working years affected the level of wealth only for men, but not for women. This can be interpreted as a result of the fact that during their working years, the labor market was clearly divided by gender, preventing the accumulation of skills and other career-related expertise for women. For their part, in their old age, the economic level of women was determined in a way that was more dependent on their spouses.

Compared to other countries, Japan still has a large gender gap, especially in terms of work styles, which remain intermittent. Recently, a majority of women have begun to continue working after the birth of their first child, but in the past, even among highly educated women, the majority stopped working. Furthermore, the gender gap in occupational career during the working years is not necessarily the same as before, since stable employment after education is no longer guaranteed, even for men. What kind of impact will the transformation of the young labor market have that is now manifesting in the middle-aged and even the elderly? We conducted a careful examination of not only the persisting gender gap and the newly emerging situation in the generational gap. Whether the clear gender gap seen heretofore will continue will require further study.

We have found that an increase in longevity in the context of population aging in Japan has occurred in the context of basic livelihood security being provided to people through family, and the family has been regarded as the main institution for securing people's lives. Our analyses confirmed that not only the relationship with the labor market but also the relationship with the family are very important in determining overall economic well-being. Men and women face asymmetrical circumstances in various ways, particularly in terms of access to wealth. In Japan, the family plays a large and critical function in providing basic livelihood security, but at the same time the heterogeneity within the family has not received sufficient attention even in social stratification studies. Households have been discussed mainly in terms of their adequacy as a unit of stratification, and I believe that it is still valid as a basic unit of analysis. However, the next important agenda is to examine heterogeneity within the family/household in the aging population.

Population aging takes place with an imbalance in the ratio of men to women, as gender differences in longevity increase with age.[17] In addition, the economic status of very old women varies significantly depending on whether they live alone or with their children. In Japan, where wealth is not just something to be created by the individual but is often inherited after the death of a parent, the process of wealth ownership is linked to conventional family norms and marital status.

Thus, our discussions about social stratification focusing on population aging and the change in the household structure could reveal the persistence of mechanisms that generate economic inequalities, and the relational situation with family and gender should receive greater attention, particularly because they are the main pillars in examining late-life inequality. It appears true that social stratification has been generated mainly by different positions and relationships with the labor market, but as people age, the demographic aspects of marital status and sibling order and relationships with other family members become important in determining economic well-being. Indeed, we were able to confirm that household situations, such as the relationship with one's spouse as exemplified by one's educational background, and marital status, such as divorce and widowhood, affect economic status in old age.

Shirahase and Ishida (2018) showed that the effect of class origins never disappears in life events. Thus, our focus on the stratification in old age revealed that the effects of one's class of origin, education, and working style during one's working years cannot be ignored even in old age, and that the pattern, degree, and continuity of these effects are essential factors particularly when examining the social stratification of the very aged society.

Notes

1. *Statistic Topics* no.126 (Ministry of Internal Affairs and Communications, https://www.stat.go.jp/data/topics/pdf/topics126.pdf).
2. *Vital Statistics* in 2020 (Ministry of Health, Labour, and Welfare, https://www.mhlw.go.jp/toukei/saikin/hw/jinkou/geppo/nengai20/dl/gaikyouR2.pdf).
3. Nihon no Tokei 2020 [2020 Statistics in Japan] (Statistics Bureau of Japan 2020) Chapter 2, Table 2.1 (https://www.stat.go.jp/data/nihon/02.html).
4. The life-cycle hypothesis states that after retirement, people maintain their livelihood by consuming the assets they accumulated earlier (Modigliani and Brumberg, 1954). In contrast, there are findings that savings are reversed for future contingencies and that retirement does not necessarily mean that assets will be consumed (De Nardi et al., 2010).
5. I use household and family more or less interchangeably in this chapter, although the definition of the household tends to be focused on the residential arrangement and that of the family is rather broader, taking into account kinship relations.
6. Jinkou Toukei Shiryo Shu 2017 Kaitei Ban [Population Statistics 2017 Revised Version] (National Institute of Population and Social Security Research) http://www.ipss.go.jp/syoushika/tohkei/Popular/Popular2017RE.asp?chap=0, Table 5.15.
7. Jinkou Toukei Shiryo Shu 2017 Kaitei Ban [Population Statistics 2017 Revised Version] (National Institute of Population and Social Security Research) http://www.ipss.go.jp/syoushika/tohkei/Popular/Popular2017RE.asp?chap=0, Table 7.1.
8. Jinkou Toukei Shiryo Shu 2017 Kaitei Ban [Population Statistics 2017 Revised Version] (National Institute of Population and Social Security Research) http://www.ipss.go.jp/syoushika/tohkei/Popular/Popular2017RE.asp?chap=0, Table 7.4.
9. Jinkou Toukei Shiryo Shu 2017 Kaitei Ban [Population Statistics 2017 Revised Version] (http://www.ipss.go.jp/syoushika/tohkei/Popular/Popular2017RE.asp?chap=0), Table 7.11.
10. For a detailed overview, refer to http://www.mhlw.go.jp/toukei/saikin/hw/k-tyosa/k-tyosa16/dl/01.pdf. We obtained approval for the use of the data for other purposes (Ministry of Health, Labor, and Welfare, fiscal statistics 0828 No. 4).

11. Because income values that the respondents answered were for the previous year. We thus will not use the survey years 2001 and 2016 but will do 2000 and 2015.
12. If one takes the logarithm of the ratio of overall average to the average of each age group, the advantage of older household heads in terms of the degree of savings decreased from −0.3220 to −0.2325 for those in their 60s and from −0.3265 to −0.2114 for those in their 70s and above.
13. Although the cross-sectional data from the present survey, in which respondents answer savings one year before the year of the survey, do not tell changes in savings with age, there are findings by Horioka and Niimi (2018) that the simple life-cycle hypothesis of consumption when people enter their old age does not apply. I would like to leave careful consideration of this issue to another paper.
14. The major characteristic and the greatest strength of SSM surveys is that they have been collecting detailed work histories of people since their last education on a yearly basis. On the other hand, its weakness is the low response rates for questions on assets, including savings. For example, only 61.8% of the respondents aged 65 and older responded to the question about their savings, and values were missing in nearly 40% of them. While keeping these data problems in mind, this paper analyzes those who responded.
15. We should further examine the relatively large impact of educational attainment for women in explaining the wealth inherited from parents, and I would like to discuss it in the other paper.
16. Among those aged 20–79 years, 25.8% answered "don't know" about their household income and 2.7% answered "unknown," for a total of 28.5% of missing values, while 27.1% answered "don't know" about their financial assets and 9.1% answered "unknown," for a total of 36.7% of missing values. Among those aged 65 and older, 61.8% answered about the amount of their savings, and nearly 30% did not know their household income. For those aged 65 and over, 61.8% of respondents answered questions about their savings, and nearly 30% answered "unknown" about their household income. Noting the problem of such high missing values, only those with valid responses were included in the analysis in our analysis.
17. With regard to the men-to-women ratio of average life expectancy, for every 100 women, the number of men is 79.9 in their late 70s and 51.3 in their late 80s, and the gap widens as they age (National Institute of Population and Social Security Research 2020), Table 2.2. http://www.ipss.go.jp/syoushika/tohkei/Popular/Popular2020.asp?chap=2&title1=%87U%81D%94N%97%EE%95%CA%901%8C%FB.

References

Breen R (ed) (2004) Social mobility in Europe. Oxford University Press, Oxford

Cabinet Office (2020) Koureishakai Hakusho [White Paper on Aging Society]. https://www8.cao.go.jp/kourei/whitepaper/w-2019/zenbun/01pdf_index.html (in Japanese)

Cole RE, Tominaga K (1976) Japan's changing occupational structure and its significance. In: Patrick H (ed) Japanese industrialization and its social consequences. University California Press, Berkeley, pp 53–95

De Nardi M, French E, Jones JB (2010) Why do the elderly save? The role of medical expenses. J Polit Econ 118(1):39–75

Erikson R, Goldthorpe JH (1992) The constant flux: a study of social mobility in industrial societies. Oxford University Press, Oxford

Glass D (1954) Social mobility in Britain. Routledge & Kegan Paul, London

Goldthorpe JH (1987) Social mobility and class structure in modern Britain. Clarendon Press, Oxford

Horioka CY, Niimi Y (2018) Nihon no Koureisha Setai no Chochiku Koudou ni Kansuru Jisshou Kenkyu [An empirical study on the saving behaviour of Japanese elderly households]. Working Paper Series Vol. Asian Growth Research Institute (in Japanese)

Ishida H (1993) Social mobility in contemporary Japan. Stanford University Press, Stanford

Ishida H (2021) Sedaikan ido to kyoiku no susei [Trends in intergenerational mobility and education]. In: Nakamura T, Miwa S, Ishida H (eds) The structure of social stratification in the early-stage of life. University of Tokyo Press, Tokyo, pp 19–36 (in Japanese)

Kitamura, Y (2019) Sedaikan Shisan Iten no Jittai to Seisaku Kadai [Intergenerational asset transfers and policy issues]. Q J Kojin Kinyuu, Spring 2019:13–22 (in Japanese)

Kitao S, Yamada T (2019) Dimensions of inequality in Japan: distributions of earnings, income, and wealth between 1984 and 2004. CREPE Working paper

Modigliani F, Brumberg RH (1954) Utility analysis and the consumption function: an interpretation of cross-section data. In: Kurihara KK (ed) Post-Keynesian economics. Rutgers University Press, New Brunswick, pp 388–436

Parkin F (1971) Class inequality and political order. Praeger, New York

Pfeffer FT (2018) Growing wealth gaps in education. Demography 55:1033–1068

Pfeffer FT, Killewald A (2018) Generations of advantage. Multigenerational correlations in family wealth. Soc Forces 96(4):1411–1441

Shirahase S (2002) Nihon no Shotoku Kakusa to Koureisha Setai: Kokusai Hikaku no Kanten Kara [Japan's income gap and elderly households: an international comparison]. Jpn J Labour Stud No 44:72–85 (in Japanese)

Shirahase S (2005) Shoshi koureika no mienai kakusa [The invisible gap in the aging and low fertility society]. Tokyo University Press (in Japanese)

Shirahase S (2015) Income inequality among older people in rapidly aging Japan. Res Soc Stratification Mobility 4:1–10

Shirahase S (2017a) Chiisana Setai no Zouka to Shakai Hosho [The increase of small households and social security]. J Soc Secure Res 2(1):4–17 (in Japanese)

Shirahase S (2017b) Social inequality in occupational inheritance and wealth accumulation in Japan from an intergenerational perspective. Paper presented at RC28 in Columbia University, New York, USA

Shirahase S, Ishida H (2018) Shoshi Kourei Shakai ni Okeru Shakai Kaisou to Life Course: Shusshin Kaisou no Life Event heno Kouka ni Chakumoku Shite [Social stratification and the life course in an aging, low fertility society: focusing on the effect of class of origin on life events]. Sociol Theor Methods 33(2):185–201 (in Japanese)

Shirahase S, Mubiyama R (2019) Gender differences in the impact of class origin throughout the life course. Paper presented at RC28 in Princeton University

Shirahase S (2020) Class inequalities in private intergenerational transfer: focusing on remittance between parents and children. Presented at the annual meeting of the 93rd Japan Sociological Society (in Japanese)

Shorrocks AF (1984) Inequality decomposition by population subgroups. Econometrica 56(6):1369–1385

Sorensen AB (2000) Toward a sounder basis for class analysis. Am J Sociol 105(6):1523–1558

Spilerman S (2000) Wealth and stratification processes. Ann Rev Sociol 26:497–52

Weber M (1946) Class, status, party. In: Girth HH, Mills CW (eds) From Max Weber: essays in sociology. Oxford University, New York, pp 180–195

Sawako Shirahase is Professor of Sociology at the Graduate School of Humanities and Sociology, the University of Tokyo. She received her D.Phil. in sociology from the University of Oxford, conducted post-doctoral research at the East Asian Institute, Columbia University as a junior researcher, and held positions of Senior Research fellow at the National Institute of Population and Social Security Research, and Associate Professor of Sociology at Tsukuba University. She is currently a director of the UTokyo Center for Contemporary Japanese Studies.

Dr. Shirahase's research interests include comparative social stratification and demographic transformation, gender and generational relations, and family change and social security system. She is the author of *Social Inequality in Japan* (Routledge, 2014) and *Demographic Change and Inequality in Japan* (ed.) (Trans Pacific Press, 2011), and her recent publications are "Social Stratification Theory and Population Aging Reconsidered," (*Social Science Japan Journal* 24(2): 277–288, 2021) and *The Structure of Social Stratification in the Late-stage of Life* (in Japanese) (ed., with S. Arita and N. Sudo) (University of Tokyo Press, 2021).

Dr. Shirahase is on the editorial board of *International Sociology* and *Contemporary Japan*, and on the advisory board of *Social Politics*. She currently serves as Vice President of the International Sociological Association and Vice President of the International Science Council. She was the principal investigator of the research project conducting the 2015 National Survey of Social Stratification and Social Mobility (SSM) Survey which has been conducted every 10 years since 1955.

Printed by Printforce, the Netherlands